AS GOOD AS GOLD

The Chemistry of Life, Love, and Business

Robert W. Killick, PhD

BALBOA.
PRESS

A DIVISION OF HAY HOUSE

Balboa Press books may be ordered through booksellers or by contacting:

Balboa Press
A Division of Hay House
1663 Liberty Drive
Bloomington, IN 47403
www.balboapress.com.au
1 (877) 407-4847

Because of the dynamic nature of the Internet, any web addresses or links contained in this book may have changed since publication and may no longer be valid. The views expressed in this work are solely those of the author and do not necessarily reflect the views of the publisher, and the publisher hereby disclaims any responsibility for them.

The author of this book does not dispense medical advice or prescribe the use of any technique as a form of treatment for physical, emotional, or medical problems without the advice of a physician, either directly or indirectly. The intent of the author is only to offer information of a general nature to help you in your quest for emotional and spiritual well-being. In the event you use any of the information in this book for yourself, which is your constitutional right, the author and the publisher assume no responsibility for your actions.

Artwork by DAVID CAIRD.

Print information available on the last page.

ISBN: 978-1-5043-0705-5 (sc)
ISBN: 978-1-5043-0706-2 (e)

Balboa Press rev. date: 03/29/2017

For Judy, with all thanks for fifty-seven fantastic years as the front lady of The Punch and Judy Travelling Show, as well as various roles, including the Beautiful Lady Alice, Cora, Gracie, and Mabel. It has been wonderful that, together, we have discovered that thanksgiving is the dialect of heaven.

Blessed to be a Blessing

CONTENTS

FOREWORD

From a Technical Perspective

I write this foreword from a hotel room in downtown Pittsburgh, Pennsylvania. Why? Bob contacted me shortly before I left on this trip, asking if I would write a foreword for his memoirs, which he was close to finishing. I said I would be pleased to help, and his work dutifully turned up on a USB. He asked me to tell him what I thought, and I am pleased to report that the read has been riveting (yes, riveting). It has also been pleasing that the book has filled in many of the blanks of Bob's life that I have for so long wondered about.

I have had the pleasure and honour of knowing Bob and Judy (also known as Alice, the power behind the crown), for an excess of twenty years. My journey with Bob has been both as a friend and the patent attorney of their company, Victorian Chemicals. I have thus shared some of the successes and the not so good patenting moments with Bob. Nevertheless, it has been both a fun and memorable journey.

As you will discover in his memoirs, Bob is a unique character. He has an uncanny, engaging, and disarming way of interacting with people.

I remember that, in the early days, we bonded partly because we shared unusual working habits. Many were the times we did our best work together between 5:30 and 6:00 a.m. As Bob would say, "The early bird gets the worm." With great chuckling, he would follow that with the running joke of "But it is the second mouse that gets the cheese." We have always jointly endorsed the advantages of the morning for clear-headed and exciting decision making, whilst "mere mortals sleep" (Bob's words). On account of my parents' inspired upbringing, which covered all the cowboy movies and musicals of the 1930's, '40's and '50's, I think I was one of the few people who could understand Bob's cryptic humour and viewing habits. Those morning discussions were magic!

Bob also taught me how valuable it is to enhance mundane things. For example, to change everyday parlance to provide the listener with an immediate lift rather than give a predictable and boring response. Take our usual morning greeting on the phone:

> WAYNE: Hi, Bob, how are you?
> BOB: If I were any better, I would be dangerous!
> (Twenty years later, that response has morphed to, "For an old man, dangerous [laughter], but then, I'm also delusional!")

I have plagiarized Bob many times and, without fail, when you say this, the recipient becomes uplifted. That's Bob! He knows people! Mind you, there have been telephone greetings and messages with my staff which have left them scratching their heads, for example:

> BOB: Hi, Deb, how are you, and is the boss man in?
> DEB: Not at the moment. Do you want to leave a message?
> BOB: Just tell him that Dr Death rang.
>
> (Deb's response was wordless wonder. The translation of Bob's humour is, of course, Dr *Kill*ick.)

The natural question from any interaction with Bob was, and is, "What is he on, and can I have some of it?" Readers of these memoirs will quickly discover what Bob is on! His faith provides an underlying approach to life, and emphasizes how much he values family, church, and other people. He is the antithesis of the modern corporate businessman who demands, rather than earns, action and respect. Bob gives respect and leadership, and, as he says, "If you want to know you are leading, look behind to see if anyone is following." Invariably, in his case, someone is.

Whilst I am not a "church" person like Bob, my family and I ascribe to Christian values. In our time together, he has provided me with the inspiration to succeed and the example of good conduct. If we all used Bob's approach, our world would be a much better place and our families that much richer. I commend this to you as a good read about someone, of which there are too few.

Wayne McMaster, LLB, Dip. Metallurgy
Registered Patent Attorney
Partner, Minter Ellison Lawyers
Melbourne, Australia

From a Societal Perspective

As Good as Gold is an apt title for the story of Robert William Killick. It has been my privilege to have known Bob, his wife, Judy, and their family for the past forty-six years. Bob is one of life's characters: unorthodox, intriguing, with loads of practical wisdom and a repertoire of quotes, sayings, and jokes that you hear multiple times and still smile in response! He, with Judy, is amazingly generous and hospitable, humble and servant hearted, irrepressible and not easily manipulated, with a great work ethic and an entrepreneurial flair that has landed some great deals. Bob has a deep commitment to his faith in Jesus and loves to help others explore what faith means.

As Good as Gold kept enticing me to read more. It is a great story of a life that seizes the day and the moments, that refuses to be kept down, that is grateful for small and large mercies. Bob's classic one-liners pop up on many of the pages, and you get insights into what makes this man tick. He is not afraid to tell it like it is, but there is tenderness to Bob that seeks the best outcome for all. He is incredibly loyal, honest to the core, and a friend who stays with you through the range of life's experiences.

If you want to be challenged, inspired, intrigued, and spurred on to have a go at fulfilling a dream, grab a cuppa and a seat, and enjoy the story of Robert William Killick. It is a great read, and I commend it to you.

Bill Brown, BScEd, BD, DMin
Senior Pastor, Syndal Baptist Church
Melbourne, Australia

PREFACE

I am an organic chemist

An organic chemist is a subset of being a scientist. This, for many in our culture, could mean I am close to being that fictitious mad scientist of renown. There is no better representation than the classic image of the maniacal lab-coated Dr Henry Frankenstein, in the 1931 film *Frankenstein*, when his patched-together monster comes alive: "Look it's moving. It's alive. It's alive. ... It's alive. It's moving. It's alive. It's alive. It's alive. It's alive. *It's alive.*" One doesn't come across a script like that every day.

Chemistry broadly splits into *organic* (the chemistry that deals with carbon compounds); *inorganic* (the chemistry of the rest of the elements); and *physical* (with the application of the techniques and theories of physics to the study of chemical systems).

The Bronze Age was established by 3000 B.C., its basis being the chemical extraction of metals from ores then re-mixing copper and tin to form bronze. There was also the manufacture of glass, soap and fermented drink. Perfumes and medicines were extracted from plants.

The Iron Age was underway by 1200 B.C. as man had developed furnaces that could produce temperatures that melted iron.

War was always a great driver, and in China in A.D. 1044, the first recorded formulation for the manufacture of gunpowder appeared.

Up until the Middle Ages, the alchemists chased two impossible goals: an elixir of life that could extend life and even provide immortality, and the philosopher's stone, which would turn base metals, such as lead, to noble metals, such as gold or silver. Modern chemistry is reputed to have begun in 1661 when Robert Boyle published *The Sceptical Chymist or Chymico-Physical Doubts & Paradoxes*.

In the early years of Victorian Chemicals, we recited our motto: "We are happy little rabbits digging six feet underground, looking for bronze with streaks of silver; for when you find gold, the vultures gather." However, with some chemical reactions, we did find gold—well, as good as gold. This used the product obtained from the reaction of a vegetable oil with an alcohol, and selling it to aid the farmer to improve the weed-killing efficacy of the herbicides being used. And, yes, the vultures did gather.

There is also the right chemistry between Judy and me. We have had the right rapport and attraction for the last fifty-seven years and happily go round as The Punch and Judy Travelling Show.

I have also been fortunate to have had the right chemistry for running a business. I could say I was in my element (pun definitely intended). People have found it easy to work for me.

ACKNOWLEDGEMENTS

When you reach the age of seventy-nine years, there are many people who have been teachers, mentors, and role models—in short, those who have made Bob, Bob. Most seem to be long gone.

To name just a few of the people who have contributed to my life and pilgrim journey: my father, Rupert, and my mother, "Topsy," both parented well in their own ways; Uncle Bill Inder, who was my role model, and Aunty Roxie, who first got me to be more skilful in writing English; four men in the National Australia Bank; Dick Hindmarsh, the NSW manager, who provided our first housing loan and let me understand the importance of the expression "Take me to your leader"; Evan Tune, our company's first Melbourne bank manager, who stood behind us when matters were really tight and taught their credit department that "Bob will be all right"; Bernie Fanning, currently a regional executive of the bank, who provided a $2 million loan for a few months, basically on the nod; and Chris Thomas, who, with strategic thinking, joined the Breakfast Club (our think tank, which I'll describe in more detail in later chapters) and immeasurably helped fund the Coolaroo purchase; Ken Knight, who caught the vision and worked assiduously to enable us to purchase Victorian Chemicals; Helmut Heymann of Germany, who concluded he could "work with Bob" and facilitated the acquisition of the Coolaroo factory complex; David Lambert, who could agree on a multimillion deal with a non-handshake; Ian McCubbin, who taught me to be a bush lawyer; and my first accountant Graeme Voigt, who drummed into me an understanding of "source and application of funds."

Another Dimension

My whole life would have been different if it were not for the Rev. Neville Horn, under whose ministry I acknowledged Jesus as Lord and whose teaching on the Holy Spirit has been invaluable; Dr Geoff Blackburn, under whose ministry at the Syndal Church I learnt the intrinsic importance of playing "second fiddle" and how to do so; and the Rev. Bill Brown, with whom Judy and I have worked for forty-six years, learning that unity in the work makes all the difference.

I particularly want to thank my Christian brothers and sisters at the Syndal Baptist Church, with whom we have shared a journey of forty-six years, and who bore with me and taught me the ways of being an effective lay leader.

Where the Rubber Hits the Road

I wish also to express my appreciation to those who were brave enough to read the earlier versions of the book and make constructive suggestions.

Special thanks to Alan Rowe, once a journalist, who read the first transcripts and encouraged me to keep writing whilst stressing I would have to change from being a "technical writer" to one for whom "prose" was second nature. Also, there was Dr Stuart Devenish, who gave his time out of an impossible workload to undertake editing. It has been a learning experience for all. Thirdly, Mrs Judy Enticott provided great instruction on finessing and providing nuances in the writing of English. She was concerned, but her fears were allayed when granddaughter Elisia said, "As I read the book, I could just hear grandpa talking."

And last but not least, and indeed the most important, my wife, Judy, who has provided fifty-seven years of the real meaning of marriage. She initiated the push for me to write these memoirs and leave a legacy for the grandchildren. She has borne the strain of living with me when I was in the middle of writing and couldn't move to do household chores: "I'm on a roll! I'm on a roll!" This has led her to comment that she was glad she had not married an author.

While I owe my thanks to each of these people and have benefited from their input, the final missive, with its errors, belongs to me. I am ever reminded of the many years when, each morning, as I was leaving for work, Judy, my beloved wife, would grab me by the lapels, shake me like a wet rat (there is nothing quite like being shaken like a wet rat), and advise, "Just remember, all wisdom does not lie with Bob Killick." *Sic transit gloria mundi* ("Thus passes the glory of the world").

Bob Killick
Melbourne, Australia
Christmas 2016

BIOGRAPHICAL INTRODUCTION

If you don't already know him, I want to introduce you to Bob Killick. Bob is a larger-than-life character; the kind of person who makes his presence unmistakably felt when he walks into a room. It's not that he was born with a silver spoon in his mouth or that he has lived a charmed life. It's more a force of his character. Bob has three things going for him which are hard to resist. The first is his quick mind; you have to move quickly to keep up with Bob. The second is his ready wit; any time Bob's around, there's a laugh a minute. And the third is that he has a plan; it's a sure bet that things won't stay the same for long before being bent to his greater sense of direction and purpose. There's more to add to be sure; such as his integrity, his ability to assess people's character ... and then there's his business acumen.

There's a lot to like about Bob. There is a certain *chemistry* about him; as an Australian born in Sydney, he has a certain way of speaking which is coloured by the Aussie lingua franca. It's not coarse, mind you, just typically direct. Then there's his business background; Bob is an industrial chemist with a PhD from Sydney University on developing new steroids. The combination of his quick mind and his business acumen has proved a handy asset over the years. Then there are his people skills; I wouldn't always say Bob knows how to manage people, per se, but he always seems to know how to choose the right person to put on his team and to work with him. The best example of this is his wife Judy, who is probably Bob's best asset ... money included. Then there's his capacity for self-deprecation, that unique skill of telling a joke against himself to make himself look bad and others look good. You've got to like a bloke who doesn't put himself on a pedestal! There's more to be said about Bob of course; world traveller, family man, entrepreneur, raconteur, man of faith, networker, leader, lover of theatre and classical music ... but I'll let Bob tell the rest of the story in the pages that follow.

To Remember Those Days of Yore

The book you are holding in your hand tells the story of Bob's life. In this piece of autobiographical writing, Bob is able to do what very few of us are able to do: tell our story on our own terms and in our own words. While it is possible for self-delusion to creep into our narrative storytelling about our own lives, all of us are to some extent experts on ourselves. We can make a case that no one knows us or our life histories like we do. So, in a sense—unless there is some great trauma or tragedy or character flaw which twists our characters so fundamentally that we can no longer see ourselves as we truly are—of all the people in the world, we each are the person best qualified to tell our own story. After all, we were there … we saw it, we heard it, we experienced it, we felt it, we know what it was like from the inside.

So here is Bob telling his own story. And what a story it is! If you dare to accept Bob's invitation to "take up and read"—which was the child's voice heard by St Augustine in the fourth century, and which led to his conversion—you might find yourself not only discovering where he lived and what he loved and how he made a success of his life … you might also find yourself being amused, appalled, amazed, and attracted to what you see in his life, his face, and his faith. In the world of newspaper journalism, editors demand that their journalists write articles that meet the public's demand for human-interest stories. And in bookshops, it is usually biography which fills the largest space on the shelf. People want to know about the lives of other people. Well, I put it to you that here is a person worth meeting, a face worth looking into, and a life worth reading. Take up and read, indeed.

Stuart Devenish, PhD
Director of Postgraduate Studies
Tabor College of Advanced Education, Adelaide, Australia

CHRONOLOGY OF A LIFE

Bob born January	1938	
	1939	
	1940	
	1941	
	1942	
	1943	Infants
	1944	Primary School 1
	1945	Primary School 2
	1946	Primary School 3
	1947	Primary School 4
	1948	Primary School 5
	1949	Primary School 6
High School 1	1950	First flight, and alone, to Brisbane
High School 2	1951	
High School 3	1952	Introduced to shipboard travel
High School 4	1953	New family home, Seaforth
High School 5	1954	
	1955	University 1
VW car for18th birthday	1956	University 2
	1957	University 3
	1958	Honours Year 4
	1959	PhD 1
Bob and Judy marry, January	1960	PhD 2; Jennifer born, December
	1961	PhD 3
Join Unilever, March, to UK	1962	Mum dies, November
	1963	Andrew born, May

Return to Sydney, June	1964	
	1965	
	1966	
	1967	Peter born, May
	1968	
Move to UK, October, by air	1969	
	1970	
Return to Sydney, April	1971	To Melbourne, Acting Dev. Mgr.
Apptd. Tech. Serv. & Dev. Mgr.	1972	Apptd. deacon, Syndal Church, Sept.
	1973	
	1974	
	1975	
	1976	Gospel Theatre - "The Dodo"
	1977	
	1978	
	1979	Appointed church secretary
Sacked from Unilever, March	1980	Joined Michaelis-Bayley, May
Vicchem for sale?, Nov.	1981	Sacked from M-B, Dec.
Vicchem for sale, April	1982	Year of negotiation
Vicchem purchased, March	1983	
	1984	
	1985	Struggle years
	1986	Struggle years
	1987	Struggle years
	1988	Struggle years
	1989	

	1990	
	1991	
Ee-muls-oyle FDA	1992	Two next door sites purchased
	1993	
	1994	
	1995	
HASTEN patent granted	1996	
	1997	Start of significant sales expansion
	1998	
	1999	
	2000	
	2001	
Dad died, March	2002	
Coolaroo negotiations	2003	Dandenong purchased, Oct.
Coolaroo purchased, Dec.	2004	
Coolaroo workings	2005	Richmond remains backstop
Coolaroo fully operational	2006	Richmond site sold, August
	2007	Sales explosion
	2008	
	2009	
	2010	
	2011	Bob retires church mgt.
Andrew appointed M.D.	2012	Bob keeps in EU mkt.
Milestone Year: Bob 75	2013	Andrew 50; VCC 80; owned 30.
	2014	

INTRODUCTION

*Merely corroborative detail, to add some artistic verisimilitude,
to an otherwise bald and unconvincing narrative.*[1]

There is an apocryphal story of a fifty-five-year-old nurse in a retirement village asking a ninety-five-year-old patient what advice she could offer for her next forty years. The old lady replied, "Make sure you build your memories, for when you are my age, that is all you will have left!" When the nurse got home that night, she said to her husband, "OK, get ready; we leave for Europe next week!"

At seventy-nine, there are obviously many, many memories, and this book can only highlight a select number of them. Some of the closer members of the family claim that they find it hard to believe what has been written, but I hold that these are my memories, for better or for worse. I could have set out to write an autobiography, but my wife, Judy, felt that an autobiography had too much of a poseur sense about it. Indeed, for her, even the term *memoirs* sounds a bit grand, when a few reflections would be adequate. She is a great believer in reflections, since she often reflects that "I am a model husband—a faint replica of the real thing," and a comedic drum roll would not go astray.

The first driver to write the book was to leave a legacy for our family. The second driver has been to respond to all those innumerable requests as we are reminded of the music hall days of yore, when the standard patter went, "At the request of thousands of our adoring fans— Judy, would you please pass me that one letter we received!" However, I do hasten to add that there really have been suggestions from many to write our story in order to encourage the wider community on how the Lord has guided our family through its earthly pilgrimage. It has been an indescribably blessed pilgrimage, even that we have been "spoilt rotten,"[2] as we Aussies like to say.

Memories

In this introduction there follows only some of all the memories that are described more fully in the Memoirs—the time at the Coolaroo factory, when the Victorian Chemicals sign replaced that of Cognis; the fact that when in negotiations, I never seem to hear the word no!; at the American Food and Drug Administration (FDA), when I changed my persona to that of "Dr Bob" of Veterinary Hospital from *The Muppets* TV show and found I had FDA approval of our product; the many joys of all those Gilbert and Sullivan nights; the many memories of fifty-seven years of marriage and the times we have been the Punch and Judy Travelling Show; the night I was an ass and asked whether Victorian Chemicals might be for sale; the jokes that I have told during serious discussions and which have been able to maintain equilibrium to reach the best result; the happiness at work of being in my element; the joys of being in musicals when I don't have a singing voice; the afternoon I was a genius and from which several patents flowed; the times I jumped layers of management to get to the top decision maker ("Take me to your leader"), with critically positive results; the afternoon we sold the Richmond plant which was on the "wrong side of the tracks" for top dollar; the days at major meetings when I would tell a joke against myself ("What is the difference between an Australian man and the yoghurt you eat for breakfast? Well, the yoghurt at least starts with some culture!"—not that it is that exciting in print, but it certainly has great acceptance at these types of meetings); memories of the bank meetings with laugh-a-minute PowerPoint presentations through which we kept a strong working relationship; the hours spent in leadership at God's work at our local church; the late afternoon purchase of a 4.5-hectare factory site, with a nodding agreement between the seller and myself. These are but some of the events that have formed the warp and weft that has been my life.

A Scientist

To be called a scientist may sound a little highfalutin; I could preferably say I have been an organic chemist all my life. This has involved me with the study of, and work with, organic compounds.

These materials form the basis of all earthly life. The simplest organic compounds are based on carbon and hydrogen and are known as hydrocarbons. The compounds can also contain many other elements, but, particularly, oxygen, nitrogen, and sulphur, in descending order of importance.

Carbon has a specific atomic structure, by which it forms covalent bonds with other elements as well as itself. This allows carbon to form long "chains" of carbon atoms. Vegetable oils, such as olive oil or canola oil, are made from a specific combination of 57 carbon atoms, 102 hydrogen atoms, and 6 oxygen atoms. For thirty years, the company has been manufacturing and selling products derived from these oils. It has kept us off the street.

It's Ever "Sho-o-o-ow" Time

There have been many ways that my life could be described over the past seventy-nine years. With the streak of showmanship that runs through both Judy and me, our preference has laid with The Punch and Judy Travelling Show. Another description would be to say that we have journeyed on the Hallelujah Trail,[3] whilst, to mix the metaphors, we have been granted the privilege of always feeling that we have been sitting in the best two seats in the house (theatre). It has been the ride of a lifetime—"and loving it."[4]

All life stories finally seem to come back to the balance between who you are and what you actually did. This is more evident in the types of stories that occur during life and which differ depending on your occupation, whether an airline pilot, a heart specialist, a garbage collector, or a missionary. My gift has been to have a technical/scientific trait and to hold closely to calling myself "the Mad Scientist of Renown." This was quite evident at times, since it was absurd that I should set out to purchase a chemical company that had "one foot in the grave and the other on a banana skin," with very little wherewithal to complete the transaction. The book records how we reached the point where the grave was filled in whilst the banana proved to be a good fertilizer.

For any reasonably successful businessman, it can be guaranteed that there will be stories involving the movement of money. Whilst money is integral to the flow of society, to talk about it in Australia is not really done. In most cases, Australian society does not flaunt its wealth. But for a memoir covering a business life, somehow a balance has to be struck between an overload of unnecessary financial detail and sufficient explanation to provide a continuity of how the business survived in the early days and blossomed in the later ones.

As we move to the book, let the thespian provide the call to the audience—"I-i-i-i-it's sho-o-o-ow time!"[5]

1 Can a Soufflé Rise Twice?

No man steps into the same river twice?[1]

It was 2003. I was sixty-five years old, happily married to Judy for forty-three years, healthy, and ignoring retirement. We had three children, all of whom were either approaching or already past forty. They were all married and—wonderfully for us—had produced six super grandchildren. We were the owners of the comfortably prosperous Victorian Chemical Company (Vicchem), which provided everything material that we needed. There were also the added extras, like twice yearly round-the-world trips to liaise with business partners and promote our products. And, most importantly, we belonged to a vibrant church community, where we could express our thankfulness to God for all His goodness to us. If this was not success, then I didn't know what was.

Perhaps facetiously, the publishing world advises that in order to double book sales, you must make sure that the word *success* is in the title. There are many who crave success in their lives and seem willing to pay whatever price to learn how to achieve it. I am reluctant to say that this book holds the gold-plated secret to success. All I can do is recount how I got to where I have in life, and from that, you may discern signposts to provide guidance for your own life's journey.

Anyone looking at our Vicchem chemical business today might presume that we came from a well-credentialed business family with an impeccable and impressive history of wealth production. But that is not how it happened. I would like to tell you about our rock-solid, platinum-class business pedigree, but it just isn't there. The fact is that we have had to work hard to turn difficulty and disadvantage into accomplishment and success. (The story of our purchase of Vicchem in 1983 is recounted in chapter 2.) The major challenge we faced in 2003 was to transform our seventy-year-old company, whose inner-city factory in Richmond was well past its use-by date, into a productive and profitable enterprise. We had looked around spasmodically, but nothing had come to hand—it was crunch time for our business. Providentially and out of the blue, we heard that a 3.5-hectare, 35,000-square-metre chemical manufacturing site situated at Coolaroo, Melbourne, might be available to purchase. It was the Golden Ball of Opportunity. The photo of the factory, below, was taken around 1990.

The Golden Ball of Opportunity

Let me say from the outset that I enjoy the challenge of competition, and I suddenly got hungry to win this manufacturing site. I might be the "Old Boy," but it could still be said that I had "it" in me. It would be the so-called icing on the cake of my life's work. The breakthrough came after a long and frustrating nine-month series of negotiations with Cognis,[2] the multinational German owners of the site. It had taken persistence, above all, with a touch of bravado on our part, as a small and fledgling enterprise, to get so far. However, a small steamroller is still a steamroller, and Cognis indicated that we would be given *one hour* to present our case for the purchase to one of their company's top three directors, who happened to be passing through Melbourne in coming weeks. Yet, as we prepared our presentation for the German director's visit, advisers from our family and senior management gave counsel that, during the meetings, I should hold myself in check and not tell any of the quirky jokes for which I am well known. "Germans are serious people!"[3] they said. Was I so whimsical that when convention demanded a serious approach to life, I would break into a series of jokes? This book tells the life story that leads up to and follows this life-changing one-hour meeting, which represents one of the most challenging and exhilarating moments, not only of my life personally, but also of the Victorian Chemical Company.

Some Background

One of the earliest motivating points in my younger life was when my mum pushed hard to get me to go to university: "At least one year, Bob; it will be a good experience for you." That one year started in 1955 and ended seven years later, in early 1963. I drifted out of Sydney University with my doctor of philosophy (PhD) degree in organic chemistry. By that time, Judy and I were married, and daughter Jenni was learning to walk. Judy had been my typist for the 223-page thesis, which was crammed full of chemical technical jargon, most of which she had never previously heard. I already knew I did not want to stay in academia, as many of my friends had done. Instead, I chose to go into business, which offered a more conducive environment for my creative and innovative tendencies to flourish. What followed was my eighteen-year-long apprenticeship in the Unilever Company, which I joined almost literally as a walk-in off the street. I started with two years at their Port Sunlight Research Laboratories on the Wirral, Cheshire, England.

We left Sydney in April 1962, with our little family. Jenni was then sixteen months old, and our parents doubted they would ever see her again. Andrew was born in May 1963, in our rented three-bedroom English terrace house in Port Sunlight. We had another stint in England for eighteen months, from 1969 to 1971, which by then included Peter, a two-year-old, living in Bromley, Kent, thirty minutes by train to the London head office. Our return to Australia took me to work in Melbourne, but after eight years, I was pushed out into the wide, wild world. After eighteen months, I spent a three-month-long sojourn among the unemployed. My personality is such that I didn't fall into depression or hysteria, but instead took it philosophically as something I could mark down to experience. Indeed, in later years, that period of unemployment provided me with the great story of how an unemployed chemist was able to buy an entire chemical company while he was out of work!

In 1983—by a series of events that still amaze me even today—I was able to buy a company called the Victorian Chemical Company (Vicchem) based in Richmond, Melbourne, Australia. (The story of the purchase of that company will be explored in chapter 2, as noted previously.) The task of this chapter is to provide an overview of how all the various parts of the story fit together. The thing to note about the purchase of the Victorian Chemical Company is that it represented our first glimpse of possibilities that lay some years ahead of us. It tantalized us with the prospect of the possibility of owning our own business, yet the very deep challenges we faced in establishing a functional base for production, market share, and, most important of all, a financially sustainable future. Thus, almost out of the blue, I was able to buy a chemical company that represented our first soufflé, in the form of the acquisition of the Victorian Chemical Company, along with its manufacturing plant, warehouses, laboratory, and offices of 1,612 square metres in Richmond. The factory had been built around 1933 to 1935, and was now in need of urgent and extensive repair and upgrading. We all joked that the factory, if not the whole company had "one foot in the grave, the other on a banana skin!" In its later years of production, it had received no regular maintenance, and was now rapidly turning into a pile of junk. The photo, below, shows just some of the decaying ambience of the plant.

Vicchem factory (1983)

Malcolm Fraser, the Australian Liberal prime minister during the 1980s, is famous for observing that, "Life wasn't meant to be easy!"[4] Our experience of owning a chemical factory bears that out. Nothing was easy for us, and those early days were particularly challenging. We often consoled ourselves by observing that "We were happy little rabbits living six feet underground, digging for bronze with streaks of silver"—because there was always the warning—"for when you find gold, the vultures gather!" We hoped that one day we would find some streaks of gold, but we never dreamt we would strike the mother lode. But, through hard work and perseverance, we were able to turn the enterprise around in the first ten years under our management regime, and had generated enough income to purchase the adjoining properties to our factory in 1992, from a distressed mortgage sale. This additional land also offered us some all-important breathing space in the form of a warehouse where our additional stock could be housed. This was particularly important at a time when sales were picking up. The total size of our factory complex was now at 5,175 square metres. However, by 2000, it was becoming increasingly obvious to everyone, even those with a cork eye,[5] that our capacity to sustain our rising levels of demand for production and sales out of our Richmond factory was impossible. We had to find new facilities, and we had to find them fast.

A Plant, a Plant, My Kingdom for a Plant

With that kind of pressure weighing on us, the meeting with Cognis was crucial to our survival. When we bought the Richmond factory years before for a steal, even though it was a pile of junk, we were minnows in business terms. But our dealings with Cognis meant that we were moving into the big league. On the one hand, it meant we could develop a larger and more sustainable manufacturing complex. But on the other hand, it represented a serious threat to our financial base, and we wondered if we could pull it off. If we were to survive into the future, we believed we only had two options available to us. Both would require us to move away from the existing Richmond plant. The first option was to design and build a brand-new manufacturing complex from the ground up on a new green-field site. The second option was to purchase an existing industrial complex that suited our purposes exactly.

The first option was daunting. Even though commercial land was available for building a new manufacturing complex, the enormity of the project was overwhelming, and the cost was likely to be prohibitive. Peter Wrigley, our general manager, our son Andrew, who was the company's marketing director, and I visited several sites in Melbourne's western industrial corridor. The immediate concern was the high level of capital required and the knowledge that we would be paying top dollar for the kind of development we needed. Compounding this was the time and energy required to obtain the regulatory approvals we needed from the various governmental bodies, such as obtaining council planning permits, the stringent Environmental Protection Authority (EPA) requirements, WorkSafe and Water Board permissions.

The second option was equally daunting. The problem for us was that we simply did not know of any manufacturing companies that could be approached. There were a few smaller companies whose manufacturing processes only had a few chemical reactors as the main drivers of their production base. In our case, the Richmond factory was already running ten different-sized reactors, and we knew we needed more capacity. We had identified four or five larger enterprises, but such was their size and volume of production that we thought it a joke to approach them in a takeover bid. But then, as the old hymn states, "God moves in a mysterious way His wonders to perform."[6] South Australian academic Stuart Devenish expanded this, saying, "As Christians we 'read' circumstances in such a way that we attribute events and circumstances to the purposeful actions of a loving God rather than to a meaningless unfolding of random events."[7] We found ourselves in the market for a property we could not possibly afford, with a budget we could only describe as less-than-satisfactory. It was impossible; it couldn't be done.

Three Warnings

When trying to explain how we find guidance, it is easier to start with a story. Preachers often tell the story as follows: It was reported that a man in Bangladesh was in his village, listening to the cricket on the radio, when the commentary was interrupted with the warning that a flood was coming and everyone in his village should leave immediately. *Not to worry,* he thinks to himself. *God will look after me!* The next time we see him, he is standing on the kitchen table, with the water lapping its edges. Rescuers come to his door in a boat and call out, "Come on board, we'll save you." "Not to worry," he tells them. "God will look after me!" The next time, he is on the roof, with the water lapping at his feet, when a helicopter hovers over him. "Climb up the ladder; we'll save you." "Not to worry," he tells them. "God will look after me!" The last time we hear of him, he is standing before God, complaining,

"Why didn't you look after me?" To which God replies, "You had the radio warning, the boat, and the helicopter! What more did you want?"

This story about far-off places and unlikely people became our own story in 2002. We experienced three events that helped concentrate our minds on the reality that our Richmond days were over. The first event took place in August, with the collapse of a full thousand-litre tank spilling one of our products onto David Street. Over the years, David Street had been our private loading dock on account of its lack of use by the general public. The incident took place when loading a truck with a one-tonne IBC shipping container. As the result of rotten wood in the base pallet, the container fell off the forklift, the plastic walls of the container split, and the industrial fluid spread across the road. Fortunately, the product was viscous, and our staff was able to contain the spill before any materials entered the storm-water drains. This was critical because, once in the drains, there was nothing to stop the product reaching the Yarra River to become an oil pollutant, the bête noire of the EPA. When the shouting and tumult had died, we contacted the EPA to report the incident. The EPA complimented us for stopping a significant incident, but they queried how long we thought we were going to continue manufacturing on the Richmond site, which was experiencing residential encroachment into the previously industrial eastern end of the suburb. The radio had given its message.

The second realization was that Richmond was no longer an industrial suburb—it was now a desirable blue-ribbon suburb. The gentrification process came as a result of large numbers of educated and articulate yuppies moving into Richmond for the purposes of living adjacent to the city centre, within easy reach of employment, education, entertainment, and restaurant facilities. Houses that had sold for $250,000.00 ten years before and which were considered to be an unbelievable price at the time, were now selling for more than $1 million. Of more immediate concern was the construction of the large Victoria Gardens shopping complex that backed onto the other side of

Doonside Street, which meant they were in effect our neighbours. As we sarcastically used to say, we couldn't understand why anyone would object to having a filthy, as described by them, chemical manufacturing plant next to a new pristine shopping complex. This was our second warning. The boat had been sent to tell us something important.

The third warning came as a result of an industrial accident. It could have been tragic but fortuitously was not. Engineering works had been authorized for the back warehouse to be undertaken on August 20. However, when the ordered pumps did not arrive at the designated time, the engineer charged with the responsibility of carrying out the work decided to save time on the next day's work. Without the appropriate authorization, he proceeded to service the next vessel on the list. He began cutting with an angle grinder through one of the vessel's external pipes. But the vessel was live from the reaction underway in the pot, and the whole vessel exploded. The pressure was such that the top lid had all its thirty bolts, each the thickness of an index finger, sheared apart. The top lid then lifted several inches, with such force that the worker was thrust onto the gantry a few feet below. He was knocked around as if he had been involved in a really bad football stoush. Thankfully, he recovered, and returned to work after some time off to allow his bruises to heal. We were fortunate there was no fatality. This was our next warning. Our helicopter had passed through.

The backwash of the work accident was the partial closure of the Richmond factory by WorkSafe, under its government-sponsored legislative requirements. In order to supplement our limited production, we commissioned another third-party company to produce and supply our product. One of those companies was Cognis, which became a supplier of products for our company from their Coolaroo factory. The first ethyl oleate was received from Coolaroo on September 4, 2002. Later, during the purchase negotiations, Cognis indicated that the ester would only be available until Christmas, as the Coolaroo factory was slated to be mothballed. There were muted discussions among our brains trust as to whether there might be any chance of buying out the Cognis plant, but we had picked up negative vibes that Cognis would rather "put a screwdriver" through the plant to destroy it than sell it to another chemical company. This may have been a passing comment. It should have sent warning signals to proceed no further, but it did not. One thing was certain—if the factory was to be ours, it would not be delivered on a silver platter.

How Serious Are Germans?

We accepted the growing evidence that the life of our chemical plant at Richmond was limited. Our first soufflé was sinking. What did this mean for our future? Unbeknown to us, the explosion in our factory forced us to contract third-party chemical companies to supply product urgently needed to fill our orders. We saw God's hand at work in putting us in contact with Cognis, which was making plans at that precise time to mothball its factory. Was this the opportunity we needed to resurrect our future? Against all odds, could our soufflé rise twice? If we were able to buy the Coolaroo factory, we were no longer looking at a pile of junk, but a real working factory with German engineering and real value.

On September 14, just ten days after the first batch of ethyl oleate[8] had been delivered to us from the Coolaroo factory, three of Cognis's managers met with us to propose that Vicchem should join with them in an attempt to affect a management buyout (MBO). The Vicchem managers who attended the meeting later reported that watching the discussions was seeing Bob, the old lion, and a young lion, the leader from the three from Cognis, circling around the Coolaroo carcass. The MBO team felt that they were bringing a functioning chemical production plant to the table, while Vicchem was providing a solid product line and sales platform to give the projected joint new company a future. In order to avoid any misunderstandings, our Vicchem management team held direct discussions with the senior Cognis

Australian management on September 20, with Tony Popper present. Tony was the Cognis Australian managing director, and he stressed they were not leaning towards an MBO. Cognis's head office had been badly bitten in the MBO of their English factory, since it had not adequately covered confidential sales and marketing information. This allowed the MBO to take over Cognis's English market. This disaster, we were assured, was not going to happen on his watch in Australia.

Judy has never had the opportunity to receive an education in chemistry, but that has not prevented her from making important contributions to the success of Vicchem. Her insights were often wise, deep, and timely, and she has been invaluable in the kind of advice she has given, both worldly and spiritual. At this stage, she strongly queried whether we ought to enter a tight partnership through the formation of a joint company. As we would commonly do in these sorts of situations, we talked over what biblical principles might apply. The first key instruction, couched as a question, is by the prophet Amos: "Do two walk together unless they have agreed to do so?[9] For those who would prefer a variant everyday proverb: "Birds of a feather flock together." Psychologists such as Donn Byrne, with early classic experiments, followed by further studies in 1961 by Theodore Newcomb, built up in their discipline, the Laws of Attraction, mainly based around the proverb "Like attracts like." This is much criticized today, but I have yet to see a skein of Canada geese flying in formation with a murder of crows.

It is the norm these days when interviewing candidates for a company position that cultural fit is central in the decision-making process. The second key biblical instruction, couched in a negative style, is "Do not go into partnership with those who have different values."[10] As discussions continued, we began to realize the extent of the cultural and management gap that existed between ourselves and the Cognis buyout team. On September 30, we took the bull by the horns and indicated we would not join the MBO. Instead, we set ourselves the task of wooing Cognis alone, and on our own terms.

By mid-October, Tony Popper, Cognis's managing director in Australia, informed us that he had no interest in our overtures. At that time, I remembered that when buying our first home and when obtaining my first employment, I had in both cases achieved success only by working through the top man of the respective organizations. Tony Popper was the Australian head, but he was answerable to the head office in Germany, which was overseen by venture capitalists who were seemingly driven by the accumulation of money. They were selling assets as if there was no tomorrow, and, apart from Coolaroo, there were complete factories for sale in South Africa, the United States, and Europe. From a distance, Coolaroo was looking more and more like a sweet honeypot. In an effort to overcome the impasse in the Australian office, I wanted to prove what could be achieved with the catchwords "Take me to your leader,"[11] and if that meant going to Germany, then to Germany we would go. After some heart searching among the Breakfast Club as to whether this might offend Tony, we agreed that we had nothing to lose but to bypass Cognis Australia and see what we could achieve with the European head office. At that point, I emailed my few European connections to see whether they knew anyone in the upper echelons of Cognis. The only one to reply was Joor de Bruyn, whom I had only met once for coffee at the Dordrecht railway station on our way from Amsterdam to Brussels. I had been sooled onto him a few years previously by Geert de Boer, my previous Unichema managing director. Joor was a networker par excellence, who knew the oleochemical world and its people like the back of his hand. He had worked in the upper levels of Unichema and indeed was intimately involved in the selling of the Unichema company to the English-owned ICI. It may have been the only reply, but he was able to take us right to the top, as he was a personal friend of Antonio Trius, the leader of Cognis's ruling triumvirate. We could go no higher, and we would win there or not at all. It was time for a trip to Germany.

A Meeting of Minds

On Thursday, November 21, 2002, I left Melbourne, bound for Frankfurt via Singapore. This route became a well-worn track in the years that followed. On arrival on Tuesday, November 26, I caught the 12:04 afternoon train to Dusseldorf, staying at the Courtyard Hafen Marriott. That afternoon, Joor arrived at the hotel, and we laid our plans. The next day, Joor and I had two hours with Dr Alfred Meffert, Cognis's worldwide production manager. It was a friendly meeting, though no real outcomes came from it. They were keeping their cards close to their chest. I flew on to the United States the next week, for business, and arrived home to Judy and the family on Monday, December 9. A full review of Australian operations by the Cognis International Board was to be held on December 11, and the next day a business plan was hatched. The year finished with the receipt of the last ethyl oleate manufactured for us at Coolaroo. The factory was then closed and mothballed, and the EPA licence handed back to the authorities—something that was to return to dog us three years later.

The year 2003 began with our hearts set towards buying Coolaroo; indeed, it had become a real hunger. In late January, we received a letter from Cognis Deutschland, forwarding "some more information about our location in Coolaroo." A CD-ROM containing a description of the hardware and plant drawings was enclosed. The letter finished, "Hopefully, this information will enable you to provide a non-binding bid." The positive note sounded by the correspondence indicated that the sale was a goer, but we later learnt how little we knew! Our hopeful offer was presented to the Australian office of Cognis on February 1. What we learnt much later was that the Australian and head office parts of Cognis were living in different worlds.

The Cognis German head office protocol was that it did not second-guess or override the actions of their country managers in their respective countries of production and sales. Thus, it was expected they should follow Tony Popper's advice concerning what would be best for Cognis in the Australian setting. We later learnt that Tony strongly argued why it was not in Cognis's best interest to sell Coolaroo. The main cogent reason was that Cognis was still planning to sell products in Australia by importing their needs from their overseas production units. We would be a locally manufactured competitor from their previously owned plant. The apocryphal story was that they would rather have the plant lay idle in mothballs than have another company using it and running in competition.

However, the venture capitalists based in the Dusseldorf head office continued to push for capital and the need to turn their realizable assets into real money. This meant that pressure fell again on the team charged with maximizing asset sales throughout the world. In this team was a Mrs Antje Scaglione, and we heard through the grapevine that this lady, whom we had never met, was pushing our case with the simple statement, "Maybe we should reconsider the possible sale of Coolaroo." Whilst we had maintained contact with the Dusseldorf office, the word came from Australia that one of the leading men of the triumvirate, Helmut Heymann, would be visiting Melbourne at the end of a round-Asian tour of Cognis's offices. We would be given one hour to present our case to him for the purchase of Coolaroo.

With this once-in-a-lifetime opportunity, it was agreed to cover Joor's return air fares to Melbourne from Amsterdam so that he could participate in the negotiations, knowing how the European business culture worked. It was much appreciated that Joor was prepared to fly economy class. Some of Vicchem's management team queried the wisdom of bringing him out to Melbourne, but, in my mind, it provided a person on our team who understood the European mindset.

Joor de Bruyn

As mentioned earlier, Joor had been embroiled in the billion-dollar sale of Unichema to ICI several years prior and was experienced in such negotiations; but, above all, it signalled to Cognis that we were serious. It may well be that you might sometimes use a sprat to catch a mackerel, but when important matters are involved, never send a boy to do a man's job. We needed a big hitter on our team to help us get the winning home run, and Joor was the man to do it. Helmut knew that Joor knew Antonio Trius. We would have to pay a few thousand dollars for the plane fare, but this was relatively minuscule to the few millions we were going to outlay for the purchase. The decision to bring him was a no-brainer.

The different managerial and cultural worlds within Cognis were continuing down their own tracks. Cognis Australia never seemed to move quickly. On March 27, after nearly two months had passed since our offer, Tony finally informed us that our offer had been rejected and that Cognis Australia would not be proceeding with any sale. Helmut from the head office was, however, already working his way across Japan. On the day after Joor arrived in Melbourne, Vicchem's management team met to discuss strategy. This think tank had started months earlier, consisting of myself, son Andrew, Peter Wrigley (our general manager), Graeme Voigt for financial and business experience, Ian McCubbin (our company's legal mind as well as a provider of further business experience), and Chris Thomas (our bank manager, who helped put together our bank proposals; not surprisingly, these proposals were always approved). We like catchy titles, and as we met traditionally at 7:30 a.m., close to the factory at the Richmond Rydges Hotel, the title of our group quickly became the Breakfast Club. In the same spirit of catchiness, one of the drinks served at our working lunch times was Passiona, a yellow-coloured drink based on the purple edible fruit called the passion fruit. Thirty-plus years later, banker Chris likes to talk about it to this day. The morning of the meeting with Helmut, the Breakfast Club dutifully met to ensure that everything, as much as possible, was in place.

Helmut and Tony reached our factory at 11:55 a.m. After the sale, Helmut reminisced in private conversation that he had never seen anyone drive as slowly as Tony did from the airport to Richmond. Helmut remembered that during the journey Tony never made disparaging comments about me but only expressed kind words. There was nothing personal in his decision not to sell the Coolaroo site; it only revolved around the future place of the manufacture of Cognis products. After their arrival and sociable greetings, Helmut was taken on a tour of our factory. On the walk around, it was not hard to perceive that he had a good sense of humour, and there was a twinkle in his eye. Yes, I had been warned not to let loose a volley of jokes, but it is hard to keep an old comic in control. During the factory inspection, I threw out the bait that it wasn't really me who was in charge of the company—the real manager was my wife, Judy! Helmut rose as a fish from the water, saying, "We in Germany have the story of the husband under the kitchen table, and his frau says, 'Get out from under that table.' He replies, 'I'm not getting out, and let people know that you are in control!'" It may not have been the best joke I have ever heard, but we both laughed. For the remainder of the factory tour, we told joke for joke to each other, and got on like a house on fire.

Helmut Heymann

It was obvious there were disconnects within the Cognis team itself, and without doubt there were also some cultural misunderstandings at play between us, the Vicchem leadership, and the very European Helmut. However, Helmut had come from Germany wanting the money from the sale of the Coolaroo property to meet the demands of the venture capitalists back in Düsseldorf, and did not anticipate going back empty-handed. During the discussions that took place over our sandwich lunch, a classic conversation ensued that would forever change our fortune and the fortunes of the Victorian Chemical Company.

> HELMUT: I don't see why we can't sell to Bob, do you, Tony?
> TONY: (Long hesitation) No, I don't see why we can't, Helmut.
> HELMUT: How long would it take to arrange, Tony?
> TONY: (Long hesitation) Three months, Helmut.
> HELMUT: That seems a long time, Tony.
> TONY: No, no … no! It will take that long.

It was clear that Helmut wanted the sale but did not want to ride roughshod over his Australian manager. After forty years of service and within twelve months of retirement, Tony was well established in the way the company worked. Whilst his opinion would be considered, he also knew he couldn't beat the European city hall. Thus, an agreement in spirit was reached between Helmut and me, and we both knew that we were going to make it happen.

Tony had got his three months to revert with a proposal, and when he did, it was annoyingly only for half the site—it did take another year and three quarters to reach the day of settlement for the whole site. It then took another year to resolve difficult-to-obtain regulatory approvals, particularly with the Environmental Protection Authority. On January 1, 2006, the Coolaroo plant was once again fully operational—and under our control. Twenty months later, we sold the Richmond property, after full site remediation. (The latter activities are told in chapter 11.) It was with a great deal of relief that the Victorian Chemical Company took control not only of the Coolaroo plant but also of our own destiny. We can only express great thankfulness to God, and to all those who helped us on the continuing journey.

And for those desperate to know
> **—our soufflé did rise twice.**

2 To Buy a Wasted Gold Mine

There is a tide in the affairs of men which, taken
at the flood, leads on to fortune ...
... And we must take the current when it serves, or lose our ventures.[1]

We have always believed that God has been weaving His will through the fabric of our family life. In the realm of business, the *pièce de résistance* has to be the enabling us to buy the Victorian Chemical Company at the right time, at the right place, and at a price that was right. What a delightfully intricate thing life is!

The beginning of that story was in 1971, when we were providentially moved to Melbourne from Sydney. Without us knowing we needed to go and without us ever wanting to, Melbourne became God's place for us. This in itself was an interesting exercise in that it occurred during our second posting to the UK, when my English boss and I failed to see eye to eye. It was a traumatic experience which lasted eighteen months. He did not like colonials, and he considered himself a wine connoisseur. The problems began when he discovered that I did not drink alcohol. Mum and Dad had introduced me in my mid-teens to handling alcoholic drinks through what we called shandies (mixtures of beer and lemonade) or weak mint juleps (blends of spirits, water, and mint). Judy's initiation was through shandies. But that was that, and from our late teens, alcoholic drinks have been alien to both of us. In the Australian vernacular, we are teetotallers. The boss liked to go into long discussions on the merits of a particular wine. But my failure to participate seemed like a slight to him. I have claimed over the years that my non-drinking of alcohol has never affected the successes in my business life. My English boss was the one exception that proves the rule;[2] however, this failure did get us to Melbourne, and that was a good thing.

Robert W. Killick, PhD

Learning to Write English at Age Thirty-One

The key problem at work was the publication of a fortnightly newsletter in which I reported all that was happening in Unilever's Industrial Detergent world. As discussed later (see chapter 5), I had to have coaching in English to obtain my leaving certificate to go to university. Despite being better technically educated than my boss, English was the stumbling point. I cannot remember one paragraph that he did not see necessary to critique and correct. He was pedantic in the extreme. For example, if I started a sentence with "In contrast to ...," it would be returned to me, heavily crossed out and with a replacement inserted: "By contrast with ... ." My immediate boss, Hans, took it upon himself to become my mentor to improve my written expression. It was most appreciated that a Netherlander was teaching English to an Australian. My fortnightly examiner hovered above the whole process. The most positive aspect of this traumatic saga was that by the time we returned to Australia, I knew how to play with words and write English. Not appreciated then, but this was to become an invaluable asset to me personally, and to Vicchem when, for example, I was preparing proposals for the bank. A trivial example of wordplay was the composition of a poem on a recent cruise. The family was more than bemused that the poem was placed second. (For the record, it is in the notes section[3].)

The posting was to have been for two years, after which I was to return home to Sydney, to the position of General Manager, Industrial Detergents, a Division of Unilever, the total company being one of the world's largest marketing multinationals. But that was not going to happen; we were on our way back after eighteen months. (The machinations on whether I would have a continuing job at all are discussed in the "Move to Melbourne" section in chapter 7.) Suffice to say that the Managing Director of Unichema, Unilever's Chemical Division, said he would take me on to see if I could fit into the role of the Technical Service and Development Manager, as the current incumbent planned on retiring within the year. The problem was the position was in Melbourne, and when I told Judy we were going south, it was the only time that I ever saw her shed a tear during our marriage. She had been so looking forward to being back in Sydney, with our families all together with the grandchildren. We can, however, both look back and praise God for pulling us, ever reluctantly, out of Manly and its beautiful beaches, to the colder climate of Melbourne.

The next step in the process was eight years later, when I had to be shaken out of Unilever itself. I am not easily shaken—"limpet" could be my middle name, whether in my job, in our marriage, or in the church. The operation started on Friday, December 7, 1979, when, after seventeen and a half years and two overseas postings with Unilever, my managing director, Geert de Boer, told me that I had no future in Unichema. His reason was that I had become a blocker, having sat eight years in my role as Technical Services and Development Manager. He tried to help find a new outside placement, but almost four months later, without a job in hand, I finally said goodbye to Unilever on Wednesday, March 26, 1980. *Sic transit gloria mundi*—"Thus passes the glory of the world."[4]

I went into overdrive hunting for a job. On April 9, 1980, I had my first interview with the managing director of Michaelis Bayley. I was appointed and finally commenced work six weeks later, on Monday, May 26, as Corporate Development Manager. It was, however, only to last for eighteen months; nevertheless, it was another of the Lord's necessary appointments, as Victorian Chemicals was not ready to be acquired. The Michaelis Bayley Company was sick, and the expectations were for me to somehow pull it all together operationally. In reality, it was already passed the tipping point. It was a season when corporate raiders bought undervalued companies, broke them up into their respective parts, and sold the various assets at a profit. Michaelis Bayley had been saved in a previous raid with four so-called white knights taking over 80 per cent of the ownership. This worked well until the white knights[5] decided they would take full ownership. The role of corporate development in the head office was of no interest when these shenanigans commenced. However, on account of the earlier manager's abrupt departure, I was able to transfer over to one of the subsidiaries, Australian Hostess Industries, as operations manager. This was another moment of change for me. Michaelis Bayley was an interesting personal interlude of watching the machinations of business acquisitions, mergers, and takeovers of companies. I learnt the lesson that—if possible—it was best not to become beholden financially to business or banking third parties who were running their own agendas. This was further backup to Judy's belief of the dangers of becoming involved in partnerships outside our own ilk.

A few months later, as part of building its defences, the directors decided to combine Australian Hostess Industries with their Fowlers-Vacola Bottling Division. The more critical decision was to sack the Hostess management team, where I was working, and keep the Fowlers-Vacola management to run the combined operation. My tenure was extended for a few brief months longer than the other Hostess managers, as I was required to fill in for their existing manager, who resigned in search of a better appointment. This was all in the Lord's timing.

The Victorian Chemical Company (Vicchem)

Recognizing I would be released in a few weeks, I began the search for a new job through the standard employment agencies and the *Saturday Age*'s work advertisements. Over the period from October 1981 to February 1982, Judy typed 132 job applications. Out of all of these applications, I made the short list only three or four times. I was never offered a position. I did, however, paint the outside of our house while Judy went back to teaching on a casual basis, to provide cash flow.

To return to teaching even on a casual basis, Judy had to undertake a ten-day refresher course over the three weeks from February 23 to March 12, 1982. Her first working day was at Clayton North Primary School, where she was thrown in at the deep end of grade 6. Judy stands a petite 5 feet, 2 inches (157.5 centimetres). We have always claimed that the 1925 song "Five Foot Two" [6]was a foretaste of Judy, the little lady who was to come. It epitomizes Judy to a tee and has been included in almost every concert we have run:

> Five foot two, eyes of blue
> But oh! What those five foot could do
> Has anybody seen my girl?
>
> But could she love, could she woo
> Could she, could she, could she coo
> Has anybody seen my girl?

Now, some of the schoolboys were taller than she was. One was really obstreperous, and Judy told him to go to the headmaster. She then saw him walking towards the exit gate. She rushed to the headmaster and told him. When she got home, Andrew queried, "How was your day, Mum?" The shattered reply was "It was terrible!" As a gallant son, he responded, "That's good, Mum; the rest can't get any worse." Thankfully, they did not.

I was continually running lists of possible companies through my mind, in my search for suitable employment. In November 1982, I remembered the Victorian Chemical Company, which I had visited only once in my early eight years at Unichema. By contrast with almost all the rest of the possible jobs, it was the nearest to my oleochemical field of knowledge. For those with some chemical background, Victorian Chemicals used to take oleic acid from Unichema, sulphonate it in the presence of naphthalene, and sell the newly produced Twitchell Reagent back to Unichema. This was a crude but adequate emulsifier which was used in their fat-splitting operation. The Twitchell Reagent was no longer required in the late 1970s, after Unichema moved to high pressure splitting, which did not require any emulsification. I had not visited Victorian Chemicals after that time. As I look back over fifty years, blind chance does not statistically provide answers for the directional flow of my life. For us, we see the hand of God, not as a voice but as an inner witness guiding us in kindly ways to achieve what is best for us. The shepherd's Psalm puts it so succinctly: "Surely goodness and love will follow me all the days of my life."[7] At that time, I was being led to follow, and follow we did, by chasing every rabbit down every burrow.

In order to learn more about Victorian Chemicals before making any contact, I acquired the microfiche from corporate affairs, showing the details of the company's shareholders, directors, and creditors. The only place to read a microfiche was at our local library, and with a lingering respect for librarians, I awaited the hand on my shoulder to be politely asked, "Sir, what are you reading on our microfiche unit?" It was my first time reading company documentation, but I suddenly saw that a Ken Knight of Birralee Street had been interim company secretary of Victorian Chemicals for about six months, during 1967 and 1968. *That guy lives in our street,* I thought to myself. I sort of knew him and his wife, Elinor. We had had our first supper with them back in late October 1971, at a neighbour's house, as we were settling into the local community. Elinor had often helped Judy over the years with Bible study mornings in our home.

Ken Knight

Always believing in moving fast when you can, I went up the street that night to meet with Ken. Interestingly, this date was not recorded in my diary, but it would have been in the late-October to late-November period of 1981. After exchanging pleasantries, there came another of those life-changing conversations that have played a key part in our lives:

> BOB: Ken, is there any chance of getting a job at Vicchem?
> KEN: The way Vicchem is travelling at the moment, Bob, I wouldn't put my worst enemy in there, let alone a neighbour!
> BOB: Would Vicchem be for sale?

Reflecting on that moment of banter later, I was reminded that God once spoke to an erring prophet through the mouth of an actual ass.[8] Obviously, He had not changed His method of communicating even in 1981, choosing my wry sense of humour to open doors. I had never thought through the implications of the question. I had never run a company; at the most, I had supervised a few people in a development department. Judy and I had no serious finance available to us, and, anyway, why would someone loan money to an eccentric scientist who would be unemployed within weeks? It might have been a question from an ass, but there was no need to worry. Ken replied, "Over the years, we have had enquiries, but the company is not for sale." With more pleasantries, the night was over. But the seed had been sown in his mind.

I was finally sacked from Australian Hostess Industries on Friday, December 11, 1981. The next months, spent among the unemployed, were of modified interest, to say the least. On December 13, we drove to Adelaide to spend a few weeks with our daughter, Jenni, for her twenty-first birthday, and to stay on for Christmas. After arriving home, I tried to apply for social benefits, but CentreLink was closed for the Christmas holidays. We drove to Sydney for the summer holidays, and our journey took us to the usual watering holes, including South Steyne, Queenscliff, and Aunty Roxie and Uncle Bill Inder's house on Whale Beach. While there, I continued to look for work in between swims at the beach, as my diary notes: January 20, RK application letters." I applied for social benefits after our return to Melbourne, on Tuesday, January 26, 1982. Their agent was a charming lady, very sympathetic in looking after this middle-class applicant who had come upon hard times. I was granted the dole, although Judy did not consider we should take it. My debating points of having paid our taxes over the years and that we wouldn't have been granted it if we were not within the guidelines did not cut any ice with her. I think the payments lasted for two to three months, but definitely finished in April when I started working on a paid project with the Baptist Union of Victoria. Neither of us can remember the amount we were actually paid.

On January 27, another six job applications were posted at the post office. This may sound exciting, but filling applications does not leave one with a sense of fulfilment or fill out the day. It doesn't work well for my temperament. Some suggest I am a workaholic, but I will only concede I'm a modified workaholic. The best suggestion was to do something—anything—to keep me occupied. So I set to painting the outside of our white brick house. We likened it to the American President's White House, replying to enquiries after our well-being, "The president is well, and the husband isn't bad either." On Tuesday, February 2, my diary laconically records, "Start garage"; and then on Wednesday, February 3, "Paint fascia boards."

I have always appreciated the cliché "Meanwhile, back at the ranch."[9] It is a great reminder for me not to think that I have everything under control. At all times, there are many people working in many other settings who make decisions which will impact me, for better or for worse. So, back at the Vicchem ranch in the first half of March 1982, the directors of Vicchem decided to put the company up for sale, and the letter of offer would be issued on April 1, 1982. We heard this through a surprise phone call from Ken Knight. It was now four months since I had visited Ken at his home and enquired whether Vicchem might be for sale. In the meantime, Ken and I had met socially, but nothing was ever said about the company. In my own mind, I had certainly discounted Vicchem as a job opportunity, let alone a purchase. Writers of fictional romance and tellers of religious conversion testimonies like to tell of "the day that changed my life."[10] The day Ken called me on the phone to say Vicchem was for sale was truly a life-changer for me. I also like the quirkiness of life and the fact that the letter of offer was dated April 1, 1982: April Fool's Day. Surely, God has a sense of humour!

Vicchem for sale

Intermission

But then, everything went strangely quiet. During the next five months, we seemed to take two steps forwards and three backwards. There was, as it were, a clearing of the decks, getting rid of the old to make room for the new. In my naivety, I had anticipated the negotiations would be all over in a month or two, but we finally bought the company just short of one year later, on March 18, 1983. This was to be a serious learning period which made sure I understood patience and persistence. In early April, we received the letter of offer, and promptly replied, expressing our interest in buying Vicchem. But then … silence!

April was a desultory month, when our lives seemed to be waiting, waiting. We were fretting over the lack of communication from the Vicchem directors. I now realize that I had the taste in my mouth to win the deal. There was also continuing frustration in my search for a job, should the Vicchem deal collapse. The push to finish painting the house also continued and this did finally end on Friday, April 23, with this terse comment in my diary: "Touched up white walls." Thereafter, no mention of house painting appears. Christian friends had become increasingly concerned about us, as the months drifted on, with no certainty of a job. They organized a paid position with the Baptist Union of Victoria, for several weeks, carrying out market research. The question I was to investigate was whether there was any future for locally produced Sunday school materials. The simple answer was no. The Sunday school movement, as we had known it for a hundred years, was fading. Its last hurrah was the American All-Age Sunday School, which did well in the American environment, but never took root in Australian soil. However, there are parents who still want their children taught the basis of the faith, and whilst the name of Sunday school has disappeared, the Syndal Church still maintains its emphasis on teaching the substance of Christian truth, albeit under different names, such as the Cubby, the Teepee, the Treehouse, the Tribe, and the Lounge.

We pushed on with the job search, to the end of May. Companies that gave me an interview were as follows, in alphabetical order: ACW, Aerosol Industries, ALCOA, APASCO, Boyden, Gibson Chemicals, Hunter Douglas, MEECO, Nicholas, Nylex, Poly Pacific, SACS, Triton Paints, UCB, Unichema, and W. R. Grace. There are many more than I remember or would have believed! The next Vicchem contact was on

May 3, when their accountants, Deloitte, presented us with the balance sheet containing all the wonderful points of value of the company. A sarcastic comment for thirty years later: there were only two valuable points to remember. The first was the Ee-muls-oyle trade mark, for which we paid $15,000.00 (this is further discussed in chapter 8). The second was the land, valued at $170,000.00, which, twenty-five years later, was worth in the low millions of dollars. Graeme Voigt, who had been doing our yearly tax work and had been our church's treasurer, joined us as our financial advisor. At the cup-of-coffee review meeting after the Deloitte's presentation, Graeme stressed, "All they have done is to put a wallet on the table, but we don't know if there is anything inside!"

The one month's delay in hearing from Vicchem's directors should have been seen as a sign of the drawn-out negotiations that were to follow. On August 27, 1933, Vicchem was birthed, with five founding directors, by the NSW-based Crown Chemical Company. There were some interesting characters among them. One of them had a photo of a meeting of the combined boards of the Crown Chemical and Victorian Chemical Companies, around 1937. When each of his fellow directors died over the following years, he would put a mark on the man's forehead in the photo. This photo had become an heirloom to be displayed to all and sundry. Someone later whitened out the marks. On our purchase of the company, it was handed down to us as an heirloom of ownership.

Vicchem & Crown Chemicals Board

The Vicchem directors' choice of the Richmond site was determined by its central location to the Melbourne CBD and the port facilities. These were important factors seventy years later, when it came time for us to sell the property to enable us to relocate our manufacturing facility. The strength of Crown Chemical Company, the founders of Vicchem, was its oleochemical products sold into the textile and tanning markets. They had set up camp in the industrial eastern hub of Richmond, one of Melbourne's inner-city suburbs. The factory was two streets back from the Yarra River, but thirteen tannery factories to which Vicchem could deliver its products by forklift ran along the river edge. The 1930s were the days when river water was used more than viewed. To the west lay Collingwood and Abbotsford, in the hub of Melbourne's clothing industry. The site itself was surrounded by housing to the south, metal manufacture to the west, steel product manufacture by Vickers Ruwolt to the north, and Hadaway, the steel forgers, to the east. Immediately further to the north were other major metal manufacturers, such as Ajax Fasteners. By the time we bought Vicchem, all manufacturing had departed, except for Hadaways, whose site was used by television production units for shows, such as *The Sullivans,* when they needed a factory scene set in the 1930s. It finally disappeared around 1995, to become three boutique warehouses.

The major stumbling block for a smooth sale lay in the proliferation of shareholders over the fifty years of Vicchem's existence. By 1982, the share ownership had twenty-three disparate shareholders, including widows, children, grandchildren, and trusts. The last of the founding directors died in 1980, and this marked the end of what had always seemed to have been a fragile consensus. Divisions among directors came first from the long-standing inter-city rivalry between Sydney and Melbourne, quaint though it may sound to those who have not lived in either city, particularly during that time period. The second was religious, between two families, one Catholic and the other Protestant. There was the problem of wealth concentrated in the hands of a few families, such as one director's family owning its own yacht on Sydney Harbour and on which some directors' meetings were held.

The directors struggled to obtain consensus at any time, and this showed up as a lack of decisiveness, which thence resulted in a year of tense negotiation. They had struggled long to decide whether or not to sell the company. The straw that finally broke that camel's back was the rapid approach of yet another year of losses. The company had been bleeding losses for some years, which meant cash pouring into the proverbial black hole, and none of the shareholders were prepared to invest any of their own money. The company coffers were empty.

Everything was empty

The directors elected not to sell on the open market, since it would have meant letting all and sundry know that their enterprise was sinking. They thus made direct approaches to BASF, Ciba-Geigy, Croda Chemicals, ICI, and Sandoz, with a view to sell. They also approached us, but only because Ken Knight argued that they should do so. The other contenders slowly fell away for a variety of reasons. The classic excuse summarized by one of the companies was "I already have one pile of junk, why do I want another one?" Never were truer words spoken. But, as they say in Yorkshire, where mining is a profitable activity, "Where there's muck, there's brass."[11] Not only was I small fry, compared to the multinational companies, I was a nothing. I was just an unemployed person receiving social benefits from the public purse. The only reason we were kept in the process was through the continuous support of Ken Knight.

Nearly another month later, on May 25, our accountant, Graeme, and I were given a full factory inspection of the Richmond site. It was a greasy mess! The steps were slippery with embedded oil and grease;

there was a sense of chaos and grime. It was obvious this factory was a cot-case. The next step was a meeting on August 9, with the Sydney contingent of the board. This was a critical meeting, as the Sydney contingent still considered itself as the power base that determined the company's future. This was rooted in history, since Vicchem had been spawned out of Sydney when three families were sent to Melbourne to set up an independent outpost of the Crown Chemical Company. The unwritten understanding was that the Sydney shareholders had to retain 51 per cent of the vote. This was highlighted during the appointment of a general manager in the 1960s who demanded five hundred shares to take the position. The board then issued another 522 shares to the Sydney cabal to maintain that 51 per cent line in the sand. When the general manager left in 1967, it was claimed the company "lost the only management talent who understood anything about costing." With all the inter-city rivalry, the most serious question that I was asked at the meeting was "Why should we sell to you, a Melbourne man?" We now look back in bemusement at the smallness of this question. The meeting was held in a room overlooking Sydney Harbour. I nodded to the north and said, "I was born and bred in Manly." I think they still considered me suspect because I had been living in Melbourne for twelve years. Philosophically and theologically, one can ponder that one's future can depend on a nonsense deal-breaker like your place of birth and current abode!

The Main Attraction

We continued to make all the right noises directly, while, in the background, Ken Knight continued to champion our family's cause. In the meantime, Judy had called our church to pray for us in order to break the deadlock. She said to one of her best friends, "If this doesn't work out, Marj, we may be living on your front lawn, in a tent!" After a further three months, with no interest expressed by the other third parties, it was agreed that I should go and work in the factory as general manager. This was to ensure that there could be no later argument that I was not fully informed about the status of the company and its financials. For a long time, the directors did not seem to want to discuss the price in detail. It was finally proposed that the price would be based simply on the assets less the liabilities. There would be no goodwill because there was no goodwill. On the figures that we had available to us, it appeared that the price would be something around the high $300,000.00s. But we simply did not have that sort of money. This was the first time I began looking for loans other than when we bought our own three homes which occurred when we got married, when we returned the first time from the UK, and when we came to Melbourne. It reminded me of the story about America's most famous Depression-era bank robber, William Sutton.[12] When asked why he robbed banks he observed, "Because that's where the money is!" The first bank we visited was the one that had given us our housing loan. I know how corny it sounded: "I'm an unemployed scientist who has recently been on the dole. Would you please lend me more money than I can imagine, to buy a company with a run-down factory? Oh, and by the way, I have neither run a company nor a factory in my life!" Well, stagger me, no, they wouldn't lend! Where is the spirit of Anzac when you need it?

Some people love them, some people loathe them, but in the business world, you certainly have to live with banks. Leaving aside any attempted jocular sarcasm, I have been very fortunate to have had a fruitful and enjoyable working relationship with our bank for more than fifty years. Our first bank experience was when we were looking for a loan to buy our first home. Mum and Dad had used the Commonwealth Bank, so we went there. They tripped up over their own rules and could not lend to us because I didn't have an existing account. They weren't willing to take Mum and Dad's several accounts into consideration. Dad was not happy, and the Commonwealth Bank was in the "bad books." Dad worked for the wholesaler S. Hoffnung & Co., and its senior management pointed him towards the company's main bank, the Commercial Banking Company of Sydney. With Hoffnung's backing, my father took me to meet the NSW manager, Dick Hindmarsh. We talked pleasantries, but not being a patient man, Dad burst out, "We've come to talk about a house loan for Bob!" To which Dick Hindmarsh simply replied, "That was a given, Mr Killick; it's just nice to have time to have a chat." We got the loan, and the rest is history; but I learnt the lesson that if you want anything done, you must deal with the people who have the authority to make decisions. As stated in chapter 1, "Take me to your leader."

Learn to Love Your Bank

In 1982, the Commercial Banking Company of Sydney was acquired by the National Bank of Australasia and became the National Australia Bank. So, when we arrived in Melbourne, uncertain of where we would live, we set up our account at NAB's Melbourne head office, in Collins Street. This accidental but providential choice became strategic when we began to seek financing for Vicchem's purchase, as the managers we were dealing with had higher lending limits. But, from 1971 to 1982, our life had been uneventful, and we were always ahead in the repayment of our loans. We had bought our Mount Waverley house, and it has been our "Castle"[13] for forty-six years. However, by 1980, our house's windowsills had well-established wood rot. I wrote a bouncy letter to the bank manager, whom I had not met, suggesting that I would be in need of up to $2,000.00, to replace the wooden sills with aluminium. I indicated my preference for the bank to extend the mortgage—and please don't even think about sending an application for a personal loan! The manager, Evan Tune, did the most sensible thing: he picked up the phone, and rang. The conversation was bouncy, we got to know each other, and the personal loan application turned up in the post. By the time I contacted him several years later about a loan to buy Vicchem, we were old buddies. There was still no capital to allow us to purchase the factory outright, but he was prepared to set up an $80,000.00 overdraft on two-thirds of the bank's valuation of the two units Judy owned at Dee Why, Sydney. These had been bought by realization of other property from Mum's estate.

A few years later, when our overdraft was sitting on $140,000.00 for months on end and the bank's credit department was demanding action, Evan stood behind us. "Bob will be all right," he assured his managers. (We don't think that Evan would have been able to get away with it these days, with the tightening of credit lines.) In the meantime, Judy continued to call our church to pray for us. On July 5, we approached Graham Byrnes, our contact director, with a general offer to purchase the net assets of Victorian Chemicals. The land was a key part of the total value of the deal, and a revaluation was undertaken on July 21, with a value of $176,000.00. Following a meeting of the Vicchem directors on August 9, we received the stupendous news that they were willing to sell the company to us. As businessmen always wanting to do a deal, it was incumbent on them that there had to be some final haggling over the price. By August 24, we had completed the fourth schedule, which allowed us, on July 26, to offer $14.80 per share. It is noteworthy that they had changed our offer from buying the net assets to buying the shares. This upped the risk for us in that we were not just buying the business; rather, by taking the shares, we were acquiring the company as a "job lot." This left us open to any hidden liabilities the company may have had, such as from the Australian Tax Office, any environmental problems at Richmond, or disgruntled farmers who wanted to sue for crop damage caused by our products. These thankfully never eventuated, but we did think about them.

In his haggling over the price, Vicchem's key negotiator claimed that our bid was low and that we had to improve our offer. We reverted on July 30, with an offer of $15.00 per share, a total $390,330.00. It was only a gross increase of $5,204.40, but he had saved face to go back to his board. This was accepted, and in principle, on August 31, we were the de facto owners of a chemical company. So we finally had acceptance, but that was where two real difficulties raised their ugly heads. The first was that we now needed to find the funding to pay for the loan to buy the company. The bank had gone strangely silent on our loan applications, so we began talking to anyone who might have money and who would talk with us. Once we held the acceptance of offer letter, dated August 31, in our hands, while we didn't have the money to consummate the deal, we proceeded as if we did own the company. On September 1, the Vicchem Management Committee was inaugurated. That week, we met with Peter and Andrea Wrigley to discuss whether Peter would be interested in joining the company after the sale was consummated. He was interested and joined our team in May 1983. He became our general manager in May 1992, and provided dedication and expertise.

Matters were now getting serious, and the legal advice was that, as we were to buy the company's shares, we should purchase through a trust. This would provide an element of a protective wall around us. To this end, the Killick Family Trust was set up in August 1982, with a company, Bob Killick & Associates Pty Ltd, as its trustee. In 1993, the latter entity changed names to Victorian Chemicals International Pty Ltd (VCI). The trust holds 98 per cent of the company's shares, with each of the five family members holding 0.4 per cent. Its role is to provide managing and technical services mainly but not limited to Vicchem.

Acting the Role

As managing director designate, I began meeting our customers, from the middle of September. I had appointments with BP, Shell, George Pitt, Fibremakers, Record Leather, and Comalco. The following week, there were meetings with Keys Development, Bill Waldie, BP, Dulux, and Avon Sheepskins. A fortnight later, I travelled to Sydney, to meet with Harrisons, Genkem, Harcros, Ciba-Geigy, Gordon Radford Industries, Sybron Gamlin, Revlon, Paykel, Castrol, Metal Manufacturers, Surfactant Services, Colgate, and two individuals Brian

Cartwright (a friend from Lever & Kitchen days) and Mike Corlet (an agent for several companies). In early October, we had our first meeting with Ron Gordon, who was an old-school union representative. His mantra was "if one non-union person touches one button in the factory, then a strike will be called."

The money hunt continued unabated. On Saturday, September 18, 1983, I spent all day working on a finance proposal. This was obviously not all that "crash hot," for we had no success with Getty Finance, the Commonwealth Development Corporation, private financiers, the Chase MB Bank, and the Australian Development Corporation. There were ever the problems that I was unemployed and buying junk. As the day of settlement drew nearer, the Vicchem board agreed that the purchase price could be split as follows: $208,176.00, to be paid on the day of settlement, and then two equal instalments of $91,077.00 on the first and second years following. The interest rate on these loans was to be 15 per cent. This may seem inordinately high, but ninety-day commercial bills had peaked on March 1, 1983, at 17.62 per cent. On the day of settlement, March 18, the rate was 14.28 per cent.

Given the levels of interest we were paying in those days, I find it particularly quaint that as I write this paragraph in May 2016, there is continuing pressure from economists and the media that the Reserve Bank of Australia should reduce interest rates to stimulate Australia's economy. The current interest rate on ninety-day bank bills is 1.75 per cent, and on August 3, 2016, it was reduced to 1.5 per cent.

So, what assets did we have available? We were paying off our home, but this was not going to give us anything exciting. There were, however, two low-value units at Dee Why, one of the beach suburbs north of Manly. We purchased them in 1964 for £4,500.00 and £4,000.00, respectively, from what Mum had left us in her estate. When Australia's currency decimalized, these became worth $9,000.00 and $8,000.00, respectively. Twenty years, later the bank's combined valuation for the two units was $120,000.00, from which the NAB would provide a bank overdraft facility of $80,000.00. We had no other assets with which to buy the company. We simply had to wait to see if someone would loan us money for the purchase and then hope we could trade our way into existence.

With a few weeks to go, there came our female knight in shining armour. Sandra McCubbin was a lawyer and the wife of our solicitor/legal advisor, Ian. Sandra made contact, having heard of our problem over dinner talk. She said it would be worthwhile to contact her boss, David Geer, a partner of Herbert, Geer & Rundle (HGR). For the next two years, David became our banker, with solicitors' trust money. Ian was annoyed that he hadn't thought of this possibility earlier. David would jog to and from his Hawthorn home to his city office and would pass the factory to confirm that everything was going to plan. Our own solicitor, Ian, who knew David, stressed that there would be no trouble as long as we paid our interest on time at the end of each quarter. "Bob, he will have no hesitation to sell you up if you aren't on time," Ian told me. We kept to the arrangement. We were to borrow $160,000.00 from HGR at the then-acceptable going interest rate of 15 per cent.

Control of the Board

The next big problem we faced was whether Vicchem's board would ever reach a consensus from their shareholders for the sale of the company. The various family shareholders had their own agendas, and there was subsequently much division and dissonance among the board. If there were to be a sale, it was necessary for consensus among the board. As soon as they agreed to proceed, one particular family would pull out at the last minute. The frustrations came to a head around the meeting proposed for November 5, 1982. Everyone was in agreement that the sale should proceed, all our monies were in place, and my appointment diary for November 11 read, "All systems go."[14]

The high jinks climaxed when, once again, just before the November meeting, the same particular family was advised, from the brother-in-law who was the most astute in the family, "not to sell the land to Bob, but to let him lease it." They pulled out, and the consensus was lost. Interestingly, our ownership of the land was one of the keys to our later long-term survival, and thereafter to our future company's prosperity. Fortunately, holding on to the land was not what the rest of the directors wanted. They wanted out, preferring the money rather than the obligations that go hand in hand with owning land—especially industrial land. My diary note at the end of November simply read, "Things still messy with Sydney." Realizing they were not getting a unanimous requirement—nor would they ever—the frustrated majority obtained fresh legal advice that if a private company had sixteen or fewer shareholders, they could proceed with a majority, not a unanimous vote. They therefore set out to combine the number of shares within their families to obtain a majority. Ultimately, the family which had always seemed to disagree, recognized that the others were serious, and an in-house revolt was under way. They could see they would be left as minority shareholders among the Killick family shareholding. They realized that if they stayed, they would have no say in the running of the company and no guarantee of the future value of their shares. They finally agreed to sell, with no ability to revoke their decision. So, there was a flurry of appointments with the finance providers, and the legal gentry were certainly ready to have their pound of flesh. My diary records twenty-two legal appointments over the last six months of 1982; plus, a multitude of long and short phone calls.

The Last Flurry, or How to Buy a Company for $15,676.00 Cash

Although this may sound trite, the main thing I learnt on buying a chemical company was that it was just not the same as going to the local Woolworth's store to buy a litre of milk. Trite but true. With the milk, there were only two of us involved, but in our purchase of Vicchem, there were ten entities involved, each of which wanted its own opinions vented at some time, and, for some, at several times. There were Judy and I; Ian McCubbin, our lawyer; Graeme Voigt, our financial advisor, the Victorian Chemical International Company as trustee of the Killick Family Trust; the estate of my late mother; the NAB; the solicitor providing his solicitor's funds; the Victorian Chemical Company; the twenty-three vendor shareholders; and two or three solicitors to cover their interests. The day had to proceed in tight order:

- For weeks, our bank had been primed, ready to go, and at 9:30 a.m., on Friday, March 18, 1983, I collected a bank cheque made out to the vendors' solicitors, Maddock, Lonie, and Chisholm, for $150,000.00, as a short-term loan to me. The second bank cheque was for $42,500.00, which was the fund from my mother's estate, on which Dad was to receive the interest for the rest of his life, whilst I was the remainderman when he died. The third bank cheque was for $15,676.00, and represented our entire family cash wealth that Judy and I had saved, including what had been given me on leaving Unilever. With Graeme Voigt in tow, we went to the solicitors' office. We loaned this money to the Killick Family Trust, which was going to buy the Vicchem's shares.

- At 10:00 a.m., we gathered at the vendors' solicitors' office, and I put the cheques totalling $208,176.00 on the table. The original plan had been that the Killick Family Trust would purchase all the shares, but the purchase would be payable in three steps: half the value on the day of settlement ($195,165.00), a quarter ($97,582.50) a year later, and the last quarter a year after that. Because among the twenty-three shareholders some allotments were small, it was later agreed that these few would be paid in full on the day of settlement. This meant that the first outlay came to the tabled $208,176.00, and the remaining quarters would be $91,077.00 each, carrying an interest rate of 15 per cent.

- I remember some kerfuffle among the vendor's solicitors on whether some of their powers of attorney were in order, but peace settled, and the vendors' solicitors settled into filling out the transfers of share certificates.

- After midday, and with the share certificates and minute books in hand, we went to one of Ian's spare visitors' offices. Once ensconced, Judy and I, as directors of VCI and thus in control of the trust which was the owner of Vicchem, elected Bob, Judy, Jenni, and Andrew to form the new Vicchem board. Peter was elected to the board in 1992. The newly elected Vicchem board held an immediate meeting to ratify all the corporate matters needing attention.

- It was agreed that Vicchem would borrow $160,000.00 from HGR, using the Appleton Street property as first mortgage.

- It was then further agreed that Vicchem would use these funds to purchase the dossier of intellectual property which I had accumulated over the previous years, covering technical, marketing, and general expertise in the oleochemical world. During the ensuing years, this proved of immense value to bring Vicchem up to scratch and make it the successful business it became.

- With a $150,000.00 cheque in hand, we returned to the bank, and I repaid the short-term six-hour loan.

From a historical perspective, our $15,676.00 cash was a low outlay to pay for what has become a successful oleochemical company. But very few thought we were going to be successful, and looking at the photos of the plant, beauty ever remains in the eye of the beholder. However, our Lord could tick the boxes: He had moved us to Melbourne, He had extricated me from Unilever, and He had organized us to buy Victorian Chemicals.

Is "that" a factory?

And this is the moment when I would like to wax lyrical, for it had come to pass that by the night of March 18, 1983, the Killick family had ownership of the Victorian Chemical Company.

**"For better for worse, for richer for poorer,
in sickness and in health."**[15]

3   In the Tailing Dumps

Beauty is in the eye of the beholder.[1]

On March 18, 1983, our ugly duckling was hatched, but not one of us believed it would turn into something swan-like and beautiful. I think we were just pragmatic and would simply have been pleased if it became a going concern—albeit much cleaner than when we had first seen it. We had often been described as the company that had "one foot in the grave, the other on a banana skin." So now that we had a factory that matched our company profile, it was up to us to make our chemical site work as efficiently as possible. The ultimate test was simple: would Vicchem's assets outweigh its liabilities on a balance sheet? I have continued to have a love-hate relationship with our company's balance sheets. Although they are simple on the surface, they are complex in practice because so much seems to depend on how we define its various parts.

For those who have run their own businesses, there is one balance-sheet element that stirs the heart: stock. I cannot remember a time when I was discussing the business with Dad or Uncle Bill and no matter how good the sales or profits may be, they only had one question: "What are your stock levels?" The one exception to this rule was when we had bought the company just one week after Bob Hawke and the Labour Party had swept to power in Canberra, replacing the pro-business Liberal Party for the next thirteen years. Dad and Uncle Bill both continued to express their concerns for several weeks, but there was no going back.

Victorian Chemicals was small enough that no policy changes made by any government, either Labour or Liberal, would impinge on our survival. The closest we ever got to Bob Hawke was that we slept with him and Blanche D'Alpuget. Admittedly, it was at thirty thousand feet, flying over the Indian Ocean on our way to South Africa from Perth. At 3:00 a.m., on our way to the toilets, Hawke and I had a limited conversation. When he got back to his seat, I could see Blanche ask him, "Who was that?" To which he replied, "I don't know, but he is a voter!"

Balancing Finances and Staffing

Business academies[2] often use the educational films developed by the well-known British comedian John Cleese. In their advertising, there are typical lines which say it all. One set goes something like this:

> RONNIE CORBETT: The balance sheet is the window through which we view the firm.
> JOHN CLEESE: It is the blind drawn by accountants to keep managers in the dark.

After thirty years, accountants still tell me different stories about how the figures should be presented. Below is a copy of Vicchem's first two balance sheets for the financial years ending June 30, 1983 (three months after we bought the company) and June 30, 1984. They represent a true expression of the worth of Vicchem, but the value was far from impressive. Someone even observed that they were a set of figures that would make an accountant weep. For those with their eyes trained at control,[3] it could be observed that Vicchem was teetering on the edge of oblivion. A few years later, when Graeme Voigt, our accountant, felt that our continuing struggles needed a pretty good survival strategy, he asked his Jewish friend Freddy Haas for advice on what we should do. Freddy had one question: "Do they own the land?" To which Graeme was pleased to reply, "Yes." Freddy's prophetic words of wisdom were "They'll be all right!"

Richmond land values in 1984 were increasing, and a revaluation

Robert W. Killick, PhD

of the land was included in our budgeting process. We also believed that the company's intellectual property was worth more than we had previously indicated, and it was subsequently revalued upwards. This all helped the 1984 balance sheet become more balanced.

FIRST BALANCE SHEETS

	06-30-1983	06-30-1984
	$ '000s	$ '000s
SHARE CAPITAL AND RESERVES		
Share Capital	52	52
Capital Profit Reserve	85	85
Property Revaluation Reserve	-	324
General Reserve	59	59
Retained Earnings	(224)	(216)
Share Capital Reserve/Unappropriated Profits	104	107
TOTAL	76	412

Represented by

FIXED ASSETS		
Land and Building (Cost)	46	46
Land and Building (Revaluation)	-	324
Plant (less depreciation)	61	55
Office and Furniture (less depreciation)	3	3
Motor Vehicle (less depreciation)	4	3
TOTAL	114	431

CURRENT ASSETS		
Cash	1	1
Debtors	175	137
Stock	184	244
Other Debtors/Loans/Prepayments	7	74
Loan to Family Trust	-	15
TOTAL	366	470

INTANGIBLE ASSETS		
Ee-muls-oyle	15	15
Industrial Property	123	245

TOTAL ASSETS	618	1161

CURRENT LIABILITIES		
Bank Overdraft	82	97
Trade/Other Creditors	167	287
TOTAL	249	385

OTHER CURRENT LIABILITIES

Personal Loans/Property Trust	37	13
Bank Bills	155	279
TOTAL	192	292
PROVISIONS		
Holiday Pay	31	34
Long Service Leave	38	39
TOTAL	69	73
TOTAL LIABILITIES	542	750
NET ASSETS	76	412

To handle the financials was one thing, but staffing became a major issue, and the takeover led to a boilover of the staff of the old Vicchem company.

- The general manager had resigned and left before the takeover was complete. We therefore decided to proceed without one, with me absorbing the role. This also provided a financial saving.
- The sales team, with the exception of Ken Allen, had similarly disappeared before our arrival. With his prior service and knowledge of the operations of the company, Ken remained a stalwart and most loyal company man for the next fifteen years, until his retirement in 1998. He liked quoting the adage "Never bite the hand that feeds you." This was a principle which he followed unswervingly. Years before, Vicchem had taken him on as a company truck driver. After several years, Ken was told, "You know where all the goods are delivered, so wear a tie on Monday, and you can go out and sell them." Wearing a tie had become the insignia of management, and unless exceptional circumstances prevailed, such as temperatures over 40 degrees Celsius, it was never to be removed. He had no technical knowledge of how the chemical products were made, but he was worldly-wise and knew when to say that he would ask those in the know for the technical answers and faithfully report back to the inquirer at his earliest convenience. This kind of

old-school dependability and trustworthiness meant a great deal in those days, as indeed it does today.

- The company secretary/accountant retired a few months after we purchased the company, and it was clear we needed someone new to manage the finances. Graeme Voigt undertook the accounting on a part-time basis, and I covered the role of company secretary.
- The technical director was one of the previous shareholders and a director of the company, and had stood down when the company was sold.
- The quality-control chemist decided to seek greener pastures.
- The production supervisor resigned in order to go to one of our competitors. He had his own way of doing things, as there was no one above him to provide training. When a production batch was out of specification, for example, he would store the material in drums and "lose" them in the warehouse without telling anybody. This covered failed reactions. Our first inkling of the situation came when I was reviewing with Ken Allen that something was seriously wrong, as we were losing $1,000.00 per week. The only answer was to recheck stocks, which led back to the production mistakes sitting up like "Jackie"[4] in the warehouse but not carrying any value.
- The operators were strongly unionized. Typically, a certain staff member sat all day reading the newspaper, and it took several years before he would undertake at least some form of warehouse work. We had an old traditional union representative on-site who kept reinforcing that if a manager pressed one factory button, the workforce would down tools.
- The spirit of the place was "Near enough is good enough," whilst the ethos of the marketing team had been, "Don't look at the quality, look at the price!" The problem lay in the fact that customers did look at the quality, and the low prices set for the products meant the company's gross margins were not adequate to provide profitability.

Sales were declining bit by bit, along with the lifeblood of the company. Even though I'd had several months to view the happenings, I am sure that when we finally bought the company, I did not realize the parlous state of its finances or the risk we were taking. Would we have bought the company, if we had known? Who knows? But, fortuitously, it never became an issue, as the old adage says, "What the eye doesn't see, the heart doesn't grieve over."

Is That a Profit?

Our first staff appointment for the new company was Peter Wrigley. He had been a cargo surveyor, which required attendance—day or night—whenever a ship arrived, for assessment of its cargo for discharge. Peter had only recently married Andrea, and Gwen, Andrea's mum, was concerned by the demands of Peter's working hours. Judy and Gwen were friends, and halfway through our purchasing negotiations, Judy indicated that if the acquisition proceeded, a position would be available for Peter. This was on May 28, 1983, with Peter starting as our laboratory manager and subsequently becoming our general manager. Peter provided much technical input and administrative oversight for more than thirty years.

We needed to build up an *esprit de corps* and a culture of cleanliness among our workforce. It didn't help that everything in the factory was grotty, with its greasy floors and run-down machinery, not to mention the poor design of the factory layout. We needed to change the polarity of things … and quickly. We set out to do three things. The first was simply to establish a baseline for cleanliness, then keep the place clean, with no rubbish left around, and the floors cleaned and safe to work on. We bought our own high-pressure steam-cleaning unit and replaced the cracked and broken windows in the first-floor laboratory. It is likely we were ten years ahead of New York City with the broken-window policy claiming that "by targeting minor disorder, more serious crime could be reduced."[5] Our problem wasn't crime—more like grime. But replacing the broken windows played a key part in fixing the defeatist attitude of the workforce and raising the quality of the products produced in the factory. It was all part of stopping the rot. The future of our factory and our company depended upon it. The second was to paint the walls. We decided on a darker grey up to waist high, and a lighter grey to the ceiling. One of our painters was Alan Rowe, who had been made redundant from his profession in journalism. He had never held a paintbrush before, and there was great hilarity when he set about his task as it sometimes seemed that he was painting more of himself than the wall. However, he became an adequate painter and has continued to thank me for the opportunity to prove to himself that he could do something other than journalism. We also provided work experience for three of the Jones boys. These are the grandchildren of the Rev. Neville Horn, under whose teaching I came to commit my life to Christ (which is discussed further in chapter 5, in the section "Full Commitment"). Neville was promoted to glory[6] in 2013, and had seen them in the bud stage of Christian work, mentoring in Tanzania, reading towards a PhD in theology for future college work, studying to become a pastor in the local church and the final son undertaking lay ministries. The seemingly never-ending job of painting was eventually finished by Peter Wrigley's father-in-law. The third action was having Peter Wrigley in the laboratory, as he set and maintained a necessary high standard for production, handling, warehousing, and delivery of our goods.

John Norman was another stalwart at this time. He was the working arm of Etonwood Consultants, whose raison d'être was the provision of market intelligence. John, however, also had production experience, which provided a significant boost to the quality of our staff in the early days. In his role as adviser with Etonwood Consultants, John encouraged me to take a two-week study trip to India, surveying the Indian chemical market and asking the question, "Is the closed door opening?" Typical of his generosity, John acted as general manager of Vicchem back in Melbourne during my two-week survey of the potential in Indian markets, and has done so at other times, as required, until the appointment of Peter Wrigley to the position in 1990.

Finally, there came a day when the business made a profit! Please don't ask me exactly when. I just remember that I came home one night, with suppressed excitement, and told Judy that in the month just finished we had made a profit! When I showed her the ledger, this ever-practical Scottish lady made the profound response, "But I don't see it!" It was there all right; it just needed a trained eye and the patience of a saint to see it—but mostly someone who knew how the company operated. Eventually, Judy agreed that it must be there somewhere, so we can give her the credit of being a saint.

So, when I returned to work early the next morning, I asked plaintively, "Where is it? Where is the profit?" There was an immediate lesson on what, in accounting terms, is known as *source and application of funds*. Keeping to lay terms, this provides an indication of the way cash is flowing through a business while the profit or the loss is hidden in, whether the amount of cash has either increased overall, which indicated a profit, or decreased, which showed a loss. The profitability/loss in any period may be simply obtained by summing up the changes in the debtors, stock, creditors, and liquid liabilities between the beginning and end of the time period under review, normally a month. Judy thinks it still remains all a little complicated and wishes it were one figure. It is the figure that appears at the bottom of the profit and loss account, otherwise known as the P & L account.

Building Up Steam

In the early years, we found ourselves in the classic situation of undercapitalization, which is recognized as one of the major causes of business start-up failures. Undercapitalization is the problem of insufficient funds for the size of the company. With the lack of cash, bank loans were generally unavailable because of unacceptable high loan-to-equity ratios. The NAB had not loaned us any capital to help purchase Vicchem. The first capital outside borrowings of $160,000.00 to buy Vicchem had been solicitors' trust funds from HGR and had a year's life. In addition to the fast-approaching deadline for the repayment of the solicitors' trust funds, we also needed to pay out the original shareholders, as agreed to in our purchase contract. We had to find other sources of finance beyond those we had already tapped. Bill Watson from Syndal Church was then running his own Watson Financials and was promoting the RESI Building Society. This society was at that time looking to expand its loans portfolio, which was only residential, to include commercial property. We had arrived on the society's doorstep, seeking funds, at the strategic time when it was intent on building up its own commercial loan portfolio. We thus took the opportunity to borrow around $340,000.00 to pay off the HGR debt, plus all the remaining owings to the original shareholders, which fully completed the purchase of Vicchem.

To keep the balance sheet in line, we were again able to revalue the property upwards by $324,000.00, which gave our company a healthier balance sheet. This operation is dangerous, particularly in a private company, where values are decided by talking with local real estate agents and directors can pick a figure. Jumping ahead to review our situation as a whole, we were with RESI for around three years when the NAB approached us to take over our complete account. After some long reflections on the wisdom of having all our eggs in one basket, we agreed.

Our other banker in the early days was Barry Palmer, owner and managing director of Tallow Products our major raw material supplier. Barry was good to us. There are remembrances—apocryphal, I'm sure—that he allowed our credit to run to 180 days. Maybe this could be a trifle high, but the length he let us run was definitely not thirty days!

During this period, the Australian Industry Development Corporation (AIDC) was inaugurated by the government to lend money to potential "winners" to expand Australia's manufacturing base. We bravely applied for around $120,000.00, which we were duly awarded and then repaid over the years. We were one of the few companies that ever did meet its repayment obligations to this taxpayer-funded scheme. By contrast, one pharmaceutical concern we heard of had borrowed $20 million from the AIDC and never repaid the debt.

As mentioned earlier, the NAB was also gracious during those early undercapitalized days, bearing with us while we sought to trade our way out of the red and into the black. Also as mentioned earlier, we had two small units on Sydney's northern beaches, at Dee Why. The conservative bank valuation at that time was $120,000.00, on which they were prepared to lend $80,000.00, which was used for our overdraft. The company ran the overdraft facility at $130,000.00 for weeks on end—something we certainly would not get away with in today's more tightly constrained fiscal environment. Evan Tune, who was our bank manager at that time, was under pressure to rein in our borrowings, but he maintained our facility with the comment, "Bob will be all right."

Evan Tune

Evan was the face of NAB over the early difficult years, and without him there would be no Vicchem as we know it today. He was the old-school banker who decided his responses on his customer's character, personality, and qualification(s) to run a business. We respected his acumen; and he, our infectious enthusiasm. Though retired, he and his wife, Mary, came to our twenty-five-year anniversary of owning the business. We also visited them several years later in their home on the Mornington Peninsula. He was inordinately pleased that the company had become so successful.

Undercapitalization

The above situation couldn't last forever, and through Heine Finance we set about factoring our debts. Factoring was where a copy of a sales invoice was presented to Heine, who immediately paid Vicchem 80 per cent of the invoice's face value. When our customer paid the invoice, the cheque was paid into Heine's bank account, which then paid us the remaining 20 per cent, less interest charges and commission. This was against all the wishes of our accountant, Graeme, and there was much wringing of hands. We went ahead, nonetheless, with an understanding that this was not a long-term option. For that particular season, it did in fact turn out to be a strategic business decision to keep the company going.

At this stage, monthly reporting of profit and loss was introduced to the boardroom, with an almost fanatical watch on gross margins and cash flow. We knew how close to the wind we were sailing. The chase to ensure minimal stock was also launched, since holding high levels of stock was a reduction of working capital. Increased sales have always been the universal solution to get out of the type of hole we were in, but that was always easier said than done. We also dreamt that the level of our selling prices might be lifted to a level equivalent to the figure obtained by doubling the raw materials and drum costs. There were a few years in the late 1990s when the canola oil price hovered around ninety cents per kilogram. With the good graces of God, a quality production and management team, and fair winds and following seas,[7] the situation did start to turn out for the better. There are times when we look at ourselves and realize how spoilt we have been. Indeed, in the Australian idiom, we have been *"spoilt rotten!"* These were our early days in the sun.

At this time in the company's life, Vicchem received a further shot in the arm. This first breakthrough came from our long-established product, Ee-muls-oyle, which was used for drying grapes into sultanas in the Sunraysia district, in and around Mildura. We did not recognize it at the time, but it was this product's increase of sales that saved the business. At the same time, it both opened our eyes and gave us a taste of the value and size for our type of products in Australian agriculture. When the company was purchased, sales in agriculture were 11 per cent of our total $2 million sales, whereas today, it is 80 per cent of a $34 million enterprise. The Ee-muls-oyle success was our ability to swing our key raw material from the animal-based tallow to the vegetable-based canola oil, with its beneficial properties. This allowed us to obtain the US Food and Drug Administration (FDA) approval. (Because of its importance in the company's history, these developments are more comprehensively expanded in chapter 8, "Ee-muls-oyle Kept us in Business.") We went on to incorporate this new raw material as the oil base in our manufacture. In production and marketing terms, we had struck silver! Our new understanding of the properties of canola oil extended our knowledge on the role that ethyl oleate, our key product of manufacture, plays on the surfaces of grapes, weeds, and insects. And, using several important contacts in the United States, we were able to meet Dr Dave Schulteis, the research and development guru who worked for the Wilbur-Ellis, a large American company. This put Vicchem on the wider map and led directly to the company's expansion of good fortune.

Finding New Markets

A parallel impetus which directed us into agriculture came with the arrival of "Eric the Red" Hawkes from the multinational Croda Chemical Company, in July 1985. Croda was in a slow decline, suffering from many of the same problems that had beset us at Vicchem. Eric came seeking a job and promoting his ability to get us into bloat products. Bloat occurs in cattle when the animals graze on lush pasture, such as clover or lucerne. Ruminant animals produce large volumes of gas during the normal process of digestion, and that gas is either belched up or passed through the gastrointestinal tract and expelled as wind. The problem starts with the cows' four stomachs; if natural foaming agents are present, they can cause a stable foam to form in the rumen. Gas is then trapped in small bubbles, and the animal cannot belch up the gas. This leads to a pressure build-up in the rumen, which ultimately kills the animal, as the swelling rumen compresses the lungs, and the animal cannot breathe. Not only does this result in great pain for the animal, it also leads to significant financial loss for the farmer.

The traditional answer to the problem has been the introduction of chemicals, such as petroleum oil, into the rumen. The oil breaks up the foam and the gas is released. This could quaintly be described as "pouring oil on troubled waters." This was right up our development alley. Eric told tales of Croda taking twenty thousand litres of oil into the factory in the morning and another twenty thousand litres in the afternoon. These were vast quantities of materials. If we could tap the market, our sales levels would increase significantly. The materials would also fill a ten thousand-litre blending vessel that was little used. We never did reach such exalted levels, but there was a marked increase in our sales performance over a period of several years. In subsequent years, the volumes of the oil-based products dropped away as slow-release products took over as the preferred agents to manage the problem of animal bloat.

The other new market segments introduced by Eric were the summer and winter oil insecticides, also known as white oil insecticides.

These are used in citrus and stone/pome fruit orchards against scale insects and mites which have the potential to cause sooty mould and are capable of virus transmission. With the simplicity of the manufacture of the insecticides, the gross profit margin is not high. However, tens of thousands of litres were produced, and the generated profits helped to cover the company's fixed expenses. Their introduction also expanded our product range and meant that we were not just a one-product agriculture company with Ee-muls-oyle.

The late 1980s and early 1990s were the hard slog years for the management and production teams at Vicchem, and without a doubt, it had become wearing. It is not easy to coherently remember my feelings and motivations twenty-five years ago, but I am pretty sure that after five years of ownership, if someone had offered to buy Vicchem, and let me clear a few hundred thousand dollars from our input, I'm sure I would have grabbed the money and run.

We had discussions with Unichema about a possible sale of Vicchem, with the interest coming more from their side than ours. Unichema urgently needed to increase local sales and saw fatty esters as the natural extension of its existing product line. This was not unexpected, as, internationally, fatty acid manufacturers had their ester ranges. Australian manufacture of fatty acids had started in the early 1900s as a parallel process to soap production, as both processes started from tallow or animal fat. The previous Unichema boards did not want to produce esters which would directly compete with their main customers. Times had changed, and esters were again being considered as a potential market. When Unichema saw the dilapidated state of our Richmond factory, the possibility of a sale came to a sudden halt. It was obvious to them, as it was certainly obvious to us, that Vicchem was just not Unilever.

Castrol has been a long-term purchaser of several of our products, and John Gribble, the general manager, again being on the expansion-via-acquisition track, made contact. I felt that this could have been a good fit, and discussions proceeded well. The last and best meeting was held at a restaurant in the old tram depot, Military Road, Neutral Bay, Sydney. Military Road is on the way back to Manly from Sydney airport, and each time I visit Manly and pass the tram depot, I wonder what might have been—or, more importantly, what might not have been. However, shortly after the meeting, John was transferred to another position, and his successor had no interest in the previous acquisition strategy. So that was that.

Steetley, which had also traded both as Harcros and APS, was one of the major chemical companies which had grown by acquisition, as shown in three of its names. Indeed, one of its earliest takeovers was the Crown Chemical Company that had already spawned Victorian Chemicals in 1933. It has now itself been taken over by the New Zealand-based Nuplex organization. Back in the 1980s, "Rocky" Stone, Steetley's managing director, had made his name for the English-owned company by this expansionism. Once again, the discussions proceeded positively until we reached the question of price. Rocky stressed that for goodwill we could not anticipate any more than three times the average profitability over the previous three years. While we were surviving, we only had low levels of profitability. This time I walked away from the possible sale.

We took these experiences as an indication that our ugly duckling was still alive and well, and the sale of Vicchem was obviously not meant to proceed. Vicchem had a future, and if the truth be told, there was still a faint gleam in my eye and a hope for what the future might hold for this company. Although in the earliest days there was no doubt that we had "one foot in the grave and the other on a banana skin," the first feelings that maybe we had our foot off the banana skin had started to occur.

Expansion and Consolidation

Meanwhile, back at the ranch, I did not have delusions of grandeur as the managing director, and took a salary just above that of the highest-paid manager. Judy and I balanced the various demands on the company's gross profitability, and when the first profits appeared, we poured as much as we could into our personal superannuation. The level of money available was at its maximum, as no company tax payments were needed because of the tax losses which had accumulated over the years. Indeed, some of these occurred well before we had purchased the company. Being savers at heart, there was never going to be a yacht on the bay, and into super it went. This personal-finance strategy has proven to be a very effective one for our business, as well as for us going forward into retirement as a couple.

In its simplest form, superannuation was introduced throughout Australia in 1983 by the then government, whereby employers were required by law to make a 3 per cent contribution of each employee's salaries into a super fund. These have taken two forms: the large commercial funds and the small self-managed super funds (SMSFs), the latter mainly run by families, such as Judy's and mine. On retirement, the accrued funds are accessed through either slow-release income streams or lump sums. The government's aim has been for people to have put aside enough money during their working lives to minimize the number of people who have to be supported by a government pension. Superannuation really took off in Australia in 1992, when increased taxation benefits were introduced to encourage more people into the system. In addition, it was permissible to have two parallel funds. Personal donations were possible whilst it all worked under a capping limit of seven times the reasonable benefits limit. The regulations became changeable under political pressures but remain valuable for our situation. The ability to run two funds was finally cancelled, and the level of money allowed to be put into a fund was capped as a fixed sum. For those early days, it was our accumulating time in the sun.

For the company, the major event of 1992 was the purchase of the two dilapidated properties that bordered the Richmond factory. Vicchem occupied the south-east corner of the island block bordered by Appleton, David, Doonside, and Burnley Streets, Richmond. The remainder of the island had originally been owned by Repco and a parquetry company. It was in a run-down condition, not too bad up Burnley Street, but decrepit up at the western end. The whole area had been mortgaged to Chinese interests who were looking to be the developers, using funding from the State Bank of Victoria. The scheme went bust around the same time that the State Bank itself was taken over by the Commonwealth Bank. The new bank owners wished to realize on this part of their portfolio. Their first attempt was to auction the entire lot in a single-block sale. When this did not raise any bid, they subdivided the area into six blocks. Harry the Hirer purchased the block with the Burnley Street frontage and those directly behind. This left the two blocks that abutted us.

Lot number 4, 36-44 Doonside Street, was on the north-east corner block. It had an old building inhabited by squatters, including a dodgy painter who made forged paintings for sale. It seems that at some time during or after the painting process, to get rid of the cleaning turpentine, he had poured it into the cracks in the concrete floor. When the investigators used the same cracks to make the boring of their test bore holes easier, the results appeared to show we were in an area of significant environmental concern. It eventually got sorted out, and the property was put on the market. The price, at $360,000.00, was a bargain, but, again, beauty is ever in the eye of the beholder. The property of approximately sixteen hundred square metres of grotty Richmond real estate that was in the manufacturing zone on the wrong side of the tracks and asbestos wall sheeting blowing in the wind was settled on October 1.

Lot Number 4: Looking towards the factory

Lot number 5, 27-35 Appleton Street, was west of the factory. If there were signs of anguish among our advisors when we determined to purchase lot number 4, this was only exacerbated when the Commonwealth Bank came to unload the last block (number 5). For this last block of 2,004 square metres, we negotiated the price down to $250,000.00. This was settled on December 1. The bankers were pleased to have found some donkey that was prepared to take it off their hands.

Lot Number 5: It's the land

We formed the RJK Property Trust, with the Victorian Chemical International Pty Ltd (VCI) as the trustee. This was a unit trust, which works on a non-discretionary basis, in that at the end of each year the income is distributed in proportion to the units that the beneficiary holds. We proceeded to the purchase of the two lots, using both our superannuation funds and separate personal monies. The superannuation regulations did not allow borrowed money to be used for the purchase of assets in the funds.

These purchases were important firstly as the factory was now protected from the neighbours by buffer land of passive non-productive use. We were able to turn the northern property into a warehouse and installed four relatively small tanks, which, for us, became our own mini-tank farm! The western property provided car parking, which had been a sore point with the council, particularly as we didn't have any car spaces for our twenty workers. There was also space for stock within the older, run-down building. While it certainly didn't look pretty, the increased space gave us the ability over the next ten years to significantly increase our holdings and our sales.

The main benefit was that we had purchased land. As the old adage says so well, "Buy land ... they are not making any more of the stuff."[8] As the land increased in value, so our superannuation fund also increased its value. By the time we sold Richmond to move to Coolaroo, these unbecoming toads had turned into princes—still ugly, but with full purses. Each was sold as a remediated clean site, and their land value had increased many times over. (This is discussed further in chapter 11.)

> **We had stumbled into owning an old wasted mine and were having fun ...**
>
> **... but one day, one might somehow stumble across a mother lode ...**
>
> **... and find "there's gold in them thar stills."**

But, before then, what were the roots of life and the soil that had got us to this place?

4 Our Ancestors

*All the world's a stage and all the men and women merely players
who have their ... entries.*[1]

You are a mist that appears for a little while and then vanishes.[2]

You cannot be too careful in the choice of your parents.[3]

As I begin this chapter, it seems appropriate to ask the question, "What makes Bob, Bob?" Many of my friends and family members would simply shrug and say the question is unanswerable! The same people would at least agree that "What you see is what you get."

Another way of asking the question could start with, "What might be the impressions taken away if meeting Bob for the first time?" I have only known Dr Stuart Devenish[4] for a short time. He was brave enough to have a lash and give me his first impressions:

> Bob is a larger-than-life character. He is one of those people who, when he walks into a room, makes his presence unmistakably felt. It's not that he was born with a silver spoon in his mouth, or has lived a charmed life. It's more a force of his character. Bob has three things going for him which are hard to resist. The first is his quick mind; you have to move quickly to keep up with Bob. The second is his ready wit; any time Bob's around there's a laugh a minute. And the third is that he has a plan; it's guaranteed that things won't stay the same for long before serious matters are being discussed. Once you get to know him, there's more to

add such as his integrity, his ability to read peoples' characters and the fact that he is a world traveller, family man, entrepreneur, raconteur, man of faith, networker, leader, lover of theatre and music.

There is something in the gene mix that makes the person. It has thus been both challenging and interesting to look back in this chapter at my family and my ancestral roots. After all, without them, there would have been a different Bob, and, indeed, who knows whether the larger story of Vicchem could have been told. A record of my early nurture, experiences, schooling, and university studies continue in chapter 5, whilst this chapter reflects on the gene pool.

My Country

Writing my memoirs has certainly stoked the investigative fires of exploring family heritage. Judy's family has Scottish roots, whilst my family roots are English. These forerunners all reached Australia as, I would describe, the "Boat People of the 1800s." The period from the 1830s to the 1880s has been seen as one of Australia's population growth spurts. Our earliest settlers from each side of the family reached Australian shores in 1837 and 1838, which was only around fifty years after the founding of the colony. We find this short time frame almost unbelievable, although strangely stimulating. Our genetic lines began here at a time that had minimal infrastructure. It was 1788 that Governor Phillip started white settlement with, according to his first census, 1,030 persons, 753 of whom were convicts. For trivia buffs, there were also seven horses, twenty-nine sheep, seventy-four swine, six rabbits. and seven cattle[5]. Eighty years later, the last 269 convicts arrived, on January 9. This made a total of 164,000 inmates in the new open jail. The country's total population had already reached 1.5 million, which indicates the importance of free settlers, such as my forebears, the Southwell family, who in their genealogy and history book described themselves as "pioneers of the Canberra District."[6]

The majority of our antecedents went bush to find their livelihood. The shock of the new country, as compared with that of England, must have been harrowing. It is best epitomized in the poem by Dorothea Mackellar. She was born in Sydney in 1885, and at the age of nineteen whilst on a visit to Britain became homesick for Australia. She penned the poem "My Country." The first verse sets the scene for those whose love of England was strong; the second verse then launches to tell of the wilful, lavish land that is Australia. The iconic patriotic description continues for four more verses. The first two verses follow:

My Country

1.

The love of field and coppice
Of green and shaded lanes,
Of ordered woods and gardens
Is running in your veins;
Strong love of grey-blue distance,
Brown streams and soft dim skies-
I know but cannot share it,
My love is otherwise

2.

I love a sunburnt country
A land of sweeping plains
Of rugged mountain ranges
Of droughts and flooding rains
I love her far horizons,
I love her jewel sea,
Her beauty and her terror-
The wide brown land for me!

These first two verses ever bring a tear to my eyelash.

The Arrivals

The following list provides the arrival date in Australia of both Judy's and my ancestors. It is based on both sets of grandparents through their paternal and maternal lines:

Antecedents' Arrivals

Our Grandparents	Notes on First Ancestors to Australia	Boat	Arrival Date
Bob's Family			
Paternal			
George Alfred Killick	Grandfather arrived as a ten-year-old in the family of George and Mary Killick	*Star of India*	**1883** November 16
Helen Bembrick	Great-Great-Grandmother Mary Ann Southwell was one and a half years old when she arrived	*Lady Nugent*	**1838** November 27
Maternal			
William Inder	Grandfather William arrived when he was twenty years old, with his brother, Percy, fleeing their stepmother	*Trafalgar*	**1882** October 19
Minnie Horn	Came with father from England via New Zealand; arrival date in Australia unknown	*Clifton*	**1841** October 3 (NZ)

Judy's Family

Paternal

John Gillies	Great-Grandfather Malcolm was sixteen on arrival with his father, Donald, from the Isle of Skye, fleeing poverty	*Midlothian*	**1837** December 12
Lily Anderson Beveridge	Arrived with her father, Laurence Beveridge, at six years of age	*Loch Garry*	**1880** September 26

Maternal

Mathew Lamont McFadzean	Great-Grandfather Mathew's date of arrival has been calculated from his death certificate	Not known	**1860**
Alice Edith Akhurst	Great-Grandfather Johann Kitz from Hanau, Germany	*Barrackpore*	**1853** February 5

In thinking about my Killick antecedents, I begin with my grandfather as a fixed point. He was alive for the first twenty-two years of my life and was the only grandparent I knew. Of particular interest were his parents, my great-grandparents, George Killick and Mary Elizabeth Tedham, who brought the Killick genes to Australia. They were married in the third quarter of 1870, at Hailsham, Sussex, England. The photo below has them dressed for the wedding. Whilst in February 1840, Queen Victoria was married to Albert, *in white*, nonetheless, the "bride in white" did not become customary until the late 1800s. Mary was thus in her Sunday best, which continued to be usable after the wedding. Although she could well expect many children, I wonder whether she anticipated there would be eleven. Nor, I doubt, did she ever envision that the latter part of her life would be in the rural backwater of Harden, in the colony of New South Wales.

Great-grandparents' wedding day

George was a journeyman corn miller by trade and had lived in at least five locales before he left for Australia. He seemed successful, so I don't know what drew him to emigrate to the colonies, but the family did so, leaving Plymouth on Thursday, August 23, 1883, on the eleven hundred-tonne Blackwall frigate, *Star of India*. It had been built in 1861, in Dundee, and continued to ply the seas until 1892, when, in mid-Atlantic waters, it had to be abandoned and later sank. The ship was the same size as the current Manly ferries, such as the *Narrabeen,* which have a gross displacement of 1,150 tonnes.

As all our antecedents came on these little ships, it is worth noting reports in the literature[7] that it was rugged voyaging, battling through terrific gales, labouring and rolling in a most distressing manner, according to many a ship's log. The life aboard was especially hard on the emigrants cooped up in the 'tween deck, fed a diet of hardtack (also known as sea biscuit, made from flour and water) and salt junk (basically salted beef or pork). They were subject to *mal de mer* (seasickness) and a host of other ills, and it is astonishing that their death rate was so low. They were a tough lot, though, drawn from the working classes of England and Scotland, and many of them went on to prosper in their new country.

The family, with its six children (Grandpa was ten years of age, as noted above) arrived safely in Sydney, on Friday, November 16, 1883. Another five children were born to them in Australia: Florence, Frederick, Lina, Eldred, and Albert, who died in the year of his birth. The family first settled in Temora, NSW. The last move for George and Mary was to the twin towns of Murrumburrah-Harden, where Great-Grandfather was the manager of Allsopp's Flour Mills for twenty-six years. In the later years, they had a store in the Harden side of the towns, and Mary was a valuable assistant to her husband.

When they arrived in the towns, they were looking for a place of worship. George's "In Memoriam"[8] recalls this:

> Hitherto, he had been associated with the Baptist Church, having been baptized by Charles Spurgeon, but his own denomination being unrepresented in the town, he joined the little company of Methodists meeting in Harden … Those were days of struggle, and no one showed greater zeal and devotion for the infant cause than George Killick and his family. Great was his pride and deep his joy, when the new church opened its

doors for public worship. His own home was denuded
of its American organ in order that the worship of
God's house might be fittingly led.

It has often been said that in Australia we live "Down Under," and we like to pride ourselves on our upside-down approach to matters. Thus, to have the status of "Australian royalty," it is required that one must have convict ancestry, and the real top level is when one's antecedents came on the First Fleet. Indeed, were the convicts not chosen by the best judges of England? In the milieu of Protestantism, there is no royalty, but there is a thrill in knowing that our heritage touches the figure of Charles Spurgeon, through the fact that my great-grandfather had been baptized by immersion by him. In Baptist circles, Spurgeon,[9] who lived from 1834 to 1892, is discussed in hushed tones as the greatest preacher of the last hundreds of years. Near the Elephant and Castle in London, he filled the 5,500 seats of the Metropolitan Tabernacle every service and is reputed to have preached to 10 million people in his lifetime. No, for us, there are no convicts back there, but there is Great-Grandfather, who was baptized by Charles Haddon Spurgeon, and that is more than enough for me.

George's son and my grandfather, George Alfred, had his first job working in the flour mills. He would routinely pick up 140-pound (63.5 kilogram) bags of flour and throw them overhead. He was well known for his strength and used it in challenge wrestling matches around the country. He regularly won, and this was a nice little money earner. In 1897, Grandpa married Helen Bembrick. Her birth was on December 4, 1871, to parents Alfred and Mary, who lived at Rye Park, NSW, about forty kilometres north of Yass and thirty kilometres east of Boorowa. Her father Alfred's occupation was then noted as postmaster, shopkeeper, and farmer. In 1875, the family moved to Grenfell, where her dad continued farming and shopkeeping. The final move, in around 1894, was to Harden, where he was dedicated to shopkeeping alone.

A year after their marriage, in 1898, at twenty-five and twenty-seven years of age, respectively, Grandfather and Grandmother opened their general store in Ryan Street, Galong. The store also included a butchery. Grandmother Helen had spent all her early years in her father's store, which training proved invaluable. Her full eulogy is recorded later but one line puts it succinctly:

> With the true spirit of the pioneer she helped her husband lay the foundations of his business in the village of Galong, where God prospered them.[10]

Galong, Our Australian Ancestral Village

The Galong countryside, situated in the northern regions of the Riverina district, was settled in the late 1820s as the home of transported Irish convict "Ned" Ryan. In 1829, Governor Darling redefined the boundaries of the colony, setting up nineteen counties as the limits of lawful occupancy of land.[11] Ned petitioned for a grant of land outside the limits, but was rejected. Unperturbed, he illegally squatted on huge acreages "beyond the limits of location," but we do prefer the expression "beyond the black stump." In the 1860s, the Crown agreed to his holdings.

During 1877, the main south railway line between Sydney and Melbourne was extended through the Galong area. The village's claim to fame was that it became the junction for the Beerowa branch line, which was just twenty-nine kilometres long and opened on October 10, 1914. It was closed sixty years later, in August 1974, along with Galong as a passenger station. The first station was constructed in 1877 and was replaced in 1916, with then, as shown in the photo below and tongue in cheek, world-class cutting-edge architecture. The hill rising to the left at the back is Big Bobbara and its rabbits, which are mentioned later.

Galong Railway Station

Over the twenty years of this period, the village settled. The Galong Hotel received its licence in 1888; the public school commenced in October 1890. By 1901, key businesses included the Friend Brothers Galong Dairying Company, T. Grimley's blacksmith shop, and a factory operating for many years freezing rabbits for export. In 1914, the last of Ned Ryan's descendants died, and the estate passed into the care of the Roman Catholic Redemptorist Order, which, in 1918, opened a monastery five kilometres from the village. It ceased to operate in 1975 and has now become a retreat centre.

Grandpa's integrity was recognized when, in 1904, he was again granted the year's licence to store and sell explosives at his shop.[12] He went on to be appointed the local magistrate in April 1911.[13] This was the time of the duplication of the main southern rail line, and there were three thousand navvies in the surrounds. The *Burrowa News*, on October 22, 1915, provided a classic report in "Town Topics," highlighting the spirit of the period:

For some time past Messers Maginnis and Jellies Bros., pastoralists, Bookham have been endeavouring with the aid of the police and others, to solve the disappearance of a number of fat sheep valued at 25 shillings per head. In all about 30 sheep had disappeared. An answer to the conundrum was supplied last week, when a deputation of departing navvies from the duplication works dumped a parcel of skins down at the business establishment of Mr G. A. Killick, Galong, with the request that they should be credited to Maginnis and Jellies. "We have" said the spokesman "ate the jumbucks, and we are off." They left by the southern train.

It was confirming to see in a newspaper the accepted use of the word *jumbucks* for sheep, as now it only appears in our second national anthem, "Waltzing Matilda," with "that jumbuck in your tucker bag." Anyway, the thirty stolen sheep did not seem to be a hanging offence, nor did the action particularly blot the escutcheon of the one-man police force, as his letter two years later exemplifies.

Galong 24 July 1917
SM Parramatta,
Dear Sir,
Under separate registered cover we are sending you a gold watch, suitably inscribed, also a cheque for £1/10/6, and we would be obliged if you would hand the watch to Constable D. Lane, of your district, and give him some suitable present. This presentation is from the people of Galong and district in recognition of the efficient manner in which Constable Lane discharged his duties while stationed at Galong. We had 3,000 navvies in and around the town when the main southern line was being duplicated and the constable

deserves credit for the able manner in which he had handled (single-handed) the men.

(signed)

Mr George A. Killick, local magistrate

Mr A. J. Rutherford, manager of a local bank

Over the years, I have often claimed that my business genes had only come from Mum's Inder side, but I have now come to appreciate that the Killick ancestors have also put in their two pennies' worth. The general stores of both Great-Grandfather George and Grandfather G. A. had done well, even prospered. A report in the *Burrowa News* on November 30, 1923 noted:

> Messrs. G. A. Killick and Sons have just installed in their business premises, Lampson's Service Co's. cash carriers from all counters to the office which will be a benefit both to customers and to proprietors. Messers Killick and Sons are to be congratulated on their enterprise; it would be difficult to find more up to date premises in any country town.

Grandpa's brother, Gordon, was one of the interviewees of the national Galong Oral History Project, and the digital master is held in the National Library of Australia. Among the many points of his remembrances were "the dances and balls in Galong and Binalong; the Grovener band; and the numbers of people who attended." This provides a little background to the doctor's advice that, after Grandma had "a turn," they should leave the social pressures of country life and retire to the city for peace and quiet! How advice changes over time. They arrived in around 1928, at their last home, 183 Sydney Road, Manly, with the country man proud of his clutch of around a dozen chooks up in the backyard, which he ran until his death.

And what of my Australian ancestral village? At the 2011 census, Galong had a population of 338 souls, a population increase of 216 since the 2006 census. Both Galong and Binalong are now the site of urban development and are at the farthest perimeter of Canberra's outer suburbs. Canberra, the nation's capital, is a fifty-minute drive away, but the housing is cheap, cheap, cheap. Last year, the local mine, with a staff of nineteen, produced three hundred thousand tonnes of limestone, a quarter of NSW's requirements.

The one public remembrance of the Killicks' existence in the country is a dead-end gravel road for farmers to reach their properties. It starts at a T-junction with Tumbarumba Road, south-east of Book Book—it's all small time, but it does carry the *name*. The first photo is the junction with the tarred Tumbarumba Road, which joins the city of Wagga Wagga and the town of Tumbarumba. The road crosses the Hume Highway, the main highway between Melbourne and Sydney, and thus provides access for Wagga Wagga residents to that highway. The second photo shows the gravel Killicks Road passing over the almost always dry bed of Kyeamba Creek.

Sign for Killicks Road · Killicks Road

And what of my English ancestral village? There are two that vie for the title. The first village that had years of Killick blood intertwined in its life is Rotherfield, Sussex. Anthony Killick, my great-great-great-great-great-great-grandfather, was born in 1657, at Nutfield, Sussex, and during his life became a citizen of Rotherfield, dying there in 1736. His descendants and my successive great-grandfathers born there were Thomas in 1690, Benjamin in 1726, William in 1761, Thomas in 1799, and George in 1850. As mentioned, my great-grandfather, George, was a journeyman corn miller by trade and seemed to live an itinerant lifestyle, as can be perceived by following the birthplaces of his children: Frances, in 1871, at Sedlescombe, Sussex; Grandpa George Alfred, on January 25, 1873, at Fareham, Hampshire; William, in 1875, at Steyning, Sussex; Rose, in 1877, at Rotherfield-Peppard, Oxfordshire; Julia, in 1881, at Rotherfield-Peppard, Oxfordshire; and Lena, in 1883, in the same village. So which village do I claim? As an old romantic, I claim title to Rotherfield-Peppard, in the Chiltern Hills of South Oxfordshire, five kilometres to the west of Henley-on-Thames, but only another thirty kilometres to London Heathrow Airport. It was there that Great-Grandfather George lived for a few years and sired two of my great-aunts; it was also from this locale that he set out for Australia. At the 2011 census, the village had 678 homes and 3,800 souls living there. With its Old World charm, it has been used thrice as the setting for scenes in the TV series *Midsomer Murders*,[14] and also in the film *Howards End*,[15] including the eponymous house.

Immediate Antecedents

My first interest in my family's genealogy was roused when I was around twelve years old. Grandpa was then seventy-five and looked very old, but the preferred word is *weather-beaten*. It was Mum's and Dad's weekly responsibility to visit Grandpa, since the rest of the family lived upcountry. It was within the generation where children were to be seen and not heard. To avoid any break-up of this "culture," Mum and Dad would leave me at the Manly Baptist Sunday School at 3:00 p.m., to be cared for by the generous-hearted Sunday school teachers, and then drive on two minutes to Grandpa's for afternoon tea. Such was Grandpa's disinterest in children that I would then be picked up from the Sunday school at 4:00 p.m. for a cursory hello and goodbye, and then we all drove home, five minutes away. The only conversation which I remember having with Grandpa went something like this:

> GRANDPA: I hear you are interested in church.
> BOB: Yes.
> GRANDPA: Well, what is the first commandment with a promise?

The expected answer was the fifth of the Ten Commandments, "Honour your father and your mother, so that you may live long in the land that the Lord your God is giving you."[16] I don't remember my response, but I do remember this one communication with my grandpa, and the question he posed.

I am sure that if Mum could see how Judy's and my life has turned out, she would be inordinately pleased. For Grandpa and Dad, I really wonder! During my school and university days neither Grandpa—nor Dad, for that matter—ever came to any sporting or school event in which I participated. However, even though there was not all that much I can remember that was particularly important, it was never going to be their scene. On the educational side, there was no way either Mum or Dad were ever going to help me with schoolwork. Modern expectations are that it is crucial for children to have adults and significant "others" in their lives to provide encouragement and to value them. But if I didn't know I was deprived, I wonder whether in fact I really was deprived. If anything, it probably made me more independent earlier and cultivated the driving force in my personality. The contrast between then and now is that today's grandparents must—it seems—be present at every school play, musical performance, swimming carnival, and dancing review. If it were possible, one may even suggest that the lot of grandparents might be said to be even more burdensome, and even more joyful, than that of a child's parents. Yet, looking at myself, I feel that there are some of the old practices lingering, since I am still content if I do not attend every activity of my grandchildren.

Grandfather Killick and his family

Grandpa (George Alfred Killick) married Helen Bembrick in 1897. The above photo, which is just over 100 years old, shows the children. As they are all Killicks, I have only included their two Christian names. Top left is Alfred Bembrick (1898–1973), who operated the general store at Galong, NSW; top right is Roy Tedham (1899–1987), who had the Allawah farm at Galong; bottom right is Thelma Mary (1902–1988), who, with her husband, Sid Ward, had a farm at Quandialla, fifty-five kilometres east of West Wyalong, NSW; bottom centre is Norman Henley (1907–1986), who had a farm at Book Book near Wagga Wagga; bottom left is Elva Southwell (1908–1986), who was married to Howard Bolton, a peripatetic bank manager around NSW; and, last but not least, the centre baby is Dad, William George Rupert (1912–2002), who was born May 8, 1912, at Murrumburrah, NSW.

Grandma Helen survived seven years in retirement at Manly, and was "promoted to Glory" in May 1935. I knew nothing of Grandmother until, in my researching for these memoirs, I came across the following tribute in the *Methodist* magazine—refer reference 10 in this chapters Notes.

MRS G. A. KILLICK

A wide circle of friends in city and country alike lament the passing of Mrs G. A. Killick, to whom the home-call came suddenly on 4th April. Daughter of that Methodist patriarch, William Bembrick, of Harden, she responded to the influences of that wonderful home which gave so many leaders to the church, and early dedicated herself to God with a quiet but deep devotion. With the true spirit of the pioneer she helped her husband lay the foundations of his business in the village of Galong, where God prospered them. That home became the active centre of spiritual life in the town and countryside. The preachers of the various churches who ministered in the little Union Church were ever welcome guests, but to Methodist preachers it was as their own home, and all who were privileged to share its intimacy, cherish the memory of its bright and beautiful fellowship. To the young probationers who were in charge of the circuit, Mrs Killick was as a mother, and inspired in them a filial reverence and affection. Her family and her church constituted her world, she gave herself without reserve, and her children have risen up to call her blessed. The last few years were spent in retirement at Manly. There also her gracious nature made itself felt. At the funeral service her pastor told how oftimes the poor were helped anonymously; blankets would be sent to the destitute and food parcels to the hungry. An elect lady has gone from us, and tender sympathy will go out to the sorrowing husband and family. – R.J.W.

A year later, in 1936, Grandpa married Mary Ann ("Polly") West. She had been a "maid of all work" living in the house. This is a quaint phrase describing someone, generally indigent, who did general household duties whilst she was provided with food and a roof over her head. We always called her Aunty Polly. She was born in Young, NSW, in 1891, and died in 1974. In our archives there are photos of her holding our baby daughter Jenni in her arms, with her Great-Grandfather alongside.

My Father

Dad was christened William George Rupert Killick, but was called Rupert all his life. His name, however, always remained W.G.R.K. for passports and important documents. The reason handed down to us concerning why Dad was called Rupert and not William was attributed to the death of his uncle William three weeks before the christening. It was considered inappropriate for Dad to use William, and thus he was called Rupert, or "Rupe," throughout his life. The problem for us as a family is that, in reality, Uncle William had died nine years earlier. This is where family history can become confusing, yet one can appreciate how certain things become either lost or reminted in the telling and retelling of the family myths and legends. There is no argument that Dad was raised at Galong in New South Wales, where his father owned the general store. Galong is the place for young boys to run wild, something Dad surely did with his horse and his dog. In later years, he had a bad back from all his falls, spills, and playing rugby union. The family is sure that the chiropractor could afford a yacht on the harbour from all of Dad's visits.

Sometimes my grandchildren think I am quaint because I always want to talk about catching rabbits. When we are leaving the house for a walk, they will hear the plaintive farewell, "Don't forget to write, but we're going after rabbits." I put this down to Dad's own fixation with rabbits. He would reminisce about his childhood, when he and his cousins would walk over Galong's two hills, Big Bobbara and Little Bobbara. So thick were they on the ground that the rabbits could be clubbed to death with knotted fencing wire. That was his story, and he stuck to it. It would have an element of truth, since the NSW government had set up primary production boards to, in part, eliminate the rabbit problem. The efficacy of the kill lay with the farmer, and this was the main problem. Under the title "Rabbit Pest," on page 7 of the *Burrowa News* of Friday, February 28, 1936, it reads:

> WARNINGS ISSUED
> The P. P. Board at its meeting held in Young on Saturday decided to prosecute in three cases where the inspectors reported that rabbit extermination had not been carried out as required by the Act. (Three people named)
> Peremptory notices were sent to 8 persons.

One of these notices went to R. Killick, Galong. This was my Uncle Roy. We had to go and see—it was a time to discover some of our roots! But the hills were not moving with rabbits any longer. By 1965, myxomatosis, an infectious disease deadly to rabbits and introduced in 1950 to control the rabbit population, had done its work well. The hills were verdant with grasses, to Dad's great disappointment, more so than mine. No rabbits could be seen.

When Dad was seven, his eldest brother Uncle Alf, an AIF gunner with the Fourth Field Artillery Brigade, returned to Australia on January 24, 1919, from the First World War, having served in France. He was only nineteen years old when he had embarked, on November 16, 1917, from Sydney on board the SS *Canberra*. Uncle Roy thought it would also be a good idea to go to war, and twice went up to Sydney to enlist. Grandpa followed both times, and, since he was underage, dragged him back to Galong. The enlistment officers didn't seem too worried about the underage country boy, a strong strapping youth who knew how to handle guns. This personal observation finds a backup through Australia's first war correspondent, Charles Bean, who helped to mould our national self-image, and lay the foundations for what became known as the ANZAC legend. In his book, *Gallipoli*,[17] Les Carolyn writes that Bean "was probably on one of his romantic flights in portraying the men of the First Australian Imperial Force as all of a kind. Bean tended to look at people the way farmers look at livestock—he had the idea of a good type. He favoured a country lad, lean and sinewy, tough but big-hearted, equally good with a horse or cricket bat but always modest."

Uncle Alf's brigade joined the European operations in early 1918 and was ready for the German spring offensive in March, ending up at the Somme. A letter from his mum told him that Dad and his sister, my aunty Elva, were arguing whether he was doing anything of value. He wrote back that his artillery piece had fired 5,565 shots while he was there—but added that one never knew what damage had been done. Alf was a messenger and was hit in the face by shrapnel. He was well appreciated at the rehabilitation hospital in England, as he could play the piano and lead the singing. The thought of him as a nineteen-year-old going to war has impacted me, as I thought back to Eric

Bogle's classic song for the diggers, "And the Band Played 'Waltzing Matilda,'"[18] a few lines of which run:

... So they gave me a tin hat, and they gave me a gun, and they marched me away to the war

> And the band played "Waltzing Matilda" as the ship
> pulled away from the quay
> And amidst all the cheers, the flag waving and tears,
> we sailed off for ...

I have lingered with Uncle Alf, since, while he was learning army discipline and responsibility, no one was interested in raising Rupert. The end result was a larrikin who didn't follow the rules or mores of society. He, his horse, and his dog roamed across all of Galong's wide countryside. In the end, the family took the easier course to send the thirteen-year-old wild boy to the boarding school at Sydney's Newington College and let them do the hard work to instil some semblance of discipline and responsibility. Both he and Dad's immediate elder brother, Uncle Norman, would recall in later years their disappointment with Newington, as the school seemed more interested in exploiting their sporting prowess for the school's glory than giving them an education. The minor level of responsibility Dad absorbed at school might be gauged in that he continued to prefer to ride home to Galong on the roofs of the country trains.

At fifteen years old, and with school going nowhere, Dad left academia, most certainly to the relief of all concerned. He was put to work sweeping floors in S. Hoffnung & Co., a general wholesaler based in Sydney (as mentioned earlier), where he remained for his entire working life. The older men thought it terribly funny to send new staff off to obtain non-existent materials. For example, Dad would be sent down, to say, the hardware department for a long weight (punning on the word *wait*); or for a can of striped paint (which of course didn't exist); or a left-handed screwdriver (which was just stupid). He could be left cooling his heels, doing nothing, for a few hours. Dad was a worker and slowly climbed the ladder of success to ultimately become a director of the company.

Dad was a sportsman, with tennis and rugby union being his preferred sporting codes. He was a cacky (left) handed player and so took the backhand court when playing tennis with Mum. They did well as a team. In rugby union, he played for Manly weekly and for the NSW state team when interstate matches occurred. The country's newspaper archives have several reports, including one in the sporting section (page 14) of the *Sydney Morning Herald*, on Tuesday, June 5, 1934:

> The visitors (Victoria) were coming again from the centre with a bright passing rush that seemed to foretell trouble when Killick flashed in amongst the dark blues, intercepted finely, and after running half the length of the field scored - Victoria 11, New South Wales 6. (Victoria was ultimately successful 14 points to 6.)

Three weeks later, he was reported gravely ill in the personals column, on page 9 of the *Burrowa News*, on Friday, June 29, 1934:

> Following an operation on Monday, the condition of Mr Rupert Killick (Manly) became so grave that his parents were called to his bedside. However, we are pleased to say, the fine condition of the big centre threequarter in the Rugby Union code helped him to withstand the test (sic), and he is now out of danger. Rupert is the youngest son of Mr and Mrs G. A. Killick.

Dad had never told me of his operation, and whether the need to have it arose from the match a few weeks before can only be speculation. He never encouraged me to play rugby, and when I did, he was even less keen for me to be in the forwards for, as he was wont to say, "That is where the thugs gather."

Dad, serial number N 233996, was a sergeant in the latter part of the Second World War, working in a district accounts office. He never went overseas. A few times he told the story of his involvement in manning an anti-aircraft battery situated on what is now known as Parriwi Park, on the southern hill to the Spit Bridge over Middle Harbour. There was no action, apart from one night when the battery heard a small plane flying north to Newcastle and loosed off a few shots. It remains encouraging that one of our own planes did not get shot down, but I don't think that there was any real chance of that ever happening.

Dad sometimes talked about what he saw as the unfairness of life. He would tell the story of Grandpa's first distribution of wealth before the Second World War. The Galong General Store was handed down to Uncle Alf, the eldest, and £1,000.00 each was given to Uncle Roy and to Aunty Thelma, which allowed them each to buy a farm. During the war, inflation ran rampant, such that by the late 1940s, Grandpa had nothing to endow the youngest three children, Dad, Aunty Elva, and Uncle Norman, although Norman did finally obtain a property near Book Book through his own resources. Grandpa found himself living in genteel poverty during his later years, in the old black-brick house on Sydney Road, Manly, which they had acquired when they came down from Galong for health reasons. It was situated opposite the Acme Tyne Laundry, the latter now long pulled down for unit development.

The Inder Family

My maternal grandfather, William Inder, and his brother, Percy, arrived in Sydney on October 19, 1882, fleeing their stepmother in England. In government papers, he was always described as a carpenter, but builder-developer would have been more appropriate. His early bailiwick was Annandale. Whereas now, Annandale is an inner-city suburb situated just over six kilometres from Circular Quay, then it was farm land.

From the earliest days Australians seem to have had their love affair with land. This typically started early when, on October 8, 1793 and in 1794, Capt. George Johnston received 57 hectares on a Crown grant in this area. In 1799, a further 133 hectares were granted on the north side of east-west Parramatta Road, which became known as Annandale. Finally in George's lifetime he acquired another 3,689 hectares, Annandale remained the centre of his empire.

On October 11, 1884, land allotments of fifteen perches, 380 square metres, became available, and 77 Albion Street was bought by James Ansell. It was sold on to Robert Richards in 1897, and to Grandpa William Inder, carpenter, in October 1900 as a joint tenancy with himself, Grandma Minnie, Uncle Bill, and Mum. Thirty-six years later, on his death, the joint tenants became Grandma Minnie, Uncle Bill, and Mum, whilst on Minnie's death, in 1948, all the property was left in Uncle Bill's and Mum's shared ownership. At that time, Mum and Uncle Bill decided to divvy up all the real estate between themselves. This is how Mum received the Queenscliff flats and the house on South Steyne. In Young Street, Annandale, Uncle Bill took four houses in a row, whilst Mum kept the other four, the last being on a corner. She claimed the land would be used one day for a petrol station—it never was.

Uncle Bill's father, William was a wealth creator. The only loss ever mentioned by the Inders' on property was a group of strip shops in Redfern. These were compulsorily acquired by the state government in the 1890's to reorganize the Redfern Railway station, for the building of the new Sydney Central Railway station. He married Minnie Horne in 1904. Minnie was one of six girls and one boy, from the issue of John Horn(e) and the second marriage of Elizabeth (Lizzie) Walker. The issue was William George (1905–2006), known to us all our lives as Uncle Bill, and Mum (Olive Minnie [1909–1962]), known by one and all as "Topsy," because of her curly black hair. The only family photo is below. For those of a former generation, Mum does give me a feel that she is ready to step into the *St Trinian's* film series[19] of the 1950s.

Inder grandparents, Mum, and Uncle Bill

Twenty years later, Uncle Bill had reached the position of the Australian Head Engineer of the American Westinghouse Corporation.[20] When the Great Depression intensified, Westinghouse pulled out of Australia, but with his repute in the company, he was invited to work in America. His mother, Minnie, "put her foot down" and told him "Australia is your home; stay here." America was off the agenda. What to do in the Great Depression? Uncle Bill saw a market gap in that, with Westinghouse gone, there was no supply of replacement parts for electric jugs, toasters, and electric radiators, and he set out to make them in Australia. Fitzall was the brand name. It was his business genius to see a need and fill it. The first practical production was undertaken on the back veranda of the family house at Narrabeen Lakes, Sydney. The following step was to rent rooms on the first floor of a building in Pitt Street, in the city. I can remember walking up old wooden stairs into rooms that can only best be described as a mess. This mess of titbits followed to each next building, but electricians recount fondly how they would go into the shop, looking for an obscure item, and Uncle Bill's staff could always find a duplicate.

Whilst he was single and working in the city, his accommodation was in the Young Men's Christian Association (YMCA). This was followed, up to the time that he was married, at the Hotel Manly, opposite the ferry wharf. One night Uncle Bill was in the Pacific hotel and saw Aunty Roxie across the lounge with Una Cato, a lady friend, both visiting from Melbourne. He sent over two glasses of sherry, and in a short course of time, Roxie and Bill were married, on March 11, 1944, at Una's private chapel, Olinda, in the Dandenong Ranges. Aunty Roxie was a medical doctor, a rarity in those days, and a keen believer in education. She joined with Mum to become an integral part of my nurture and education (as highlighted in chapter 5.)

The pivotal point for Uncle Bill's ultimate success was the purchase of 65-69 Pittwater Road, Manly, which provided a shop front on one of the principal roads of Manly and a large manufacturing area at the rear. The staff level reached a peak of fifty. Mum and Dad continued to help Uncle Bill in two areas. The first was the receipt of wooden kegs in our home garage which was under the front of the Balgowlah Road house. The kegs contained the ceramic bases on which the wire would be wound. To minimize breakages of the ceramics on their export from England, sawdust was used in the packing. This seemed to be the perfect breeding ground for white ants and borers, which poured out at the opening of the keg. To this day, I still don't know why our home was not riddled with the pests. The second was that while Uncle Bill was away overseas, he trusted Dad to pay the company's invoices. The challenge was that each cheque had a limit scrawled over it: "Not over £20/-/-," "Not over £50/-/-," etc. At each departure, Uncle Bill would pacify Dad that there would be enough cheques available until he returned. There never was! I can still remember Dad counting off the days until the return.

The final successful touch was the formation, in 1956, of Manly Lighting & Electrical Suppliers Pty Ltd, which expanded its marketing by moving into various types of lighting. The family visited Europe up to twice a year to bring home the newest light designs, which again provided a cutting sales edge. The 1960s, 1970s, and into the 1980s were the days in the sun. Fitzall elements were selling well, the European lights were ablaze in the accounts, and electric wire, switches, and the items that went into buildings were providing a solid return. At that time, Uncle Bill had obtained an exclusive arrangement to sell the latter materials through the Manly and the Warringah Shires. It was also the time when building approvals were at an all-time peak. However, the sun does set, and there were significant changes in the marketplace. No longer, for example, were electric jugs sold with a replacement heating element—in the new world, when there was a failure in the unit, a new jug was purchased.

The Oracle at Delphi in ancient Greece gave us the saying "Man, know yourself." The extent to which we truly know ourselves is often accredited to the tension between some innate ability within ourselves—what some refer to as *nature*—whereas others argue that character comes from the care and training given to us by our parents and other mentors, what the scholars refer to as *nurture*. How do we become the people we become? From my own lay perspective, I would suggest that it is nature that shapes us most. When a baby is put on show, its maternal viewers debate whether the baby has its mother's eyes, its father's smile, or some other related feature which originated from its ancestors. If the facial features are expected to come from the antecedents, then how much more will the personality? Nurture obviously exerts influences during the formative years.[5] Nurture has certainly been a strong element in my life, and Judy has always claimed that she knew what I would be like in forty years when she looked at Mum's brother, my uncle Bill. As my cousin Rod Inder said in a recent email to me, "Yep, you increasingly look and sound like my father ... even more so than my brother Bryan or myself."

Bob "Inder"   Uncle Bill

Mum, the Driving Force

Now, as the story goes, Mum's and Dad's eyes had met across a crowded room, and Dad, never described as a slow worker, swept Mum off her feet and out of the clutches of Cyrille Williams, her then boyfriend. Mum and Dad were married in the space of a few months. From one particular story that has passed down through the family, the Inder-Killick matrimonial might never have happened. Mum had decided to have a last holiday as a single lady and went for a car tour with her brother Bill up around Moree, in the centre of the Black Soil Plains, whose chief characteristic was that when it rained, the roads—unsealed in those days—became impassable! It rained. The stories became garbled as to what communications eventuated, but the message got through from Dad that, "If you don't get to the church on the set time and date for the wedding, there will be no wedding." It is a speculative thought, but it is hard to think through the theology that if Mum had not got to the wedding, I, as Bob, would not actually have existed today. What a loss to the gene pool! Aunty (as we respectfully called her) Winnie Bolden was to be the bridesmaid, with Dad's brother, Uncle Norman, the best man. Aunty Winnie was seven years younger than Mum and helped make the wedding dress. Anyway, as it happened, they were married on December 26, 1935, at the Manly Methodist Church. The Boxing Day marriage allowed them to maximize the honeymoon time between Christmas and the New Year, with the limited holiday time given in those days. To the best of our knowledge, their honeymoon was at the Carlton, at Katoomba, in the Blue Mountains west of Sydney.

Bob Arrives

Two years later, I was born, on January 4, 1938, which was proclaimed in the births section of the family notices on page 8 of the *Sydney Morning Herald*, on Thursday, January 6, 1938:

> *KILLICK (nee Inder) – January 4, 1938 at St Ronan's private hospital, Manly, to Mr & Mrs Rupert Killick – a son.*

As a result of the birth, Mum contracted septicaemia (blood poisoning). In those days, antibiotics weren't available, and she was not expected to live. Out of the four doctors, only a Dr Minnett said she could be saved and worked hard to ensure she survived. But Mum never really enjoyed robust health from then onwards, and Dad sometimes blamed me and my birth for all of Mum's future health problems. I was christened Robert William Killick in the Manly Methodist Church. My sister, Denyse Ruth, became part of the family seven years later, in 1945. Seven years was a significant age difference, and Den and I never grew up close. By the time I started university, for example, Den was still only ten, with two years of primary school to go. Our closeness began to come together after we had both married and our own children came along. The seven years' differential between forty-eight and forty-one was never apparent in the way it was when we were children and in our teens.

Mum continued to push Dad to achieve all her life. I've already described that Dad did slowly climb the ladder of success at Hoffnung & Co., as Dad himself had his own push and drive. This became evident to the senior managers, and he would be put in charge of a department with poor sales to shake it up and improve that department's figures. With job accomplished, he was then sent on to the next struggling department. In midlife he was sought out by one of Hoffnung's main competitors, Nock and Kirby, but on the night he declined the offer there was a celebratory party at home. He was a true faithful dog and believed to never bite the hand that feeds you. In the later years, he became a director of the company. This was quite something because he was the only gentile of an otherwise Jewish board. It showed the respect in which he was held by the other members. Dad, however, always felt inferior, with his lack of education, and, in particular, his lack of accounting skills, when he had to sit through board meetings talking about buying other companies with special share placements, etc. There were times when he didn't have a clue. When he expressed his concerns to the managing director, "Old Man Davis," he simply encouraged Dad by saying, "Rupert, I can hire all the financial wizards I want for advice, but you can make men want to work for you! That's something money can't buy!" It reminds me of the various variations around the basic thought: "Nobody gets to the top because they're stupid."

This trait has also appeared in me, and it never ceases to amaze me that when working on a project, I can look around and find people being heavily industrious behind me. As someone once said, "If you want to know if you are a leader, look around and see if anyone is following!" Dad's own response to his feelings of inadequacy seemed to show in his inability to give praise to me or even simply say, "Job well done!" Being often without encouragement, I sometimes felt I didn't measure up; but it never became the end of the world, and I believe it helped to foster my drive to succeed.

Dad died on March 5, 2002. He missed turning ninety by two months, but he outlived his father, which he had always wanted to do. We spread his ashes among the wave-swept rocks on the ocean side of the eastern headland of Shelley Beach, located east of South Steyne, Manly. Another locator in the Pacific Ocean is Dead Man's Surf Break, which lies about three hundred metres south-east of the shore where we had spread his ashes. Dad had been a very able body-surfer, and the Inders were wont to compare me to him. Whilst we had the same style, he always had that extra ability for the length of riding the wave. Above all, Dad had a reputation as an out-the-back man. He would be waiting as far away from the beach as possible, waiting for the Big One, the largest wave, to arrive and on which he could catch a ride right to the beach.

It is difficult to measure the influence of Mum's nurture on my life, as our time together was so limited. Through mealtime conversations, I was introduced early to discussions about property which had been brought into the family by Mum and which I understood had come down to her from her parents. Grandpa Inder had been a wealth creator as a developer around Annandale and buying property in Manly and the Warringah Shire. I remember the place on Pittwater Road, Narrabeen, whose back lawn ran back into the Narrabeen Lakes. There was a house on North Steyne, facing the ocean, and the tenant was Bridie Lewis, a name still seared in my brain sixty years later. There was the block of eight flats called North Steyne House, Pine Street, Queenscliff, which Mum owned. She was the wealth holder in the family. Dad earned his salary and never went into purchasing property. Once Mum died, he preferred to sell any property the moment it proved difficult to manage. Mum had perceived this tendency, and also believing that Dad would marry again, she did not want *that* woman to get her hands on her money. To prevent that, her will stated that at the sale of the North Steyne House property, I would be the remainderman, or capital beneficiary, of her will. This meant that Dad would receive the interest from the capital sum, but that the capital would come to me when

Dad died. This sounds reasonable until the thirty-eight-year difference between Mum's and Dad's deaths is taken into account. Inflation meant that, in 1965, we had cleared $42,500.00 for the eight-flat North Steyne House, but, in 2002, when this money came to me, it would only buy a new standard car. I learnt from this that one should never try to control from the grave, so to speak, through the will. Someone, somewhere in the family, usually finds that the originator's hopes never work out as intended.

House Trained

During my teenage years, Mum wasn't exactly an invalid, but there was a general sense of sickness in the house. This reached the point in my early teens when Dad and I agreed that with Mum so sick, one of us was going to have to learn to cook, or we would be eating bacon and eggs for the rest of our lives. I became the cook, or as we otherwise phrased it, "An organic chemist is a frustrated chef!" Over the last eight or so years, there were times when Mum could be relatively active and able to participate in life. In the latter half of 1962, when we knew Mum was dying, Unilever offered to fly me home from London. Mum rejected the idea. (Her last letter to us is contained in chapter 5.) In the vagaries of life, as it comes to each of us, Mum died from bowel cancer on November 22, 1962, whilst her brother, my uncle Bill, died in 2006, just three weeks short of 101. Mum's ashes were spread over the Rose Garden of the Northern Suburbs Memorial Gardens and Crematorium, North Ryde. There is no commemorative plaque. But we hold her near, which is something more important.

Intuition could suggest that our nature would carry half of each parent's genes. This rarely seems to occur, and in my case, it has seemed that the Inder genes have predominated over those of the Killicks. Added to that has been the strong nurture that came from Aunty Roxie and Uncle Bill. I have had Uncle Bill as my role model all my life. Some immediate traits that have come down to me from the Inder side have firstly been a thankful spirit with the ability to say—and mean it—that no matter where I am sitting in a theatre, "It was, and always is, the best seat in the house." I have had a predilection towards, and astuteness for, business. In our minds, Uncle Bill has always been associated with his company, Manly Lighting & Electrical Suppliers Pty Ltd. This was not an insignificant feature during the building boom of the 1960s in Manly and Warringah, for which he had an almost exclusive arrangement for electric wires and fittings. But it provided a good solid living for the family. There has also been a love of travel, and Judy and I have had the privilege of travelling the world many times over, copying Uncle Bill's enjoyments of being "on the road again."[21]

Judy's Family

Judy strongly queried why her ancestors had been included in my memoirs. I replied that she was the end product of their family life, and just as she has absorbed my traits over all the years of our marriage, I have been absorbing her traits into my life. It is nice to remember what I have received over our fifty-seven years together. Some people even go on to suggest that as wedding bliss extends, one starts to look like one's spouse. Judy is happy to confirm that for her, at least, the old farming adage says it best: "I have travelled with the crow, and I am certainly starting to sound like the crow."

Below is Judy's summary of her forbears.

My maternal grandfather was Frederick Lamont McFadzean (1873–1955), and he married Alice Edith Akhurst in 1908. Each family line has its own fascination, but the McFadzean line certainly has had its own quirks. My great-great-grandfather was John McFadzean (1792–1866), a factor (a person who manages a Scottish estate). His was Knockmarlock farm, Craigie, five kilometres south of Kilmarnock, which is thirty-six kilometres south-south-west of Glasgow, Scotland. A further twenty kilometres down the M77 is Alloway, the birthplace of the great Scottish poet, Robbie Burns.

John had nine children. Four of these children migrated to Australia, and the youngest of the four, Mathew Lamont, became my great grandfather. Bob calls him the black sheep of the family. He is recorded in the Scottish census of 1861 at Riccarton, Ayrshire, and the Australian marriage records of 1886 at Murrambit station, Victoria. Whilst the arrival date, the name of the ship, etc., are all available for the remainder of our antecedents, Mathew is a phantom. He was in Scotland—he was next in Australia. But exactly when he made the transition remains a mystery.

Grandmother was Alice Akhurst, whose brother, Oscar James, was married to Jessie Florence Smith. Their second daughter was Daphne Akhurst, my mother's cousin. Daphne was five times Australian tennis champion in 1925, 1926, 1928, 1929, and 1930. She is now always remembered in the family each January, when each year's winner of the Australian Ladies Open Tennis Championship is presented with the Daphne Akhurst Cup. Bob jokes that at that moment the family has to be standing at attention, with our right fists clenched and over our hearts in recognition.

Daphne Akhurst Cup

Sadly, Daphne died at thirty, from complications of an ectopic pregnancy. Her doctor had specifically told her not to play tennis, but she did, not wanting to disappoint her partner.

Returning to my grandparents, their first child was my mum, Freda Sidney (1909–1996). While they expected a boy, whom, before the birth, they had agreed to name Fred, the reality became Freda. There followed two more sisters: Hazel Lamont (1916–1992) and Nancy Alice (1918–2000). Pop, Fred, suffered from asthma and moved from Melbourne to Ballarat. He eventually moved to the country city of Orange, NSW, for the sake of his health. Mum worked in the lands department and saved hard to be able to go skiing each year at Kosciusko. She was skilled and won several prizes over the years. She was also a strong tennis player and was able to reflect back to her good genes coming from her cousin.

My mum, Freda, was energetic and effervescent. She was what we call a real goer. I can remember one fancy dress party at our Orange home: Mum greeted the guests, with two saucepan lids and one fig leaf covering the essentials. The show business streak lay strongly in her personality, but those were the days well expressed by Sir Noël Coward: "Don't put your daughter on the stage, Mrs Worthington." But, if it wasn't the professional stage, there were amateur theatricals and the parties at which the guests provided their own entertainment. A newspaper cutting from the *Orange Advocate*, January 1936, records the Apex Ladies' Night in the form of "a dinner, musical and elocutionary entertainment and dance" wherein "in a humorous elocutionary item, which has previously won for her recognition in Orange, Mrs Gillies provided what could be described as one of the gems of the entertainment." The one elocutionary item that stayed with Mum and was her party piece was "A Pleasant Sunday Afternoon at the Beach" also known as "Aggie at the Beach." (The recitation is included in the notes.[22])

Dad was Malcolm McPherson Gillies, the second to last of six children: Lilian, Winifred, Lawrence, Miriam, Malcolm, and John Frederick, who was only ever known to us as Uncle Fred. Dad was born on March 17, 1907, in the Orange Base Hospital. The family had been raised as Plymouth Brethren,[23] shortened to "the Plyms," but in the later years, three of the children—Dad, Fred, and Lil—left that group to go their own ways. From my time, he still rankled under the surface from some of the family experiences surrounding that departure. This came out when I became a Christian, and Dad expressed his concern that "Judy and Bob might become like the Plyms." We didn't. By comparison with Freda, Dad was a relatively quiet man, but he did go into the Orange amateur theatricals. It could perhaps best be described as an attraction of opposites, and Freda always claimed that, for any show, she had to know both their sets of lines, since Mal was prone to forget his, and she was always his main prompt. Mum and Dad married on Thursday, November 14, 1935, at the Orange Presbyterian Church. The three bridesmaids in attendance were Hazel and Nancy, Freda's sisters, and their adopted sister, Gwen; with two young teenagers carrying the bridal train and the seven-year-old flower girl who led the procession. Fred Gillies, Dad's younger brother, was the best man, and two friends were groomsmen.

Reverting to the Apex Ladies' Night, it further records:

> (... after presentation of a "beautiful coloured glass bowl) ... ... A motion was then carried that as the newly married Apexian of Orange, Mac Gillies, should sing a song. He obliged with a rendition of one of Richard Tauber's recent musical successes.

I was born in September 1939 and, eighteen months later my brother John came into the world. We have always got on very well and Bob has heard so many times of our exploits as teenagers sailing on Middle Harbour, Sydney, on our two-person VJ yacht. John went on to be an anaesthetist and remains my source of final medical recommendations. He married Fay Sorenson and are proud of their three children and seven grandchildren.

Dad worked in his father's men's clothing store in Orange, and it was a complete surprise when his father sold the business and Dad was out of a job. This forced the family's move to Sydney, and it was arranged for May 9, 1940, to see them off grandly with a wet farewell, the old way of saying, "with alcohol provided." Dad found work with the AMP Society and rented accommodation in the Chatswood area. In the war years, he (serial number NX 110 274) was not posted overseas, but was mainly at Tenterfield, NSW, where, like Bob's dad, he rose to the rank of sergeant.

Rental property was at a premium after the war, and the then Labour government maintained the Landlord and Tenant Act, which gave tenants the ability to retain the occupancy of their accommodation at a fixed rent. It was thus a blessing to the family when sister Hazel's bank manager husband, Harry, was transferred to the country. The Gillies quietly moved in, while Hazel and Harry moved out. When the landlord finally discovered the switch of tenants, the Gillies had been in long enough that they could not be evicted. Mum was not overly attracted to 25 Wood Street, Chatswood, and labelled it "Gillies Gully." The family wanted their own house, and Dad bought a block of land at 20 Plant Street, Balgowlah, which was happily known as "the Selection"—from Steele Rudd's Australian book *On Our Selection*. The weekends were spent clearing the block for building. It was still a time of rationing, and Dad's preoccupation was to get building materials for seemingly most of the house. Dad's ability to think outside the square was in evidence when, to capture the magnificent harbour views and against the architectural norms of the day for a two storey-house, he had the lounge, living areas, and even the kitchen upstairs, and the bedrooms downstairs. From the upstairs, there were sweeping views over Clontarf and Middle Harbour, providing a great ambience for parties. The house was finally completed and expressed in one of Freda's much-loved sayings: "with much cheers and heavy spitting!"

Changes in Life

Dad had become a representative for the Australian Mutual Provident (AMP) Society, where he remained for the rest of his working life. His professional breakthrough to become a millionaire salesman was to organize the life insurance policies of Ken Rosewell and Lew Hoad, two of Australia's greatest tennis players. For a few years after that coup, tickets used to come the family's way for the tennis at Sydney's White City Courts.

Bob and his parents used to welcome new people to the Seaforth Church with supper after the evening service. Following my conversion at the church, they had Dad and Mum for a chat at the first opportunity. Dad took a keen interest in the conversation with his biblical background picked up in the Plymouth Brethren. Mum, however, sat without saying a word. After the supper, Bob's parents agreed that whilst Dad was close to the kingdom, Mum seemed a long way off. Several weeks later, Mum also acknowledged Christ as her Lord, at forty-seven years of age. This decision had not been driven, as if there was anything traumatic, such as bad health, happening in her life—when the Lord calls someone into His kingdom, one does get up and follow Him. What was significant in her life was that, following a time of prayer, she simply stopped smoking. Dad's response to her confession of faith was that it was only a show, but Mum's life proved that it was real, and she maintained her faith until her death at eighty-seven.

To expand his retirement funds, dad built Seillig (which is Gillies spelt backwards), a block of units on Fairlight Street, Manly. It had a ground floor and two storeys, with Mum and Dad living on the top floor. This was not appreciated by Mum, having to lug the groceries up two flights of stairs—there was no elevator. Dad was a wealth creator and had a strong work ethic with an overriding desire that he and his Freda could retire without expecting the government pension. Up to around this time, to be on the old-age pension was equated with having been a failure in life. However, it was becoming acceptable to obtain the pension and retrieve some of the taxes that had been paid over one's working lifetime. Dad hoped to reach that landmark.

Dad had a genetic heart problem which ran through the Gillies family, and he suffered an attack at sixty-three. So, with climbing stairs *verboten*, Mum located a unit in the Camelot block, with a lift and otherwise flat walking. This block of units had replaced the Crescent Ballroom, where Bob and I had our wedding reception ten years earlier. Dad agreed to the purchase and spent six satisfying years there before his heart finally gave out, in 1976. He never made it to the pension.

Mum lived a further twenty years, the latter couple in Melbourne. On the week before she died, Mum said to me, "Who are you?" I was stunned and could only reply, "Judy, your daughter." Mum's sad response was the simple question "So?" She had stopped eating, and we knew the end was near. A few days later, on Sunday, we were sitting in the sun in the village's rose garden, and, whilst she had forgotten me, her mind had returned to allow her to sing the songs of her youth, such as "Chattanooga Choo-Choo," and spiritual songs, such as "How Great Thou Art," unbelievably, knowing all the words.

A New Patriarch

Judy's family origins now described, I will resume the narrative. With my own dad's death in 2002, I realized my status had risen to patriarch of our small clan. Within our culture, the title is purely nominal, but it did remind me that I was now the eldest of my sisters and in-laws.

At the beginning of this chapter, the third quotation stated, "You can never be too careful in the choice of your parents." Over the years, as Judy and I have both reflected on all that our parents did or did not do, our summation is that we could not have chosen better! For me, Bob, I could say that Mum gave me a sense of the value of property; from Dad came the ability to get on with people, and to have them work for me and with me. For Judy, her mum gave her the theatrical spirit, and the ability to stand up and perform in front of an audience;

while her Dad provided a quiet indwelling spirit. Yet behind these traits, the Bible, in Deuteronomy 8:17, does warn, "You may say to yourself, 'my power and the strength of my hands have produced this wealth for me,' but remember the Lord your God, for it is He who gives you the ability to produce wealth."

It was all the right chemistry that was going to come together from the starting genes and was honed with training to

let us lead and manage a large chemical business,

> **raise a civilized, Christian family,**

>> **participate in church life,**

>>> **and contribute effectively in the communities in which we have lived.**

5 The Year Bob Came Good

Spoilt rotten.[1]

Nothing succeeds like success.[2]

One does not normally call upon a mystery crime writer from the 1930s to provide an authoritative statement on social psychology, but it was Edgar Wallace who got right into the subject, with his short story, "Control No. 2."[3] The doctor pushing nurture claims, "With environment and training, you can make any baby [become] just what you wish." The doctor pushing nature argues, "The qualities a child has inherited, those he will develop. If my poor child had lived, he would, under God, have followed me in my profession. He would have had my code of honour, fulfilled my standard of behaviour." The book ultimately came down on the side of nature, which basically argues that we are determined by our genes, and there is nothing we can do about it. As mentioned in chapter 4, Uncle Bill has provided the Inder template, which I have followed across my lifetime.

The nurture angle has had a long rocky road to traverse. A book written around 1900 by John B Watson was still being read up to the mid-1950s. In a chapter entitled "Too Much Mother Love," the book claims:

> When you are tempted to pet your child remember that mother love is a dangerous instrument. An instrument which may inflict a never-healing wound, a wound which makes infancy unhappy, adolescence a nightmare, an instrument which may wreck your adult son or daughter's vocational future and their chances for marital happiness.

Psychologist Harry Harlow showed in some famous work during the 1950s that, using Rhesus monkeys, babies needed more than just food, water, and shelter. They also needed comfort and even love. Love soon became predominant in nurture, which led to the problems of too much, or excessive, mother love.[4] Mum was prime for that latter role.

Dad, Bob, and Mum

After my birth, Mum had travelled down the valley of the shadow of death[5] and, while recuperating, was not allowed to nurse me for my first three months. All the early photos, such as the one above, show Dad holding me to save Mum any strain.

Spoilt Rotten, Part I

The nurture angle says the quality of love and care we receive during our upbringing as children affects the kind of people we become. In my own particular case, I happen to believe that both nature and nurture have played their roles, just in different ways. I wanted to call the book, and this chapter in particular, *Spoilt Rotten*. I like the title because it reflects my belief that I received an excess of mother love and care during my upbringing. The larrikin in me wants to believe that the love that my family lavished on me during my younger years made me feel safe enough to become Bob, so that *what you see is what you get*. The over-love was present, but it did not turn me into a spoilt brat. In the end, we decided not to use the *Spoilt Rotten* title because readers from a non-English background might misunderstand my intentions and wrongly accuse my parents of producing a child who was capable only of tantrums and the worst kinds of behaviour that an overprotected childhood can produce. I don't believe I was ever that bad. I consider that I have been blessed with an equanimity of spirit which has trumped the time when I could have gone into histrionics on one side or depression on the other.

Bob and Mum in Sydney   The cowboy suit

In any case, Mum always claimed that it was her right to spoil me as her child. I don't remember being spoilt, but I do remember being made to feel special, as the only child of my parents' union. However, I did have to look special, whether we went into the city, or I was a cowboy waiting for a fancy dress party. Nor should be forgotten that brand-new red pedal car for my seventh birthday, the cricket bats and balls, and the Christmas stockings that always had to overflow.

Dad started working at fifteen, by sweeping floors at Hoffnung & Co., where he later became a storeman and thereafter a department manager, as mentioned previously. In one of the departments, it was necessary for Dad to get imported goods through customs. In the process, he got to know some of the customs agents. Each year, as a gesture of goodwill, they provided Dad with a large box of firecrackers from those which had been confiscated from illegal shipments. Dad was generous to a fault; in return, people often wanted to be generous to him. I have found that this trait, which was a part of Dad's character, has passed on to me. I like to help other people, and often find that I am the subject of others' generosity. So, each Guy Fawkes Night in November, the family would spoil me by letting me light the crackers on the Show Nights when our thirty to forty neighbours would gather and celebrate. These went well until the night of the great blow-up, when a spark got into the large box of fireworks and blew the lot up in a very intense five minutes. Skyrockets were coming through the crowds of onlookers at head height, it's a wonder no one lost an arm or an eye. I got close enough to the box to kick it over, which resulted in saving a few crackers that could be used safely the next night. Thereafter Mum and Dad were not going to have another night where I could be hurt. Dad brought no more fireworks home, and thus ended the cracker show nights in our street. It was a pity, for they had been happy times, not just for me, but for everybody.

Early Schooling

In those years, I attended the Manly West Primary School.[6] I walked there, rambling along the five hundred metres of streets to the west from home every school day. I remember the brick buildings, old even then, with one side facing the Manly Cemetery, which was also parallel to the road used coming home. One of the sports our school offered was boxing. I remember one match in particular, when, because of the way competitors were matched against each other, I was paired against a much bigger boy than I was. I got thumped, and that was the end of my boxing career, with sincere thankfulness!

Manly home

We lived at 75 Balgowlah Road, Manly, above, which shows Mum and Dad looking out over the road to the eleventh green of the Manly Golf Course. The dark chocolate-brown clinker brick house has now been demolished and replaced by units. During the early years of the Second World War, the Japanese were sweeping away all resistance as their war machine ploughed south through Asia. For Mum, in particular, fear came on the night of May 31, 1942, when three Japanese midget submarines attacked shipping in Sydney Harbour.[7] She envisaged that their follow-up army would parachute into our suburb, with the invasion using the golf course opposite our house. Because of Mum's misguided but real fear, we relocated as a family to Blackheath, in the Blue Mountains west of Sydney. The only memory from the six months or so when we stayed in that mountain town was the water authority's massive water tank nearby. During those six months, the fortunes of war changed. Just before the attack of the midget submarines, on May 4 through 8, there had been the victory in the naval Battle of the Coral Sea.[8] This was followed a month later, June 4 through 7, with the triumph at the naval Battle of Midway.[9] The most critical battle was that of the Kokoda Track Campaign,[10] which ran from July to the end of September. It was here, in Papua, New Guinea, that the Australians repulsed the Japanese army. It was the first battle in which the Japanese had been forced to retreat. By early 1943, we returned to our Manly home in Balgowlah Road, and once again I attended the Manly West Primary School.

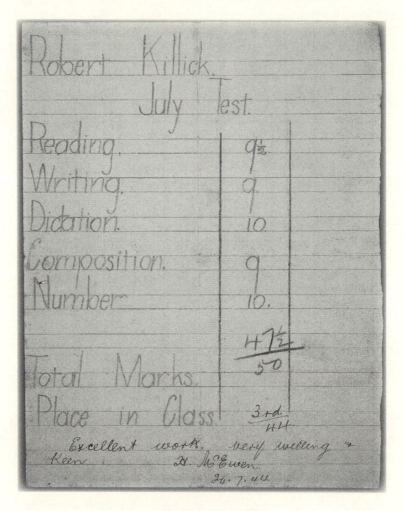

1944 school report

I still have one school report in my possession from those early days. It has sat in my small black storage box for seventy years. It is dated July 1944, and I was six. I was in a class of forty-four pupils, and came third in the tests. It seems a large class, but it was towards the war's end, and there weren't the resources we have now. I don't think that more resources would have made any difference, for, as the adage states, "Iron sharpens iron,"[11] and the iron against which I (situated fourth from right in top row [below]), would sharpen came in the package of Bob Hockey (second right in second top row), John Wilson (second right in third top row), and Alec Kilgour (far left in bottom row). The photo shows us all in the first year of primary school, and they were my key competition for the next five years. Competition seems to be an inherent way of life and built naturally into the societal air we breathe. It has always helped me.

Primary school competition

The arch striver for our family was Mum—the Killicks had to outperform and move up the class ladder. Middle class was the minimum, and if Mum could dream, upper-middle class was preferable. Dad had started work sweeping floors, but, as mentioned, by the time he retired from Hoffnung & Co., he was a director of the company, and well respected by the other board members. It reminds me of the story of the journalist who asked Hillary Clinton, "What would have happened to your life if you had married a garbage collector rather than Bill?" She retorted, "No difference, the garbage collector would have been President of the United States."

Faith Foundations

There is an old nostrum used by the Jesuits and ascribed to Francis Xavier: "Give me a child until he is seven and I will give you the man."[12] The maxim demonstrates that the training received by a child when young forms the substance and shape of his or her adult life, or, as William Wordsworth's dictum states it, "The child becomes the father of the man."[13] This only adds weight and importance to the work parents put into training and shaping the lives of their genetic offspring to guide them to become more than genetic clones, but, rather, responsible, mature adults who each make his or her own unique contributions to the world. There is no knowing how much time my first-grade teacher spent deciding on my assessment, but it makes me feel that at six I had made a good start. It reads pithily, "Excellent work. Very willing and keen." Even now, I think it is a good statement on my approach to life in the years that followed. There was also the competitive spirit which had started then at primary school. Apart from Bob Hockey for a few years at Sunday school, I have not heard of the others since we separated at twelve years of age and went to various high schools. They have been gone from my life for sixty-five years, but to Bob Hockey, Alec Kilgour, and John Wilson, I simply say in Latin, "*Saluto te!*"

In those early years of my life, another key part of my education was learning the Bible at the Sunday school of the Manly Baptist Church. I've already described how Mum and Dad sent me there to be babysat between three and four o'clock on Sunday afternoons while the grown-ups went to visit Grandpa. The church was chosen purely for convenience, with Grandpa and Aunty Polly's house just five minutes away. The Sunday school had yearly exams, and, as ever, Mum expected that I would excel if not come top of the results. The name of Bob Hockey, whose father was the Sunday school superintendent, was again there to provide suitable competition. Honour rolls were maintained on the walls of the Sunday school room, and my name did appear at least once. This was divine providence—that is, God at work in one's life, to bring what He already stated in the Bible: "From infancy I have known the holy Scriptures, which are able to make me wise for salvation through faith in Christ Jesus."[14] It wasn't always written large in my life, but the Sunday school was there in the background, teaching me that I owed my existence to God, for the universe to live in and our parents for bringing us into this life and nurturing us within it. Being thankful was what should be our natural response to Him. This theme of gratefulness became one of the most singular and important antidotes to turning me aside from my position of relative privilege, and stopped me turning into a spoilt brat.

Holidays have not been important to me. I don't want to say I was a workaholic child, but there were the signs. I will only concede that I was, and still am, a modified workaholic. During my late primary years, holidays were spent as stays in quaint guest houses, which already felt old—even back then. One town we often stayed in was Bundanoon, which lay on the main rail line between Sydney and Melbourne, one hundred kilometres south-west of Sydney, in the Great Dividing Range. The slightly larger towns either side were Bowral and Mittagong. The day's main excitement for a boy of my age was to go down to the railroad crossing to watch from only three metres away the Inter-Capital Daylight and then the Riverina Express thunder through the town, at around one hundred kilometres per hour (or sixty-six miles per hour). With a weight of four hundred tonnes, the kinetic energy emanated by the train made one's body shake. Sixty years later, I continue to enjoy the same vibrating experience when waiting on a German semi-rural one-platform train station for the local S-Bahn train to take me back to a Hauptbahnhof, such as Cologne. It only takes one of Europe's high-speed inter-city expresses (ICE) going through the station on its specific main line at over two hundred kilometres per hour. One certainly becomes "all shook up."

Meanwhile, back at Bundanoon, another pastime was to have trains flatten penny pieces. This was accomplished by laying a penny on the rail track, and then, once the train had thundered by, to try to find the flattened remains, which sometimes could have been flung metres away. I do enjoy train travel, and it was a truly special experience in my early teens to travel on the same Riverina Express through Bundanoon when we used to go south to stay at Uncle Norman and Aunty Beth's farm at Book Book, outside Wagga Wagga.

Secondary Schooling

There is an awkward age when one reaches the point at which an adult considers a conversation can be held with a child. It seemed the safest stock question was " ... and what do you want to do when you grow up?" It is interesting looking back to those earliest days, that my immediate response was that I wanted to be a train driver. There was some backwash here from Dad's stories of the Great Depression and his overwhelming desire for me to have a secure, steady, government job. Now, it might just be an old man's weakness, but reminiscing about those times and hearing the sound of a steam engine still affects me emotionally. Mum had not necessarily been innocent in providing me with a love of steam trains, for, several times when we were going up the Blue Mountains from Central Station, she would ask the engine driver and fireman if I could ride on the footplate with them—that is, in the engine cabin, for a few stations, and then return to our carriage. Most times, they agreed, and I can still remember the ambience and the smell of the steam and the coal smoke. I also learnt this at that time: always ask; they can only say no, but more often than not, it will be *yes!*

The train motif might have sounded good to me, but Mum and Aunty Roxie Inder didn't countenance the idea of Bob becoming a train driver. They soon agreed, as a first step, to get me an education that ensured I would become something, or at least, anything else. The catch cry became "If Bob could at least have one year's experience at university, all would be well." Their first important goal was to get me the best schooling available, so I was off to the Sydney Church of England Boys Grammar School, familiarly known as "Shore." This was a private fee-paying independent school located up the short hill west of the North Sydney rail station, with reputedly the best education available in that part of Sydney at the time.

Founded in 1889, Shore retained an English heritage, with sports activities high on the agenda. Rugby was the sport of choice for the boys. It is often said that "The Battle of Waterloo was won on the playing fields of Eton." I was solid for my age and played rugby union in the second row of the scrum, which was, as Dad was wont to say, "the place where the thugs gather." (You'll recall this from a previous rumination.) My sporting career, like my boxing career, offered nothing that was memorable. My sporting activities did not extend to rowing, but we were highly encouraged to attend the yearly inter-school races on the Hawkesbury River near Penrith. The first time we went, Shore won every race. We were ecstatic.

Aunty Roxie was an encourager, and when I obtained the intermediate certificate, she presented me with the 1,336-page book *The Complete Sherlock Holmes Short Stories*, with the handwritten note, "Congratulations, Bob, from Aunty Roxie (Inter. Dec. 1952)." When I want to relax, I still browse the book, sixty years later.

At the start and finish of term, the school chapel services were held, during which the same Bible passage[15] was read. Perhaps it came as a result of constant repetition from the King James translation, but verse 11 has been one of those verses which has burrowed deeply into my consciousness: "dearly beloved, I beg you as strangers and pilgrims." It reminded me of that traditional African American spiritual, "This world is not my home, I'm just a-passing through." That thought went deep into the marrow of my bones, leaving an indelible sense that in all the vagaries of life, God has been with me and is acting for me, for the time, however short or long, that we are here on earth.

The only teacher that I can recollect from the whole five years at Shore was my science teacher, Fritz Bernard. He was the one who gave me a love for mathematics and science. My fascination with maths was engendered somewhere in the first two years of high school, when I understood the truth of the equation: $(x+1).(x-1) = x^2-1$, or in layman's terms, if $(x+1)$ is multiplied by $(x-1)$, the same result will be achieved by multiplying "x" with another "x" and then taking away 1. For those not skilled in algebra,[16] this is what we know as a *general equation* and the "x" can be replaced by any number. Let's say the "x" is replaced by the number 5, then $(5+1)$ multiplied by $(5-1)$ becomes 6 multiplied by 4, which is 24. The 5 multiplied by another 5 is 25, and taking away 1 is 24. The = is an equal sign, which means that whatever is to the left or right of it ends up as the same number. I stayed up on the night I was introduced to that equation, replacing x with number after number, seeing that the equation would hold true. It may not seem to be an especially thrilling story, but it gave me a love of mathematics and the technological world. You could say in a way that it reinforced my journey exploring the mathematical beauty of the universe.

Mum had got me into Shore as the stepping stone to get me to university. This was easier said than done in those days, because to qualify for university it was a mandatory prerequisite to obtain a pass in English in the leaving certificate. But English was never one of my strengths, and the idea of passing English in the leaving certificate seemed out of the question. Nothing ever seemed to go right for me in English. A typical example I always remember was a practice English essay at school on the subject "Crossing the Harbour Bridge." The teacher stressed in his review of the composition that had got the top mark, "Note how this essay sets the scene in the night-time, with all the added possibilities of lighting, etc." I was sitting at my desk, purring, for I had set my essay in the night. But it wasn't my essay, and despite using the right words, I still received a poor mark. I was crushed, and, interestingly, I can still feel it today. I had done my best, and it was simply not good enough. If I was going to get to university, with a pass in English, then tutoring was obviously going to be the key. It came in two forms. The first was in professional coaching from a Mr Cornforth, a schoolteacher who had retired early on account of his extreme deafness and tutored to supplement his income. The classroom was in the lower ground rooms of his Mosman home, looking out onto an unkempt garden. We spent a lot of time on Shakespeare's *The Tempest*.[17] I had to read the play and answer questions posed by my after-hours teacher. The second tutor was Aunty Roxie, who would sit patiently and read over my essays, offering critique from her knowledge of what a good English essay ought to look like. My cousin, Bryan, who would have been nine years old then, remembers those times vividly.

Move to Seaforth

The Inder family consisted only of my uncle and aunty on Mum's side, and we have remained close over our lifetimes. They were also helpful in my not picking up the sin of covetousness. Why bother to be covetous when you knew that the Inders were always going to be richer? The extension to that thought was that there will always be someone better or worse off than I, in every category of life.

In August 1952, the Inders introduced my family to shipboard travel when, as two family groups, we went to Port Moresby in Papua New Guinea, on the old SS *Orion*. It had been launched in late 1934 and was ready to sail in August 1935. In its day, it was considered the epitome of modernity as the first British liner to have air conditioning in all her public rooms and an interior decor, original for the time, using chromium and Bakelite extensively. The *Orion*'s size was 23,400 tonnes, and we had an inside cabin whilst even the outside cabins only had portholes. I am sure no naval architect then would have ever dreamt of balcony cabins that surround the modern ship. In late 1963, the *Orion* was taken to the scrap yard.

All the details on the *Orion* contrast with the stupendous cruise liners launched in 2016, with sizes of 167,800 tonnes (*Ovation of the Seas*) to 225,000 tonnes (*Harmony of the Seas*). Judy and I were fortunate in our Milestone Year of 2013 to cruise as a family on the *Voyager of the Seas,* whose size was 138,000 tonnes. Judy and my feeling was that, with 3,810 passengers, it had passed by our comfort zone.

For all the travel we have enjoyed over the last sixty years, it seems wonderfully symbolic that our family was cruising to New Zealand when the telegraph message came through from the Inders announcing that I had achieved the required pass in English in the leaving certificate, which would allow me to get into university. The full results were second-class honours in mathematics 1 and in mathematics 2, an A in both physics and chemistry, and a B (which was a pass in those days) in French and in English. So, with the help of my mother and aunt, we had accomplished what we—or more so they—had set out to do. My total result was above average, but, just for the record, nowhere near those of the school's top students, who would achieve three first-class honours and two A's. By contrast with primary school (and, later, university), I had no close competition in high school. I cannot provide the name of one competitor with whom I could sit down and be sharpened further.

In 1953, Mum and Dad built their dream home, and we moved from Manly West to Kanangra Crescent, Seaforth. The prime block had spectacular views overlooking Middle Harbour. The view became even more impressive when Dad had to build a two-storey dwelling to lift the house high enough to reach the public sewer in Ethel Street. This could still only be achieved by using jackhammers to cut a two-metre-deep trench through Hawkesbury sandstone for fifty metres along a right of way between two neighbouring houses. All living was only on the higher floor, and a two-car garage went underneath, with many storage rooms that had dirt floors. There were other building problems that provided a build-up of experiences which helped me understand logistics and architecture for later in life, particularly when I was responsible for running a chemical company. Judy and I both saw our parents build, and it certainly burnt out any wish for us to do it.

By providence, the Seaforth Baptist Church had been established as an outreach from the Manly Church and was meeting in the Masonic hall not more than a three-minute walk from our new house. I rapidly became part of the furniture at the church. This was also around the time I started going to university, and Mum said words to Dad, to the effect that "Bob is a good boy, and now he is going to university, you should go to church with him to show that we are keen to support him!"

Dad came!

Mum had been really sick for what now seems like most of my teenage years. This meant that Dad and I had to do the food preparation, as mentioned previously, and I became a little more than a passably good cook. Indeed, by my late teens, I was becoming an organic chemist at university, whilst at home, a frustrated chef. Thus, when I married Judy, she found someone who could earn a living whilst being thoroughly house-trained and capable of running a household.

The white sports jacket

During the time of Mum's sicknesses, she seemed to have a need to dress me up. As a matter of course, Bob had to have sports jackets— not just any sports jacket, mind you, but a white sports jacket … and not to forget the two mustard-coloured ones. The negative impact on me from Mum's pushing for me to stand out from the crowd remains in my life today. I am not a good shopper, and I react quite negatively when some outstanding or excessively colourful clothing is suggested. In retrospect, I relate this to the example of my role model in Uncle Bill, who was slightly counter-cultural and always seemed to dress down to the oldest clothes that actually looked worn out. We would meet him walking along Manly Beach, with his reading glasses held around his neck with a piece of string. It was a great idea for Christmas to present him with a nice silver chain to hold his glasses. We only ever met him later with the piece of string still in use. Rest assured that whilst I don't use string to hold my glasses, I still often think about Uncle Bill and the kind of character he was. Whether nature or nurture, I do wonder about the inordinate power each has, running through the same family line. I resisted, basically to no avail, my mother's attempts to nurture me towards overdressing, and chose instead to give in to some underlying impulse to informality, such as Uncle Bill preferred. After fifty-plus years of marriage, Judy has finally stopped getting annoyed at the tatty throwaway clothes I wear to our local shopping village.

Full Commitment

For the week after Christmas, our Seaforth church joined with the Stanmore Baptist Church for a week of fellowship and Bible study at the base camp of the Gospel Fishermen,[18] situated at Tahlee on Port Stephens, north of Newcastle, NSW. The facilities were around the old Tahlee homestead. The leader for the week was the Rev. Neville Horn, pastor of the Stanmore Church. The typical day had a prayer meeting before breakfast and a Bible study in the morning. The afternoons were free for walks, games, and swimming behind some netting in a fairly rustic rock pool. The evening had a time of singing, followed by Neville Horn giving a scriptural challenge to commit one's life to Christ. As a means to confirm one's decision, it was considered that it should be expressed publicly by walking to the front of the room. This was followed by a time of counselling. Oh, I really did want to go forward, but I was sitting in the back row with the other boys. It was a distance too far. On the next day, I had not lost my desire to go forward publicly, and my organization skills took over, with the simplest but most effective move being to sit in the front seat. I do not remember what Neville preached on that night, but when the call was given, I was out to the front like a shot. It was a distance very close.

Tahlee house

I am sure the teaching for the rest of the week did not cover minor matters, but when I walked into home, I told Mum and Dad all the things that I was not going to do! There would be no cinema, no drinking alcohol, no smoking, no playing cards, no this, and no that. Mum and Dad fortunately played Mr and Mrs Cool. My response was the spirit of legalism, but with three questions posed by a preacher, mainly from the Bible's book to the Galatians,[19] I was brought back to the real ground: "How did your new life begin? Was it by working your heads off to please God? Or was it by responding to God's message to you?" The answer to these questions was that it was by simply responding to God's message that had come to me.

A year later, all the family came to Tahlee. Dad arrived in a big American car, familiarly known as a yank tank. To Dad's chagrin, the other campers showed no interest in his car. To stir matters further, our next contact was Fred, who sort of knew us from the Seaforth church. He brusquely said, "You can have our tent. The rains came last night, and we were washed out!" Not a good start. As Mum and Dad walked to get their morning tea, Dad noticed in one of the rooms, people on their knees praying. It wasn't part of Dad's culture. They did stay, which provided a real indication of what Mum and Dad would put up with for their number-one son. When Dad and Neville later met, Dad would recount how he threw at Neville everything nasty about God and His church that he could, and Neville only graciously responded. During the week, Dad himself committed his life to God.

Another year later, we were all there again, and halfway through the week, Mum came up from a morning Bible study, exclaiming, "Don't you know that the Bible teaches, 'Don't you know that you, yourselves, are God's temple and that God's Spirit lives in you?'"[20] This has never been considered the most evangelical verse that the Holy Spirit might use in a conversion, but, for Mum, it held special significance. Mum and Dad were both converted in their late forties, and they were going to catch up with a level of work in God's kingdom to cover all the years they felt they had lost. It was on for young and old, and they let it rip!

Rev. Neville Horn

Spoilt Rotten, Part II

By 1956—the year of my eighteenth birthday—Mum's spoiling of me came to a peak, when I was given a brand-new Volkswagen (VW) motor car after I'd had my driver's licence for a year. Mum, as always, had to have her Bob stand out, and the car she gave me had had a white stripe ducoed over the green car's luggage compartment, roof, and engine compartment. From the gasp when we saw the car at the spray painter's, I think even Mum wondered if she might have gone too far this time. (A photo of the car is in chapter 6.) The choice of the VW was not mine, but that of our Dutch neighbour, who, in discussions, told Dad, "Bob must have a VW to know the meaning of driving." I don't think I ever really thought that much of the car or the meaning of driving. As my colleagues at Vicchem have learnt over thirty years, I detest having to make the decision as to what car the company should buy for me. Since that Volkswagen, I have simply stayed within the Holden car range from General Motors.

They say that everything is relative, and as a family we were not rich, per se. I did, however, remain the key financial priority for my parents, so money was always available if something "important" was required. Mum was particularly pleased with my church affiliation. When I indicated that I would appreciate having my own copy of the Thompson Chain Reference Bible,[21] she bought it, although I think she blanched at the £20.00 price tag, which was then a significant amount of money. It was a good buy, and sixty years later, I still use that Bible in sermon preparation. This attitude of financial optimism became a blessing in later years. In my many discussions with banks or financial institutions, there was never any doubt that money could be borrowed. I always wore in my psyche an assurance that money was never an issue; it would always be available when I wanted or needed it.

Having said that money was always available, it was only because Mum and Dad had worked hard to earn it and to keep it. Our house at Kanangra Crescent, Seaforth, where I grew up through my later teenage years, was on a sloping block that provided areas underneath the house for two garages and several rooms with dirt floors. This allowed us to set up an underground cottage industry making electrical elements for Uncle Bill to sell at his company, Manly Lighting & Electrical Suppliers. I became quite efficient at my task, and the challenge was to maximize production. Sixty years afterwards, I seem to recall that I worked at the rate of one element per minute as the standard rate of production. This was a clandestine business because Mum and Dad felt it was below the status of the Killicks' to be doing piecework.[22] To this end, whenever an unexpected visitor came to the front door, whoever was upstairs would stamp on the floor as the sign to cease manufacture until it was safe to start production again. I never received any cash for services rendered; what was received from Uncle Bill went into Team Killick coffers. The other side was that Mum and Dad never refused me any requests for money. Lack of friends after school did not worry me, since, being a mild workaholic, I was most happy mining at the coal face. Once I have a project, I go for it, and other things have to fall by the roadside.

The Country Girl Who Came to Sydney

The year after the end of the Second World War, Judy's grandfather sold his menswear shop in Orange, NSW, and Mal, her father, was suddenly unemployed. To facilitate her father's search for employment, the family moved to Sydney, 520 kilometres east from Orange. He was able to sign up with the AMP Society, selling life insurance. Judy commenced schooling at age six, in first grade at Chatswood Primary. The teacher, wanting to place her in the right class level, asked her, "What is 1 + 1?" Judy sat there silently. The teacher tried again. "Judy, what is 1 + 1?" Judy sat there, still silent. The teacher said, "I know you are nervous, but do have a try. Tell me, what is 1+1?" Judy replied, "But, Teacher, you haven't told me, are we buying or are we selling?" This joke is always a good lead-in at Vicchem's business meetings, as a warning to look out for Judy's canny Scottish nature and astuteness. She did become Executive Director of the Victorian Chemical Company, jokes notwithstanding.

With their house completed, the Gillies family moved during the 1950 Christmas holidays to their new home in Plant Street, Seaforth. This was about 150 metres around the corner from our home. Judy started high school at Manly Home Science School. In the meantime, Judy and her brother, John, learnt to play the piano, but when they began to lose interest, their mother, Freda, agreed that they could learn via the Shefte method. This technique teaches pupils to play the melody line with the right hand, but then uses set bass chords for each music key for the left hand to play. This provided a much quicker learning method, and Judy and John were soon able to play the hits of the day. They both used to entertain dinner guests or party crowds at home, and it was a regular occurrence to have small coins thrown to them, three pence (3d.; or, colloquially, a traybit) or even six pence (6d.; or, colloquially, a zack) at these parties. These singalongs were so much a part of party life in those days. Interestingly, this Shefte method began to lose its popularity as a valuable teaching tool not long after Judy and John had become popular-music pianists.

When she was fifteen, Judy left school to begin work at the head office of the Bank of NSW, typing as the girl Friday (or flossie) in the Northern Inspectors Office. One of her friends from that time is Jan Rowland (née Humphreys), who continues to be a friend today. Both of them used to take part in the corps de ballet in the bank concerts, such as *Sally*. Judy did not see her long-term future in the bank, and started night school to obtain the leaving certificate which would give the necessary access to Teachers College.

The most life-changing event from these night classes started from the camaraderie among those doing night studies. One night, one of the four boys getting off the bus at Seaforth junction said to Judy, "Do you want to come to the Bappo's on Sunday night?" "Who are the Bappo's?" Judy well asked, but that following Sunday, Judy did go to the Seaforth Baptist Church. Under the preaching of layman Trevor Anthony, Judy committed herself to the Lordship of Jesus Christ. The young people were away at the NSW October Labour Day weekend camp when the word came up to us that a new young lady had become a Christian overnight at the church. Over fifty years, Judy has not wavered from that commitment she made at the Baptist church that night.

Judy's determination to always finish the course can also be recognized during the night studies, as there were those times when the family were going off to the beach to have some fun and relaxation, and she would stay home to study. She obtained the necessary four passes and went to the Western Annex of the Balmain Teachers College, situated in the suburb of Rozelle. Two years later, Judy graduated as a primary school teacher.

To University

I consider myself fortunate to have attended Sydney University. In the early days, Dad and I were driven to Hoffnung & Co., in Clarence Street, by Hughie Snaith. He was a selling agent who needed use of a car during the day. I can always remember Hughie's adventurous speedway character expressing itself when driving. After accidentally crossing a double line and, looking around to confirm that the law had not seen the indiscretion, he was wont to say, "The honest have got nothing to fear." I would finish my journey to Sydney University sedately on public transport.

During 1955, my first year of university, I was still trying to work out what my future might be. The subjects in which I was enrolled were pure mathematics and applied mathematics, because of the honours in the leaving certificate; chemistry was another of my better subjects, and geology was the fill-in. Mathematics, however, seemed to have jumped about three levels up from school, to what I could say were "infinite sets that don't exist." The argument around this difficult type of question started with Georg Cantor, in 1891, and is still spasmodically being debated to the present day.[23] Mathematics has always fascinated me. One of the quaint numbers that exists is the square root of negative one ($\sqrt{-1}$). This should, technically, not exist. However, the mathematicians have given it the nom de plume of i, and it is used quite successfully, for example, in equations for electrical engineering and control systems.

Then there is pi (π), the ratio of the circumference to the diameter of a circle, the shape of which is considered "the simplest form in the universe." A raindrop in a pool produces perfect circles of waves that can expand indefinitely. However, π cannot be expressed as an exact fraction, and its decimal representation neither repeats nor ends. It is thus an irrational number. Two Japanese mathematicians took ninety days to reach the five trillion decimal places, and they are talking of going on to ten trillion places.[24]

Another funny is infinity (∞), which is best described as an abstract concept. However, in mathematics, ∞ is often treated as if it were a number; that is, as a unit that counts or measures things. Once again, Georg Cantor formalized many ideas relating to it.

My future began to narrow very quickly, with my underwhelming first year results of three passes and a credit in geology. Geology was only a fill-in though, and, the credit notwithstanding, it was the one subject certain to be dropped. I no longer had a passion for mathematics, and maths became part of *Sic transit gloria mundi*, which then really left only chemistry. In retrospect, if I had failed a subject, it would have precluded me from going on to do a doctor of philosophy (PhD). Without being snobbish, this degree would be a key in later times, to reach appropriate technical contacts in the major multinational chemical companies. One of the other students in our year had failed one subject although he had achieved some of the highest leaving certificate results in the state, His attitude during the year had been "I am so smart that I don't have to put in the hours that lesser mortals need to; I can party all year." He rationalized his PhD rejection by giving the same response that Aesop's fox did when unable to reach the grapes it coveted—claimed the grapes were sour anyway. If there was no PhD, then he would do a double degree. The rest of us took the moral of the situation to be that work was more important than inherent talent.

Thus, in second year university (1956), I dropped both mathematics and geology, and was left with chemistry and advanced chemistry. In second year, groups began to form around the disciplines, and I was in the working competitive group which consisted of Arthur Hollis, the university medallist who sadly died three years later in a car accident; David Black, who became professor of organic chemistry at the University of NSW; Rolf Prager, who became professor of organic chemistry at the University of Adelaide; and John Hurley, who became one of the most appreciated senior lecturers of the Pharmacology College. Everyone would brag about how they never did any work each night, whilst everyone knew that each one had been working flat out like a lizard drinking, as the Australian colloquialism puts it. I was never good at night work, so I used to go to bed by 10:00 p.m., but then get up at 4:00 a.m. to work until 6:00 a.m., have breakfast, and make an early start to drive to work. We were also fortunate to have top lecturers, the best of whom was Dr Ernie Ritchie. He was senior lecturer at our time and went on to be professor. He would quietly enter the lecture hall and then open a little piece of paper, six centimetres by ten centimetres, which contained his notes for the fifty-minute lecture. It was impressive. His research work was in the isolation and characterization of the constituents of the Australian flora. He was a giant in knowledge, and that fitted in with the reference that "there were giants in the land in those days."[25]

That second year is best described as "the year Bob came good," with a high distinction in chemistry; coming third in the year and first in the organic chemistry section. The first two men were on the physical chemistry side. But second year was also the year the professors looked around to find those students who shone like sparklers in the night.

In the Lord's timing, I had been chosen, and was on the way to—dare I say it—a prestigious academic career. With the way my life eventuated, none of us obviously belonged to the School of the Prophets.[26]

God moves in a mysterious way His wonders to perform.

6 Formation of The Punch and Judy Travelling Show

There's no Punch without Judy[1]

Marriage is a noble daring.[2]

In life, there are conversations, and there are *conversations*. In April 1959, Judy and I were in the middle of one of the latter, which went something along these lines:

> JUDY (*seriously*): Please stop flying kites, Bob, and half hinting that we could end up together. If you are going to talk weddings, we must pray that it is the Lord's will ... this could last a long time!"
> BOB (*ever practical*): Well, how long exactly?
> JUDY (*after a long calculating pause*): Forty-five years?

When you are nineteen (as Judy was at that time) and deciding on taking the step to be married, forty-five years does seem a long time. We now rejoice that we have past fifty-seven years.

Both Judy and I had boy- and girlfriends, respectively, before this point, for various lengths of time. I had been courting a young lady called Margaret for two years. People used to comment about how much we seemed suited for each other. Indeed, when Judy and her mother first joined the Seaforth Baptist Church, it was their opinion that "that Bob Killick would marry that Margaret." But the courtship went awry when Margaret went to Victoria for nursing training. At that time, Victorian training was a year shorter than the four years in NSW. This would then allow her to get to the mission field a year earlier. Proverbs can be contradictory, for whilst "absence makes the heart grow fonder," it is also said that "out of sight is out of mind." In the fullness of time, Margaret married Laurie, had children, and worked for many years in Chad, Africa. Following their return to Australia, they undertook church planting in NSW, for the Brethren assemblies.

Good news travels fast, and one Monday morning in October 1956, we all knew of Judy's conversion back at Seaforth the night before (Sunday). We were mostly all away at a church camp in the Blue Mountains for the long weekend. Judy had attended on a whim that night, following the invitation to come to the "Bappo's." She heard the message that God loved her very dearly, and had sent His Son, Jesus, to lay down His life for her. When the call for commitment was given that night, Judy didn't have to be asked twice. In the coming weeks and months, she became busily involved in the work of the church and the kingdom of God. One of my first real memories of Judy was in a concert I was organizing. We had arranged that Judy would chase David, one of the youth group's younger men, out the stage window, around the church, and back through the audience, whilst she sang "You Can't Get a Man with a Gun" from the 1946 Irving Berlin musical *Annie Get Your Gun*. At the end of the item, I would like to report that the crowd rose as one for a standing ovation. This is perhaps a little exaggerated, but it was well appreciated. David was one of the groomsmen at our wedding and went on to become a medical doctor. Again, I am not saying that this song and concert was the start of our courtship, but, looking back, some of Judy's attributes swirled across the stage. Although the song said "You can't get a man with a gun," the lyrics[3] proved to be wrong in the longer term.

Courting in the Open Air

During our courting days, we continued to take part in the weekly open-air meetings run by the church. These were on the Manly Corso, which is the pedestrian thoroughfare that joins Manly Wharf, on the harbour side, with the ocean beaches to the east. Sixty years ago, reasonably good crowds would stand around those events to listen. They were not only free entertainment—they provided people with an important opportunity to think about their lives from the perspective of Eternity (capitalized intentionally). The word *Eternity* was also the copperplate mark of Arthur Stace,[4] who wrote the word with chalk on the footpaths of Sydney for thirty-five years, from 1932 to his death in 1967. Arthur was an eccentric, illiterate soldier, a reformed alcoholic who had converted to Christianity and who spread the gospel message by writing this one word about fifty times every day. His lasting impact on the city was highlighted at the spectacular fireworks display on the Harbour Bridge at the dawn of the new millennium, January 1, 2000. The thirty-minute show ended with an exploding fireball, and as the smoke cleared, and through the haze, eighteen-metre-high copperplate letters spelling *Eternity* appeared. The Sydney crowd, realizing its significance, cheered in delight as the two billion worldwide TV viewers looked on, rather perplexed and still rather bewildered.[5]

Meanwhile, back at the open-air meetings, a few of the older men would give their testimony and tell of the good news that Christ died for our sins. I also used to do some preaching and whiteboard sketching. It is a sure way to learn how to talk in front of a floating crowd that had to be retained by skill and oratory. There were songs sung, and these were accompanied by a piano accordion. Judy had a good voice to help with the singing, and she also handed out scripture tracts to those people scuttling around the edges of the crowd.

Judy and her mum used to attend the weekly Bible studies run in our home by Mum and Dad. There would be one speaker over several weeks that would provide Bible teaching for an hour, followed by discussion and then supper. We were blessed to have many formidable speakers come over the years. Rev. Neville Horn taught a series on the Person and work of the Holy Spirit, and Rev. Neville Anderson—a returned missionary from India—gave some great expositions from the Bible, in particular, the book of Romans. Unforgettable was Mr Perrett, who gave memorable teaching on the tabernacle which the Israelites took through the wilderness for worship. It was a teaching[6] which has stayed with me to the present day.

Our social lives swirled through the open-air meetings, Bible studies, concerts, and our general church activities, and Judy and I began to know each other better. Fairly rapidly, the Volkswagen car found its way to Dobroyd Head, which is situated opposite the Heads of Sydney Harbour. When one of us wasn't looking deeply and meaningfully into the other's eyes, the night views, across the harbour, of the lights of a Manly ferry plying between Manly and Circular Quay could be almost as breathtaking. It is true that Judy was not the first girl I had taken to the lookout, but she was certainly the last. To use a scientific analogy, you could say that Dobroyd became our laboratory: Judy and I spent time together there, to test whether we had the right chemistry. Reflecting on those nights more than fifty-eight years ago, I wonder how a few kisses—OK, a multitude of kisses—could give a clear indication that we would prove strong enough to stand the challenges of marriage. However, we were still the generation that was able to work out the level of chemistry between us with kisses and cuddles.

Whilst we never articulated the reasons why our marriage would be successful, the fact is that kisses and cuddles do not make up the whole marriage. Returning to those late 1950s, we now recognize that we did have several other matters running in our favour. On the spiritual side, we were both fully committed to "one Lord, one faith, one baptism."[7] We were both wholeheartedly given to the ministries of the church, such as the open-air preaching, and ever keen to learn more of the Bible in order to apply its teaching into our lives. In the social arena, we were in the middle-class milieu. We were strong in education and keen to have our own home, whilst, personally, we enjoyed sports, music, and show-time involvement. To both Judy and me, marriage means commitment, and our greatest strength is that we have commitment to the things we value. In the earliest days of continuing discussions, I would ask her to confirm that, if the marriage went ahead, she would be prepared to be a minister's wife. She might even find herself on the mission field. Judy always confirmed her preparedness to go. When life had swung completely the other way, and we were to have our house mortgaged to borrow for the purchase of a defunct company, she showed her commitment to me. The comment to Marj was re-echoed, showing her understanding of how dire the situation was: "If this doesn't work out we will be in a tent on your lawn." It was Judy's house as much as mine that was on the line. She has followed me wherever I've gone and shown complete loyalty in every situation.

When we passed Judy's original statement that she would expect our marriage to last forty-five years, I established a running joke, saying, "I'm free! I'm free!" But this was said in a manner that negated the freedom concept altogether. I would add a rider stating, "I've looked out there, and you're dreaming if you think it is better." It is interesting that I can look back now on fifty-seven years of marriage—and counting!—and claim that I have kissed nobody on the lips but Judy. There has been one exception, and that was organized by Judy herself. As a surprise for my fiftieth birthday, she arranged for a French maid to come and do a party piece. This included being tickled by a feather duster; a poem of my life; and a parting kiss on the lips, to much jocularity among the partygoers, who were clearly relieved that the shenanigans had not gone over the top as they often do. French maids have a reputation of being risqué, so Judy had heavily stressed with the booking agent that her Bob was the church secretary of a Baptist church! The maid did take the message on board.

Lone overseas travel reputedly brings temptation, but one has to be in the byway of tantalization. Not being allured by any nights on the town, I was never tempted to go to clubs or pubs. The one exception was after a late conference session. Four of us entered the hotel lift to return to our respective rooms when a provocatively dressed girl jumped in and said, "I'm off to Club Roman for a great night—who's coming with me?" We all began to make excuses, so at the next floor, she exited with the parting shot, "Party poopers." Such as it was, this was the only overt incitement in all the times that I have been away from Judy on travel for the company.

The Engagement

There was a slow and steady build-up before I had the courage to ask Judy to be my wife. I have never been a bull at a gate in matters in which the answer must be positive. Indeed, my style of negotiation, to get the answer I want, is to fly kites. One of those, for example, was for me to talk about places one might go for a honeymoon, when we had not yet agreed on whether the marriage would even take place. Understandably, Judy found this frustrating.

Yet I really did want to marry Judy, and I could only "fly kites" for so long. By April 1959, I could read the signs that the time had come when I had to stop cackling and lay an egg, so to speak. It was time to get serious, and propose. One Sunday evening, after the usual church service, I drove Judy out to Oxford Falls, just off the main road from our homes at Seaforth, through Frenchs Forest, towards the Narrabeen Lakes. Still uncertain, I kept praying to the effect that, if this should not go ahead, Lord, then let the car break down. I still believe it skipped a few beats, but the car delivered us to Oxford Falls, and with no more hints or flying kites, I simply asked her to be my wife. I would have preferred to have written that she grabbed me by the lapels, shook me like a wet rat, and said, "Listen, Bob, stop beating about the bush, and tell me you are going to marry me. It's yes or no, and you might as well learn now for the rest of your life that the answer will always be 'yes, Judy,' and then we will both lead a happy life!" But that isn't Judy. Returning to the more prosaic moment, Judy did marvellously agree to be my wife. I have never regretted asking, and Judy has never regretted saying yes.

Dad was in more than full agreement, and on the Monday night after the proposal, brought home about fifteen diamonds worth several thousand pounds for Judy to choose her engagement ring. Several were already set in a ring, and although some of the unset diamonds were of greater value, they did not have the look of the set diamonds. Judy chose the prettiest one and has loved it ever since. At the Bible study on that Friday night in April 1959, she wore her ring, and there was the growing whisper among the attendees, "She's wearing a ring!" Judy and I had known each other for about three years through the various church activities, but we had only been seriously courting for three to four months. We then had our engagement period of nine months, during which Judy turned twenty, in September. It now seems young to be married, but Judy already had had five years in the workplace. In those days, it was also a customary age to be married.

When Judy and I became engaged in April 1959, it was only a few days before the last of her Teachers College exams. But even with all the excitement of the engagement, Judy still passed her exams with flying colours and was posted to her first teaching position at Cooerwull Primary School, in Lithgow, NSW. She boarded with a Salvation Army family living close by the school.

It was at this time that I started calling Judy what has become the all-pervasive nickname of Alice. We have heard back that when several of us had all been on the same outing together, one of the group trying to describe us would say, "You know, the guy who called his wife 'Alice'!" Use of the name has come from several sources:

- It first started in our courting days, during which we would watch the American TV sitcom called *The Honeymooners,* based on the story of Ralph and Alice, who had been married for fifteen years.[8] The plot mainly centred on Ralph's unworkable get-rich-quick schemes, and Alice who brought him back to live in the real world, with much bluster and chagrin from Ralph. Alice ran his life for him, which was fortuitous. Typical scripts, after she had told him what to do, would run along the lines:

  > ALICE (*in tones of steel*): I'm not askin' ya, Ralph, I'm not askin' ya. I'm not askin' ya; I'm tellin' ya!
  > RALPH (*storming out the door*): You're tellin' me? You're tellin' me? You're tellin' me? You're tellin me? All right! I'll go! But I'm not goin' to your mother's tomorrow.

- Another Alice who has become a part of our psyche was the mother of Tarzan of the Apes,[9] of whom we read, "The beautiful Lady Alice," replied Clayton, "of whose many virtues and remarkable personal charms I often have heard my mother and father speak."
- Then there were the genes provided by Judy's grandmother, Alice Edith Akhurst,[10] whose photo on her wedding day shows that commanding—dare I say it—imperious glance.
- The most appropriate Alice was, of course, Alice in Wonderland.[11] The photo shows how early she was practising for the role, taking it to herself, and has continued to do so all her life. Known as Alice, there ever is Judy, who, above all, has remained the real sweetie.

Grandma Alice   Alice in Wonderland

Love is grand, and young love especially. On several occasions, I took the opportunity of leaving university around 1:00 p.m., collecting Mum from Manly, and driving the 150-odd kilometres over the Blue

Mountains, using the Bells Line of Road to Lithgow, to meet Judy after school. Sometimes, when I arrived early, I would look in through the window. The children would draw me to her attention, saying, "Miss Gillies, your father is at the window!" Mum, Judy, and I would then share afternoon tea together, followed by long talks into the evening, and a light tea to follow. Mum would then go to the local cinema for the first film, with two films being shown in those days for the price of one entrance fee. Judy and I went to study the stars in the clear evening mountain air. I would collect Mum at intermission, we would farewell Judy at her lodgings, and Mum and I would drive back home. They were great days. It was good to be young and nice to be keen.

The Wedding

In the six months before our marriage, Judy continued to teach at Lithgow, so the planning for the wedding fell to the two mothers. In fact, it fell mainly to Judy's mum, Freda, which she relished. My mum's health didn't allow her to exert the physical and nervous energy needed for wedding preparations at the level that was necessary. Everything proceeded smoothly. Once the 1959 term 3 was finished in December, we had to bring Judy back to Balgowlah for the last time, but this time it was with the three-tier wedding cake which had been made by a well-known Lithgow cake identity. It was an extremely packed car with Judy's chattels. As we set off, Judy, Freda, and Mum each had a tier of the cake on their laps, and with every bump there came the cry to drive more carefully!

The wedding was at 4:00 p.m. on Saturday, January 2, 1960. It was a particularly hot day, and our officiating pastor, Albert Kronert, had perspiration running down his face during the ceremony. Long before it became fashionable for others to do so; we had prepared our own order of service. Judy felt that it was biblical for her to promise in her vows "to obey (her husband)." Some ladies take umbrage at this and don't realize that the biblical passage that says "to obey" has the earlier verse "submit to one another,"[12] which bully men seem to ignore.

The sanctuary of our Seaforth church was decorated to a tee, with flowers that Freda purchased at the markets early on the morning of the wedding. Across the aisle, there were three spectacular bells.

The wedding was reported on the following Wednesday in the *Manly Daily*, our local paper:

"Teacher weds at Seaforth"

Judy, the only daughter of Mr and Mrs M. M. Gillies, of Seaforth, was married to Robert, only son of Mr and Mrs W. G. Killick, of Balgowlah, last Saturday afternoon, at the Seaforth Baptist Church.

A schoolteacher, the bride was attended by Margery Abbott, of Mittagong: Nancy Beveridge, of Gulgong: Jan Lillie, of Seaforth and Denise Killick of Seaforth, sister of the bridegroom.

Best man was David Black, of Kogarah, and the groomsmen, Arthur Hollis, Portland, David Bradford, Seaforth, and John Gillies, of Balgowlah, brother of the bride.

Robert Killick is a BSc, with honours, the best man David Black, and groomsman, Arthur Hollis, have the same BSc passes: John Gillies and David Bradford are both medical students.

The bride's gown was of guipure lace top, with four very full skirts of nylon net, the top skirt appliquéd with guipure lace flowers and seed pearls. It had a large train of nylon net frills. The head-dress was a small crown of guipure lace, with seed pearls backed by pleated nylon net.

The four bridesmaids wore turquoise delustred satin, with white flower headdress, carrying white sprays.

Mother of the bride wore mushroom chantilly lace, with small satin hat to match. Mother of the groom, Mrs Killick, had gold shadow paper taffeta, with small hat and flowers to match.

The reception was held in the Crescent Ballroom, Manly, and the honeymoon will be spent at the Hydro Majestic, Medlow Bath.

The wedding party

There are always intricacies in the organization of the wedding reception. We were in the middle of a pleasant afternoon tea at the Lane Cove National Park as Freda waxed lyrical on the Bridal Waltz. I indicated that we would not be having the Bridal Waltz in particular, or dancing in general. Freda was upset and stalked away, back to the car. This was the only difference of opinion that Freda and I ever had. I was not a dancer then, but life has changed from the honeymoon, when Judy started teaching me. We have also learnt some showy moves at classes on the ocean cruise ships. The highest accolade which we received, completely undeserved, was on the *Mississippi Queen* when we were sailing down the Ohio River, from Pittsburgh to Cincinnati, for a meeting with Procter & Gamble. One of the three professional dancers, a Canadian, said to us, "I do enjoy the way you Australians dance; you happily mix the styles of the Japanese and the Europeans." I know that our parents would never have believed that Judy's dance teaching would take us to that level, where, for me in particular, "praise from Sir Hubert is praise indeed."[13] We had built up a little routine wherein we were just having fun in our own little show time!

Meanwhile, back to organizing the reception, I managed to develop a compromise whereby, whilst there was no dancing, we ran a concert for the night's entertainment. I have continued to produce shows throughout my life, and I truly believe that what I was doing in my youth fully blossomed in the later years. One item had the best man and groomsmen play a piano duet, another was a soprano soloist, and, as the *pièce de résistance,* Judy and Dad sang two duets: "Jesus Is the Sweetest Name I Know" and "No One Ever Cared for Me Like Jesus." It was a novel and noteworthy reception, and has been the only wedding we have attended that has not had the Bridal Waltz, but a full-blown concert.

The wedding reception was held at the Crescent Ball Rooms in the Crescent, Manly. A marriage in 1960 was still in the era when the parents asked all the older relations and their friends to the reception, leaving about 10 of our friends, for a total of around 110. Although I can't remember exactly what the cost of the reception actually was, it has been rumoured around the family that the total price was twenty-seven shillings, six pence per head. As there were no alcoholic drinks, Judy's Dad, Scottish Mal, made a real saving. A few years later, the building was demolished, and the Camelot units were built on the site. Judy's parents bought unit 10, in 1970. Coming full cycle, it is now owned by Judy.

Mum had property most of her life, and there were always stories of their disbursement when someone had died without a will. This was not going to happen to her son and new bride. To this end, during the reception, Judy and I were taken aside in order to sign our wills. It was a strange event and should have provided an omen for Judy. In our later lives in business, we have both signed many documents. Judy only has to look at a bank now to get that feeling of "pass me a pen; there must be more documents to sign."

The Honeymoon

After the reception, it was the practice to change from our wedding attire to our going-away clothes. Judy wore a light-pink, close-fitting short-sleeved frock, with matching hat, whilst I had a brown shot-silk suit. I had tried to avoid having the car doctored by our young friends, but the boys had got to it, and sprayed our car with Santa Snow and marked it with lipstick to tell all and sundry that we were just married. There was also the obligatory string of rattling tin cans attached to the back bumper bar and stones in the hubcaps. We had planned to honeymoon at the Hydro Majestic Hotel, Medlow Bath, on the far side of the Blue Mountains. It was a terrible trip, with fog forming in the small valleys, providing dangerous driving conditions on the way up and over the mountains. I always have that feeling when something is going well that some surprise event will occur which will wipe the winning cup from my lips. Later in my days of working for the Unilever company, I was doing a psychological test which required me to provide an ending to five short stories. In three of the five, I had introduced an event, in the last paragraph, where the cup of success was swept away from the hero. The psychologist told me I had one of the highest scores he had ever seen, which showed to him that the drive I had to succeed ran deep. As I was reviewing chapter 14, "Heading for Home," I suddenly saw the same streak pervading the memoirs. They tell of a successful life, only, as happens in the story of Ozymandias, I feel that somewhere in the future it will all be swept away.

The Hydro Majestic Hotel was already sixty years old and had been built as Australia's first health resort. It clung to the western edge of the Megalong Valley, and we had a room with a view. However, the hotel was dated, and there was no thought of an en suite bathroom.

The honeymoon car

After church at Blackheath on Sunday morning, we had morning tea with Barbara Wadson, who was one of Judy's close friends from Teachers College and who was ministering in Papua New Guinea. The car received a cleanup. I was more than a trifle annoyed that the Santa Snow that had been used to write "Just Married" on the green duco had broken the outer-surface sheen. That Sunday was diarized as a "rest" afternoon, but looking out the window, I could see a rain shower passing across the valley. "Quick, Judy, look at the rain!" Judy replied from rest-time on the bed, "I'm not getting up for any rain shower!" And I realized two things. Firstly, like all Killick husbands, I was going to be controlled for the rest of my life. Judy, when she hears my recitation of this story, simply says, "Ha, ha!" Secondly, I recognized that Judy was not carrying any farmers' genes. Over the years, I have changed Judy's name, depending on the situation we were in. Mabel is another one among the many. It is used whenever we are associated with the country and comes from this old traditional song:

> My Mabel waits for me underneath the bright blue sky
> Where the dog sits on the tucker box, five miles from Gundagai.
> I meet her evr'y day and I know she's dinky di,
> Where the dog sits on the tucker box, five miles from Gundagai.
>
> I think she's bonza and she reckons I'm good-o
> She's such a trimmer I've entered her for the local show.
> My Mabel waits for me underneath the bright blue sky
> Where the dog sits on the tucker box, five miles from Gundagai.[14]

Judy had made a fruit cake for my twenty-second birthday, on that first Monday of our honeymoon. In the excitement of Saturday's wedding day, the cake was not packed for the honeymoon. Freda made sure the cake was left at the hotel the following day by using one of the cars that was returning wedding guests to their homes in Orange, as Medlow Bath was on the route.

The hotel ran with the old traditional night dinner fare of soup and a roast, and finished off with a pudding, with all the good old traditional titles, such as Queen Victorian, Golden, and Sticky Date. Then there was the good old style of entertainment, with the hotel on Wednesday nights running a fancy dress ball, plus a guests' concert for an exciting prize, the value of which has been completely forgotten. The newly formed Punch and Judy Travelling Show rose to the occasion!

Fancy dress— Liberace   Fancy dress—*Mikado*

On the first Wednesday, we acted in the roles of Liberace and Mom. Liberace[15] was then a well-known concert pianist with his own unique flamboyant musical showmanship and a leaning towards the honky tonk, ragtime musical styles. Judy was good at playing music of that ilk, such as "The Black and White Rag" and "The Harry Lime Theme." Controlling our modesty, we must admit we won on the night. It has been facetiously suggested that cross-dressing by the fifth night of the honeymoon has surely something to say about the nature of the marriage. It certainly said that a new show team had come together— one that played to win. On the twelfth night, we were on again, doing a musical skit on the Mikado and Katisha, his daughter-in-law-elect,[16] from Gilbert and Sullivan's operetta, *The Mikado*. We came second, but the emcee on the night came up later to apologize that we had come first, but the management liked to spread the prizes around.

First Home

Fifty-seven years ago, £4,500.00 ($9,000.00) purchased our first basic two-bedroom house, at 19 Urunga Street, North Balgowlah, NSW. I was then receiving £1,000.00 yearly for my Commonwealth Scholarship. Today, however, with those fifty-seven years gone and inflation compounding, these types of houses are fetching around $1 million, which is not just a lot of money—it is real money. Over the years, we have been quite ready to undertake renovations.

First house

In this house, the living room area was inadequate for the level of hospitality we needed to offer family, friends, and church ministries. Out came the front wall of that section of the house. For those with an eagle eye, two chairs can be seen in the photo (above). We still have one of those chairs today, albeit recovered several times; it sits in our bedroom. It was a comfortable first home. When we went for our first working trip to the UK, it was rented to a senior staff family of the Indian High Commission. On our return to Sydney in 1964, we sold it to purchase 77 Woodland Street, North Balgowlah.

In our first year of marriage, we were soon into hospitality which has continued throughout. Our first major event was a farewell surprise party to David, our best man. He was to go to Cambridge to undertake his postdoctoral research work under the noted organic chemist Lord Todd, who had been awarded the Nobel Prize for Chemistry in 1957. David had a quiet meal with my parents, whom he knew well, and was preparing to watch television, when around twenty of his friends arrived. A few days later, David dutifully left on the SS *Oronsay* for England.

A report of the party appeared in the *Australian Women's Weekly*. Mum must have pushed hard to get it published, but how she achieved it neither Judy nor I can now recall.[17]

Thus began what has often been called the Punch and Judy Travelling Show. It has been a show with a latent energy and a chemistry between Judy and me. We have the ability to bounce off each other in conversations, in shows, and in life.

For us, any and all times can be "sho-o-o-ow time!"

7 End of Training

After the Lord's provision of one's wife, one's work selection is all.[1]

Jesus replied, "My father is always working and so am I."[2]

As the twig is bent, so grows the tree.[3]

Early in our marriage, Judy began the long, slow process of teaching me many of the basic lessons of life that I was not to forget. One of the key ones required maximum input, and so, as I was going out to work each morning, she would grab me by the lapels, shake me like a wet rat—there is nothing quite like being shaken like a wet rat—and say, "Remember, all wisdom does not lie with Bob Killick!" (I mentioned this in the preface, you will recall.)

Postgraduate Studies

Second year university had been the year I came good (as described in chapter 5). In third year (1957), I only achieved a distinction in chemistry, not repeating the previous year's high distinction. I could have made the excuse that I was really sick with the flu in the days leading up to the exam. Despite the result being one level lower, it did not matter, as I was still part of the selected ones. I was now ensconced in the third year, with the students who were setting out to make organic chemistry their lifelong work. As a believer in taking small steps to reach my goals, I decided to spend the year of 1958 reading chemistry under Professor Shoppee for an honours degree rather than immediately jumping to a two-year master's degree.

Cholesterol

For the next four years of my life, the base material of my work was cholesterol, the chemical structure of which is shown above. In the years that followed university, I never worked with cholesterol again. The cholesterol we used was normally obtained from sheep brains, which contain about 2 per cent of the material, approximately the same level of cholesterol found in the human brain. My honours thesis was typed up by Fay Sorenson, who became my sister-in-law when she married John, Judy's brother. My thesis was a short and snappy sixty-four pages, entitled *Studies in the Steroid Series* (December 1958), and awarded the grade of first-class honours. The laboratory work covering the first two sections was difficult because it used the so-called aggressive halogens, chlorine and bromine, the former known as poison gas[4] when used in the First World War. The third piece of the research attempted to replace one of the carbons with a nitrogen atom—a task which continued later and became the basis of my doctor of philosophy thesis.

Following completion of my honours year, Professor Shoppee organized for two of his students—David Black and myself—to have vacation scholarships during January–February 1959, at the Australian National University's John Curtin School of Medical Research. We lived in University House, which provided meals with our accommodation. I worked with Professor Adrien Albert; David, with Dr Des Brown, the reader. Mum let everyone know—that is, everyone who would listen—that this scholarship was further evidence of the brilliance of her son. She ever believed I had been chosen for great things.

Dr Des Brown wrote Professor Albert's biography for the *Australian Dictionary of Biography,*[5] in which he states that the professor was irascible, temperamental, and plagued by health problems. As the result of a botched emergency gastrectomy, he was unable to get to work before ten o'clock in the morning, but worked late into the night. He had a very complex personality—even to his senior staff and colleagues he could be flatteringly courteous one day and hypercritical the next. Professor Albert and I never got on.

David had foreseen this at our introductory meeting: Bob, being Bob—open, frank, and boisterous—would likely never mix with Professor Albert's morose temperament and way of doing things. (These were David's words, pretty much verbatim.) David remembered the morning where I was whistling while I was working in the laboratory, and Professor Albert stormed in, emphasizing, "One does not whistle in my laboratory!" After we had finished our time in Canberra, Professor Albert wrote a scathing letter to Shoppee, claiming I didn't even have the ability to take a simple melting point.

Now, some people in business have observed that the business world is cutthroat, dog eat dog, and hard to stomach. Such people abandon the business world for the relative safety of academia. However, in my case, my—shall we say—unstable relationship with Professor Albert and other niggly incidents led me ultimately to step aside from work in research and academia, for the much more fun world of business— beauty ever being in the eye of the beholder. At least I might have thought I would be master of my own fate, and would be less dependent upon others for my future. Apart from this being suspect theology, it did not actually work out. Later in this chapter, circumstances led me to be sent home from England, with minimal job prospects in the company that had sent us to the UK with high hopes.

Whilst Professor Albert mainly worked with nitrogen compounds, particularly adenine,[6] which had four nitrogen atoms, two in each of the joined five and six heterocyclic rings, I find myself being unable to remember what I worked on during my two-month project at the university. I do recollect that most of the work was undertaken using fume cupboards. The most interesting cupboard was set in a corner room on the top level of the building, with the two outside walls missing in order to maximize air flow in the room. The view was towards the Brindabella Ranges—a view to stir any Australian's heart.

Accidents That Happen

The other event which I always associate with Canberra was the only serious car accident I have had in my life. It occurred when David Black and I were rushing to get home to Sydney for a weekend, halfway through our time in Canberra. Going round a corner on the highway, I overcorrected, and then slammed into the rock cutting on the passenger side. We were all badly shaken, the worst being David, with a lump on his forehead which was later removed by surgery. Fortunately, it did not affect his mental prowess, and he went on to obtain the Chair of Organic Chemistry at the University of New South Wales

The most critical car accident that never happened was around 1975, during our trip to Sydney for the holidays. We normally left Melbourne around 4:00 a.m., and at dawn, we were north of Albury, on the single-lane carriageway to Holbrook. The Hume Highway was not a real highway in those days, and the road undulated, resulting in minimal sightings of the vehicles approaching on the other single carriageway. In a flash, we had a truck approaching, and a car moved out across the double lines to overtake, directly facing us. My natural instincts could have had me swing onto the gravel to let the other car go through in my lane. However, I stayed in my lane, and the other car swung onto the gravel. Judy, who had been dozing, woke with a start and saw the truck on her right and the car on her left, and then it was all over, with a clear road ahead. I still contemplate that the family could have been a road fatality statistic if I had swung onto the gravel and crashed head-on, or if the other driver had stayed in my lane with the same disastrous result.

On returning to Sydney after my brief time in Canberra, I had the opportunity to join the Karoiboi Club. This was a group of senior university members who met each month over a dinner. Members of the group were supposed to have deep and meaningful discussions during the course of the evening, but the real purpose of the gathering seemed to be to sample and compare the standard of the wines being served. Because I am a non-drinker, I felt like a fish out of water. Some of their conversations at times were, I felt, indiscreet, and it seemed that I was watching snatches out of C.P. Snow's novel, *The Masters,*[7] with its descriptions of the political manoeuvres of the people campaigning for their preferred candidate to be elected master of an unnamed Cambridge College. Mum remained ecstatic that I belonged among the intellectual elite. But I had a growing sense that my life was not going to be in academia.

Having achieved my honours, the decision was easily taken to proceed with my doctorate of philosophy as a three-year research project, from 1959 to 1961. The government provided me with a £20.00 weekly Commonwealth Scholarship. I read for my degree under Professor C. W. Shoppee, and described routes to 4-azasteroids based on the Beckmann rearrangement of A-nor steroid ketoximes and on various other transformations. Specifically, 3-azasteroids were synthesized by two unambiguous routes. Molecular rotation relationships arising from the introduction of the azasteroid grouping were investigated, and this necessitated the preparation of previously unreported steroids for comparison purposes. My PhD thesis was entitled *Azasteroids and Steroids* (January 1962).

The thesis ran for 223 pages, and Judy, who was by then my wife, used her accurate typing skills to type the document as one original and five carbon copies. The days of computer cutting and pasting were still a long way off into the future. There was no way to suddenly announce to Judy that we were going to take a paragraph from, say, page 44 and paste it back in on, say, page 23, because everything in between would have to be retyped. Daughter Jenni was about to turn a year old, and she was practising her walking at Whale Beach, where we were holidaying in the Inders' beach house. Many long hours were spent in typing up the thesis.

As Shakespeare said it, "Parting is such sweet sorrow,"[8] and after seven years at Sydney University, I said goodbye to a world I knew so well. The legacy I left was in the form of three scientific papers published in the prestigious English *Journal of the Chemical Society*. The first of these is now already fifty-five years old, and I can only imagine them in some stuffy archives, gathering dust. The words from Dorothy Sayers' *Gaudy Night*[9] make me maudlin:

> She developed an acute homesickness for Oxford and for the "Study of Lefanu"—a book which would never have any advertising value, but of which some scholar might someday moderately observe, "Miss Vane has handled her subject with insight and accuracy."

I console myself, believing the papers may have been used as stepping stones in someone else's studies and at least in the overall increase of knowledge. The papers were:

Shoppee, C. W., Howden, M. E. H., Killick, R. W. and Summers, G. H. R. "Steroids and the Walden Inversion XLII: 5α-Cholestan-4-one and some derivatives thereof." *J. Chem. Soc.* (1959) 630–636

Shoppee, C. W., Killick, R. W. and Kruger, G. "Azasteroids IV: 3-Aza-5α- and -5β-cholestane and related compounds." *J. Chem. Soc.* (1962) 2275–2285.

Shoppee, C. W. and Killick, R. W. "Steroids XXXVI: Some 13, 17-seco androstanes." *J. Chem. Soc.* (1970) 1513–1514.

The legacy which I took from seven years at university was a trained technical mind and the fact I could be called Doctor Bob Killick. Mum made sure that the full title was used whenever and wherever she could arrange. Other than Mum's pride in me, the title did open doors, for in the 1960s, those of us with a PhD were a rare breed indeed.

Early Thoughts on Guidance

By this stage of my life, the teachings of the Christian faith which formed the basis of our life's primary purpose were making us sensitive to doing God's will. At one extreme, the teaching emphasized that only by laying down all one's desires on the "altar of sacrifice" could we be really blessed as disciples of Jesus. At the other extreme, was the thesis of Augustine of Hippo: "Love God and do what you like."[10] Having earned my PhD, and with Judy as my wife, it was now time to launch into the very competitive business world, to find a job where God wanted us to be. Some people venture that Christianity is for lily-livered weaklings; but, far from being a crutch, Christianity was to prove to be the compass which enabled Judy and me to launch out into the real marketplace and embrace whatever was God's adventure for us.

A part of our background experience over the years has been in the production and direction of church concerts and shows. As the director of these shows, I learnt the importance of people doing what they were directed to do. This became a practical application to our lives, in recognition that God was in control. He was the Prime Mover, the Top Director. This gave us comfort, knowing that He does all things well and our job was to look out for His direction. There were times when matters did not seem to be going as we would want, and yet, afterwards, we were able to look back and see that God had guided us towards a better outcome than we would have chosen for ourselves. It reminded us particularly of the story of Joseph in the Bible, when he said to his brothers, "You determined it for evil but God worked it for good."[11]

Looking for a Job

With the final typing of my PhD drawing to a close, I commenced job hunting in late 1961. My early forays were not at all exciting. The first appointment was with Davis Gelatine, a prominent medium-sized company based in Mascot, which manufactured gelatine, glue, stock foods, and ancillary products. It was absorbed into the Goodman Fielders Group in 1995. In retrospect, I consider that I was given an interview more out of curiosity and courtesy than anything else. Their response—something I heard several times in subsequent interviews—was that because I had a PhD, I was overqualified for the position under offer. It soon became apparent that, in regard to my academic qualifications, there was a great gulf between the attitudes of the smaller Australian businesses and the larger multinational companies. Strangely, the Australian companies appeared to show disinterest in postgraduate academic qualifications, but the international companies offered healthy respect. At that time, anyone holding a PhD was rare in this trade and industry, whereas in today's world, there are many more sprinkled on the grass.

Davis Gelatine gave me my first interview and my first no. Apart from considering me overqualified, most of the Australian companies thought my personality to be somewhat too forward for their liking. I like the word *forward* because it is decidedly more neutral than *brash*, which was how I felt Unilever saw me by the end of my time there. Many of my academic compatriots were going overseas to broaden their experience, and Judy and I thought England did sound nice. I was now moving away from Mum spoiling me, and it was the time for the Lord to start spoiling us, for we would go to England, not once, but twice—fully subsidized.

When it came to the interviews with the multinational companies, my second gambit was "I am looking for a job that will take me to England." This was not met with spontaneous enthusiasm; indeed, in the interview with Shell Petroleum, the response, understandably, was "Who do you think you are? We have many long-term staff looking for that privilege!"

Unilever and the UK

Whilst the Bob-to-UK campaign seemed to be bogged down, I now look back on the old hymn "God Moves in a Mysterious Way His wonders to Perform," to the fourth verse, "Behind a frowning providence, He hides a smiling face." Dad was talking to one and all of his business connections, and was reminded that the then Australian Chairman of Unilever, Garth Barraclough, knew the Killick family through Dad's elder brother, Norman, both of them having attended Newington College in the same years. Garth was happy to meet Dad and me, and the Bob-to-UK campaign moved into top gear. Unilever was a noteworthy international company with global reach. Their UK headquarters had sent letters to the various countries to be on the lookout for prospective employees with doctorates, who could go to their research laboratories[12] at Port Sunlight on the Wirral Peninsula in Cheshire.

It was soon agreed that Unilever would use me as the Australian experiment, and I was passed over to the technical director, Stewart Cousins, to make the practical arrangements for our transfer to the UK. Liking to be ahead of the game, I found that the ship taking the shorter journey through Suez was booked out. However, I also noted that in April, the *Orsova* was sailing through Panama to England. I told Mr Cousins that I had looked ahead and the Suez ship was full. He replied in the true Unilever spirit, "We can always get you on the ship." I then slipped in, "But there is room available on the *Orsova*, through Panama." Although the cost was over what would normally be allowed, Mr Cousins said, "Oh … well, I enjoyed Panama coming back from the war. I'm sure you will too." I joined Unilever on March 5, 1962. We left on April 10, 1962, the six-week trip calling ashore at Auckland, Fiji, Honolulu, Vancouver, San Francisco, Long Beach (for Los Angeles), Acapulco, Panama Canal, Port au Prince (Haiti), Bermuda, and Le Havre (France), reaching Southampton on May 22. We then caught the train north to London, with the amazing observation, "The grass is green, real green!"

Port Sunlight

After a few days' sightseeing in London, we were on what became a well-worn train track of Euston Station, London, to Liverpool, Lime Street Station. Unilever had organized accommodation in the upstairs rooms of a house belonging to a Miss Ison. Jenni was a fast-moving and noisy (particularly at night) two-year-old who wasn't the best sleeper in the world. We knew this accommodation arrangement was not going to work out.

399 New Chester Road

The travel department of Unilever located 399 New Chester Road, New Ferry, for us, which, when we arrived, was not painted white but had the colour of the original cement-coated gravel walls. It was unfurnished, at £3/5/- per week (pre-decimal pounds, shillings and pence). The long-term residents living in the strip of houses were under rent control and thus paying seven shillings and six pence per week.

They strongly indicated we were being robbed, but we were not going to argue about £3/5/- when we were then receiving over $A100.00 per week for our North Balgowlah property back in Australia. We were simply pleased we had the accommodation that was going to be our home for the next two years.

On our voyage to England, we had a rover at our table who loved repeating the old adage "My home is where I hang my hat." We were determined to make that true for us, even though the house was rudimentary. There were three bedrooms upstairs. Downstairs, the front door opened facing the stairs; to the left was the lounge/dining room with the one coal fire that was in use. Hot-water pipes circled the chimney. Although there was a holding tank, hot water was mainly limited to when the fire was lit. Judy would contend that this was most of the time. This water was for the bath, for there was no shower. The lounge room opened into the kitchen, where one stove and one copper for washing the laundry had been left for our use. A partition in the kitchen separated a bath over which hung the washing line. It was not easy to coax visitors to have a bath, and when my dad and Judy's mum visited, a shotgun with both barrels cocked almost had to be used to get them to have a bath. The *pièce de résistance* was the only toilet, which was located outside. One had to go out through the kitchen door, turn right along the wall, and thereby access the toilet through a door in the back wall. This toilet door was not flush fitting but designed with the top and bottom cut out for air circulation. This also allowed for snow to settle on one's lap when sitting on the toilet. During the winter, a candle was left burning overnight underneath the cistern to keep the water from freezing.

Our bedroom window looked across New Chester Road to the Port Sunlight factory. It was a fifteen-minute walk through the factory to the laboratory. A sight that has ever remained with me was at 8:00 a.m., observing ice that had formed from a puddle, with the same ice still being there on the way home at 5:00 p.m. These were temperatures we colonials had never met before. Another observation was the seemingly low financials the UK ran at that time. The laboratory cleanup girls earned £20/-/- per week, and from this they put aside £1/-/- to build up to £50/-/-, which gave them a week in a Spanish or Portuguese holiday camp. For Judy, there was the Liverpudlian accent, because of which, she claimed, she never could understand what the butcher was saying when she ordered the weekly sausages.

Judy had a ball at the local used-furniture auction where she bought our requirements at ridiculously low prices. This included a double bed and mattress for eight shillings, the single bed and mattress for sixteen shillings, and some rectangular carpet for five pounds. When we left two years later, the only item that would be taken back for sale was this carpet, more threadbare than ever.

My employment contract with Unilever Research Laboratory, dated May 28, 1962, was as a research scientist, to be remunerated at the rate of £1,025/-/- yearly. Ken Durham, head of research, kept a keen interest in how the International Doctorate Experiment was proceeding. I did not meet any others who had taken up the opportunity. My starting task was to carry out organic syntheses of perfumery materials, such as rose oil; studies into foaming and detergency of the then newly emerging biodegradable detergents; and the development of mathematical models to relate calcium detergent dissociation constants. It also included a search for possible phosphate replacements, such as EDTA (ethylene diamine tetra-acetic acid), and work to safeguard the factory by eradicating the potentially explosive potassium chlorate from crude glycerine brought in from the Sri Lankan plant.

We had arrived in May 1962, and Mal, Judy's dad, took the opportunity to visit us and see some of Europe. He arrived in England on July 18, and at our home, "399," the following day. From Saturday to Tuesday evening, we visited the Lakes District and southern Scotland, including Glasgow and Edinburgh. He left for London and Europe on Thursday, July 26.

Mum's Promotion to Glory

The news from home concerning Mum's health continued to be grave. By August, we had talked it over with research's senior management, who encouraged me with an offer to fly me home to be with Mum for the last time. I wrote to tell Mum and Dad of the possibility, and her reply letter follows. It just seems like the last letter[13] of Paul, both of them knowing that death was approaching.

Paul wrote:

> I'm about to die, my life an offering on God's altar. This is the only race worth running. I've run hard right to the finish, believed all the way. All that's left now is the shouting—God's applause! Depend on it, He's an honest judge. He'll do right not only by me, but by everyone eager for His coming.

Mum wrote:

3rd. September, 1962.

My Dear Family,

It was a wonderful thought of you wanting to come home to see me Bob, but I would rather you stayed with your family. Coming home wouldn't make me better and I feel if you came home the parting would feel like a parting. I said goodbye to you on the wharf feeling may be I will see him again, but it seems that may be I wont. As I said in a letter before, we will all meet again. By the news on the wireless of Persia I think we should be looking up. Don't get worried and upset of how Mum is feeling. I am feeling good. Enjoying being an invalid. Everyone has been wonderful. Its a strange sickness, I get very sleepy so I sleep a lot. The infection from my bowel has spread through my body and there is nothing they can do. I suppose you would say it is slowly poisoning me. All I think will happen is I will just get weaker and weaker, and when you are weak nothing worries you. If you came home I would really feel then that I was finished. Thank Judy for being willing for you to come home. I haven't missed you Bob, but I think Dad has. Please don't get all upset and think if you had been home things would have been different. I am glad you got away when you did, it was meant to be so. Thank your firm very much and say I appreciate it but I am happier you being over there working. Thank you for the scarf for my birthday, it is really beautiful. It arrived the same day as your letter. The photos of Jenny are lovely, she is getting to be a real little girl. I like your back fence. Better get some tools from Dad and do some mending. We are having the Douglas Bradfords Mrs. G. next Friday night for McMacIntosh to show the slides. He thought Judy had done wonderful buying. He said your house was as good as any other in England. Take a bow Judy. Each Sunday night after Church the young ones go to different houses to have supper. Last night it was Morriss. They had a sing song and Allan J. is down on holidays from Tahlee and he spoke. Denyse said they had a good night. Allan Johnston has started to take Alan Bull's old girl out, Dawn. Dawn de Russett has left us again. She has started teaching down at St. Paul. She had the children baptized C.E. What a girl. You know me Bob, whats to be, will be, but keep in England life still goes on. It was a wonderful thought, I am so thrilled you got away when you did. I suppose you had a wonderful time in Scotland. Did Judy get her birthday present. Thanks once again,

Love,

Mother.

Mum's last letter

We would not have received this last letter until September 10, and Mum died twelve days later, on Saturday, September 22, 1962. We had no incoming phone, and the telegram was received that Monday: "Mother gone." Mum was cremated at the Northern Suburbs Crematorium, and her ashes spread on the Rose Garden. There is no plaque indicating her details.

Following Mum's death, Dad decided to have Christmas with us and was booked to arrive at London Heathrow at 10:00 a.m., Friday, November 30. Judy and I started organizing a babysitter for Jenni whilst she and I drove down to meet Dad at the airport, leaving at

4:00 a.m. The English response was interesting, with the unanimous expostulation, "No one here drives two hundred miles down to London to pick someone up from the airport!" To which my standard reply was "What is four hours when Dad will have travelled more than ten thousand miles?" We were there, early as ever, just after 8:00 a.m., and saw the plane land right on time. We came home through Coventry and saw the bomb-destroyed cathedral. After a few days at home, Judy was agreeable for Dad and me to have several days in Europe together. On Friday, December 7, Dad called in at the English office of Hoffnung & Co., and then we went to Continental Europe. We had a good time around the classic tourist spots, but only two standout features have stayed in the memory banks. The first was the simple meal of German sausages at a little cafe in Salzburg. I took Judy back a few years later, and the little cafe had become a big restaurant—and the sausages, regrettably, had become run of the mill. The second was the purchase of a set of black lingerie from a shop on the Avenue des Champs-Elysées in Paris, for Judy's Christmas present. It was a struggle, from my lack of French and the shop attendant's lack of English. Then there was the question of moving from thirty-two inches to the equivalent in centimetres. Anyway, within twenty minutes, I had a black silk slip, half-cup bra, petite panties, and stocking-suspender belt. While paying the bill, I attempted to be gallant and asked where the attendant had learnt her English. She misunderstood and appeared embarrassed. The French lady behind spoke quickly in French; it was all smiles, and the answer was "school." It has fascinated me also at other times that the French almost take a perverse delight in letting the English struggle with the French language until its own people are in an English-speaking contretemps.

As soon as we arrived in England, we had queried our friends there as to when it was going to snow. "It never snows on the Wirral" was the response, because the Wirral Peninsula is surrounded by three bodies of water: the Irish Sea to the north, the Mersey River to the east, and the River Dee to the west, forming the border with Wales.

Notwithstanding the protection, it was the coldest and snowiest winter in a hundred years. The snow came with a vengeance, with people skating in front of Buckingham Palace, a man cycling on the Thames River near Windsor Bridge, and the whole surface of England seemingly white with snow. It certainly added to the atmosphere of Christmas. As well as Dad being with us, Judy's mum and her close school friend "Aunty" Lucy were there for what was a simply good time. Judy's lingerie present was a howling success. Both parents left for Australia early in the New Year.

Andrew, Home Delivery

Our second child was to be born in mid-May. Judy's doctor indicated that, as there had been no birth problem with our firstborn, Jennifer, Judy would have a home birth. There was shock and amazement in Australia. Both sets of our parents and Doctor Aunty Roxie thought England was still living in the dark ages. Anyway, the home birth it was to be. The main help was the midwife, and she was the contact point. Sunday, May 12, 1963, in the gloaming, we participated in a Walk of Witness to celebrate the three Methodist churches in the town combining to one, called "Trinity." Before we settled down for the night, Judy strongly suggested that I had better go and get the midwife. I had to walk about one hundred metres up the street to the public phone box. She apologized that I would have to come in my car and collect her, which I did. After an inspection, she said, "I'm giving Judy a sedative, and the baby won't be coming till the morning." I drove her home and got back to Judy, who said, "You will have to go back and get the midwife, as the baby is definitely coming!" Back to the public phone box, and the midwife said she had got her car out and could drive herself. Judy and the midwife were upstairs, and I was relegated to the downstairs fire to keep it alight and the water boiling. "It's a boy!" came the cry down the stairs. The doctor came five minutes later and confirmed that all was well. The home birth did save a lot of trouble, since the hospital where Judy would have gone was in the middle of a golden staph infection crisis. Mothers were being admitted, having their babies, and being sent home as quickly as possible.

Our first tourist trip took us south, down the English-Welsh border and out to Watergate Bay, Cornwall, to see one of England's surf beaches. After Manly, we were not impressed. We then had to visit Land's End, but, above all, Penzance, in case we might see the dreaded pirates[14] that dwell in that locality according to Gilbert & Sullivan.

For further work experience, before we returned to Australia, I was sent for four weeks (from February 22 to March 21, 1964) to Unilever's research laboratories at Vlaardingen, on the westerly outskirts of Rotterdam, The Netherlands. To maintain low costs, I went from Liverpool, to London Euston Station and over to the Liverpool Street Station for the two-hour train to Harwich International Port. Another six hours and forty-five minutes on a ferry had me in the Hook of Holland, thirty kilometres from Rotterdam. Nothing comes to mind as to what I did in the laboratories, but on Saturday nights I went to the cinema. One night the film was in German, with Dutch subtitles. I still claim that because I knew neither language I was able to pick out the murderer, as I wasn't confused by false statements. At the end of the film, the detective said to the murdering doctor something like, "Why did you do it?" The reply was *"Brüder,"* which I could translate into brother, and this basically explained the movie. Another Saturday night there was James Bond's *From Russia with Love,* advertised as "original English version." With Bond's dry sense of humour, I was laughing, whist the serious Dutch around me were obviously wondering who the ushers had let into the theatre.

Meanwhile, back at the ranch in England, it was still cold, and Judy was pouring coal onto the lounge room fire. A knock came on the door, and the neighbour said, "Your chimney is on fire!" Judy replied, "All those sparks up in the air are pretty." The neighbour, realizing that Judy did not comprehend the seriousness of the situation, said, "You had better call the fire brigade." Judy soon had four firemen in the house, feeling the walls to make sure the woodwork behind was not on fire! Everything was all right, and we could only muse how long it had been since a chimney sweep had been used.

The Bob-to-UK campaign trial was a two-year test, and I believe it could be treated as a success, since we were asked to stay another year. However, with the weather and missing grandparents, it was a time too long for Judy, who could only say, "You promised two."

Goodbye, England

Sydney Intermission

We left Southampton on June 2, 1964 on P & O's *Arcadia*. We called in at Gibraltar, Port Said, and passed through the Suez Canal. It has no locks and, surrounded by desert sands, contrasted greatly with our previous experience of passing through the Panama Canal, with its three sets of locks and surrounding lush tropical vegetation. Our experience with major canals was complete. Mount Sinai lays roughly fifty kilometres inland, to the east from the southern end of the Gulf of Suez. It is surrounded on all sides by higher peaks of the mountain ranges. At least we had euphemistically seen the area where God had given the Ten Commandments to Moses. We felt Aden, the next port, was quite dilapidated. Its duty-free shopping was its one claim to fame, but, for us, it was definitely overrated. Robust bargaining was still required to obtain the best price. What I did find tiring by the end of our stay was the frivolous boasting of the other passengers: "If only you had gone around the corner of the street, you would have been able to purchase your roll of photographic film twenty cents cheaper." I wanted to respond, "Give the canary another seed."

The last foreign port was Colombo, the capital of what was then called Ceylon (now Sri Lanka). The ship had a selection of arranged tours, and we chose the one highlighting Colombo and its surrounds. As part of the traditional ending to these tours there was the mandatory visit to the shops, the professional way to soak up the tourist dollar. The country being known for its sapphires, our tour ended at the sapphire shops on Mount Levinia, a suburb of Colombia. We were definitely not inured to selling pressures in those days, and we remain pleased that, with semi-robust bargaining, I managed to buy Judy a sapphire ring which is still worn fifty years later.

The first Australian port was Fremantle—only highlighted because, after two years away, we found the Australian accent grating. The trip finished by calling in at Adelaide and Melbourne, then reaching Sydney on Wednesday, July 1, a clear, sunny, winter's day. During the ship's passage, Judy and I used our long-standing sporting abilities and entered all the on-board competitions. It was almost embarrassing when, at the last night's prize-giving ceremony, we were presented with about ten prizes each, which we had won over the previous four weeks. It was a joyous return to Sydney and Australia, with our now two children. Dad had remarried within four months of Mum's death, and he and his new wife, Jean, had joined the ship for the Melbourne-to-Sydney last leg home to get to know the both of us and their grandchildren, Jenni and Andrew, just that little bit more. With the marriage, two stepsisters joined the extended family, Margaret Jean (who became Mrs Harper) and Judith Elaine (who became Mrs Caradus).

On arriving back in Sydney, we sold our Urunga Street house to buy the larger and more family-friendly 77 Woodland Street, Balgowlah. For the next two years, 1964 and 1965, I was a product development officer for Unilever's Lever & Kitchen Company. This was a technical position. It was treated by the company as a time of training, which included the position of acting transport manager, during which I restructured the administration control of goods in and out of the factory; a time in industrial engineering; and time as a production supervisor. This was good training for when we took over Victorian Chemicals in later years. We always said that Unilever gave us the training that equipped us for all that was to follow.

I was then promoted to product development manager for Lever & Kitchen. This was a technical position and covered the maintenance of the technical competitive edge of the company's product range, from powdered detergents (Surf and Omo), to liquid surfactants (Handy-Andy) and toilet and laundry soaps, such as Lux, Sunlight, and Solvol.

I was promoted in 1969 to become Lever & Kitchen's new product manager, which was a marketing function to evaluate new retail market areas into which the company could penetrate. Subsequent to my short stay and following my transfer to the UK, the company moved into a range of aerosol products.

Back to the UK

In 1969, Unilever sent me to London for training and to garner experience in preparation for my future appointment as industrial detergent manager in Australia, answerable to the global coordinator of industrial detergents.

The jet age had now fully arrived and provided the option of a lower-cost fare to London than to go by ship. Unilever had provided a farewell room at the airport for the family to bid us au revoir. Judy was dressed in white and wearing a hat, and I wore a suit. There were no air bridges, and as we came up the stairs to board the plane, the air hostess mistook us for a honeymooning couple … until our three children came into view, bringing up the rear. We all had a good laugh.

We left on April 10, with the journey taking us from Sydney via Darwin, Bangkok, Athens, Thessalonica, and Vienna, to London. We found accommodation at 8 Quernmore Close, Bromley North, Kent. This was to the south-east and just outside the London postal districts.

I had achieved success! This was our family's second overseas UK company posting, with all travel expenses paid. It was London, and after two years, I was to return to the role of General Manager Industrial Detergents for Australia. My London role was that of Technical Information Officer for Unilever Ltd. It was both a technical and marketing function, and coordinated the flow and dissemination of information through Unilever's Industrial Detergent Technical Centre to companies across Europe and throughout the world.

But success is ephemeral, and my posting became a disaster. What we thought was a position of success leading ever upward became one and a half years of tears. Looking outwards, the problem lay in the fact that my English boss and I never saw eye to eye. He particularly did not like colonials. Added to this was the fact that I did not imbibe alcoholic drinks, whereas he considered himself a wine connoisseur. Long discussions would be held on the merits of a particular wine, without my participation, which appeared in his mind to be a slight against him. Looking inwards, my written English was not up to the standards of the Queen's English, which my boss demanded for the newsletter published fortnightly throughout Unilever's industrial detergent world, telling of all that was happening in our bailiwick. It still rankles that I would start a sentence "In contrast to …" and it would be rejected and replaced with "By contrast with …"—time and time again. My line manager, a Dutchman called Hans, took it upon himself to spend extra time with me to improve my writing skills to produce proper English, whilst my overall boss examined my written work for every flaw and mistake. Looking back, it was certainly quaint that there was this Dutchman teaching an Australian how to write English. (I described the foregoing in chapter 2 as well.)

Nevertheless, the die had been cast almost from the beginning, and my writings were never going to come up to pass level. After eighteen months, everyone decided to cut their losses, and although the posting was to have been for two years, it was all over. I was sent home, with no real prospects of a job. Spurgeon[15], the well known London preacher of a former generation, did have an encouraging word in one of his sermons: "We cannot always see the hand of God in Providence, but we may be always sure that it is there."

Hans remained sympathetic to me and arranged our return on a pleasant sea voyage rather than rushing home by air to a job that would no longer be mine. This did not mean that I sulked and did nothing on the way home. I was often to be found ensconced in the ship's library, preparing a proposal for the launching of a research and development facility in Australia, and modesty forbids me from indicating who would be the person to manage such a facility.

The company booked us on the *Galileo Galilei*, built in Italy in 1963 for the Lloyd Triestino shipping company to be mainly used on the Italy-Australia route. The family left London on Wednesday, March 24, 1971, on the 10:30 a.m. train from Victoria Station, travelling overnight to arrive in Pisa, Italy, at 9:15 a.m. I can guarantee that we would never do it again with young children. After touring the Leaning Tower and its surrounds, we went on to Florence. The next morning was the city tour, and we then went on to Genoa. The ship left at 6:00 p.m. the following day, Saturday, March 27.

Naples was the first port reached on the next day, whilst the following day we called in at Messina, on the northernmost point of Sicily. The Suez Canal was in its eight-year closure following the Six Day War, and this forced the ship's route to follow the two thousand kilometres-longer way around the Cape of Good Hope, on the southernmost tip of South Africa. After three days from Messina, we had a few hours stay at Tenerife on the Canary Island, thence the nine-day sea voyage to Durban. This was followed by seven days to reach Fremantle, and during all these sea days there were the shipboard activities, which included the fancy dress ball. Eleven years from our honeymoon, we were on again as Liberace and Mom, but we only cracked the second prize. It has been said that the first rule is not to blame the adjudicators, but let me encourage myself that the Italian sense of humour is different from the Australian. Apologies for the lack of sharpness in the following photos, but they were taken during the performance by the ship's photographer, to be included—rough and ready—in the next morning's *Ship's Daily Programme*.

Best legs in the business   Judy in full flight

The penultimate port was Melbourne, and in a frenzy of tourism, we carted the children around the highlights: Captain Cook's Cottage, the Myer Music Bowl, the War Memorial, etc., since we anticipated we would not be returning soon. Once again, this proved why we were not in the School of the Prophets.

We berthed at Sydney, at 4:00 p.m. on Sunday, April 25, 1971, a beautiful day. We were accommodated at the Manly Hotel, opposite the wharf, and that first night had a welcome home party at Judy's parents' unit, which they had bought while we were away. Dad and Jean, my step mum, were living at Glenbrook, in the Blue Mountains, and we caught up with them a few days later.

The only asset that I brought back to Australia was a knowledge of writing English—something not to be sneezed at.

Move to Melbourne

I reported for work at Unilever's offices, Circular Quay, on Tuesday, April 27, 1971, and was told with no uncertainty that any future job was "up in the air." I just walked around Manly that afternoon, feeling the sword of Damocles[16] above me. I had my proposal typed and presented Wednesday. For a week, I hovered around the phone. On Wednesday, May 5, Unilever reported there would be no news until the following Monday, at the earliest. Actually, the meeting was not until 9:00 a.m. on Friday, May 14. The first point made by senior management was that I could forget about setting up any research facility. The one possibility for a job was in Melbourne, for which Fred Pott, the then managing director of Unichema, Unilever's Australian Chemical Division, said, he would take me on to see if I could fit into the role of technical service and development manager, as the current incumbent, Dave Noy, planned on retiring within the year. I was flown to Melbourne on Australian National Airways flight 11, at 9:15 a.m. the next Monday. There were long discussions, and I returned on the flight from Essendon at 5:20 p.m. on Tuesday, May 18.

Fred Pott was OK with me, and on Wednesday, May 19, I was officially offered the position of acting development manager of Unichema Australia. This was to allow them time to see whether I had the right stuff. Judy came home with me on the ferry, and I said, "I have good news and bad news. I still have a job, but it is in Melbourne!" It was the only time in our marriage that I have seen Judy shed a tear. She was looking forward to being back with our families. However, by this time, we had reached a basic understanding that wherever the Unilever company directed us to go was the direction that our Lord would have us travel. We can, however, both look back and praise God for pulling us, ever reluctantly, out of Sydney, out of Manly and from its beaches, to Melbourne. Melbourne was to be a blessing to us all.

We arrived in Melbourne on Friday May 21, and stayed at the Brighton Savoy Motel. The key was to find a home, and the company's recommendation was that the three suburban areas which should be suitable for us were Brighton, Waverley, and Balwyn. On Friday, the fourth day of the house hunt, we believed we had the house, in Mount Waverley. It was easy to inspect, as the owners were already on their way back to the United States for the husband's new appointment.

"The White House"

The deposit was put down the following Monday, the contract was signed on Thursday, June 3, and the day of settlement was Friday, June 11. It has been our home now for coming on forty-six years, and the place in which our children have grown and matured. Part of my dad's homilies on property was never to purchase a white-painted brick building. The background for this in Dad's generation was that, firstly, builders had been known to build with shoddy bricks and let the paint cover same. The second problem was that inferior mortar could be used. It was a habit of Uncle Bill to run his car key along the mortar line of a house to test whether it was up to scratch. The final and practical problem with a white-painted brick house was the regular outside painting in order that the house would always look bright and sparkling. None of these ever became a problem for us—it has always been home.

My managers must have thought I was management material, because in 1973, when Dave Noy retired, I took over his role of technical service and development manager. This was both a marketing and corporate development function, charged with the future expansion of the Unichema's chemical business. There were three major development projects undertaken at that time, covering:

- Market surveys and product development, which included coordinating research and promotion of chemical products throughout the Australian mining industry in order to expand the company's interests in this burgeoning market. Later, I made a public relations visit for Unilever to South Africa and Zambia.
- Preparation of major recommendations, which would alter the type of raw materials used in the detergent industry to those available from renewable resources.
- Preparation of proposals for company diversification via value-added oleochemicals and acquisitions. Commercial aspects were an integral part of the above work, determining the viability of capital works through discounted cash flows, etc.

From late 1978, I was involved in preparing Operation Persia, which was an Acquisition Proposal—Steetley, for that company's purchase. Our senior Dutch boss, Lambert van Hout, called in to Melbourne on his way to Sydney for the final negotiations. He gave me a farewell pat on the back: "We'll do the best that we can." In the end, the operation was abandoned on account of Steetley's product range being dominated by high volume but low margin products, such as ammonium sulphate, a flocculating agent. It was all good training for what was to come later at Victorian Chemicals.

After eight years with the Unichema chemical business, the then managing director, Geert de Boer, suggested I should leave the company. It was strange that he should get me to leave when I wanted to stay, whilst Mike Newton, the then technical manager, wanted to go and Geert got him to stay. (This departure and my stay in Michaelis Bayley Ltd have been told more fully in chapter 2.)

It now seemed that the formal part of my training was over.

Below is my unexpurgated 1997 Personality Assessment:

THE TOTAL PERSON
(Hawkins Consulting—April 18, 1997)

Note: The Total Person is a combination of all aspects of the Prevue Assessment incorporating an explanation of Abilities, Interests and Personality.

You have roughly equal needs for solitude and companionship. Though determined and competitive, you enjoy meeting new people.

A somewhat conservative individual, you are a person who responds best to change if it is gradual. You would probably work best in a well established organization.

You have the ability to remain relaxed under pressure and are reasonably calm in a conflict.

You are an individual who prefers to deal with information or physical objects. As such, you are well suited to solitary work operating tools and machines. However, you are also capable of abstract thought, and could work well with symbol manipulators such as computers or electronic instruments.

You describe yourself as a motivated, competitive and driven person. You willingly put forth your own views and have no fear of confrontation or controversy. Although you have a strong need to succeed, on rare occasions you can achieve this success as part of a team. You will work hard and actively to reach your goals.

You probably feel that an ability to organize and your dependability are your strongest traits. While you will happily work in a traditional manner and follow the rules, you can also be flexible when needed.

You work best from a plan, and are most comfortable when your affairs are organized. You cope well with change as long as you are given some chance to think through possibilities before acting. You prefer to work with other people who share these qualities.

You need social stimulation and enjoy periods of high activity by talking to people. You find yourself refreshed by occasional excitement.

At work, you are happiest in situations where there is a reasonable amount of contact with other people. You are likely to become bored with routine work if it is continuous.

You are able to cope with life's pressures in a relaxed and civilised manner. You are also quite a trusting individual. Only rarely do you interpret a transgression personally, and even then you are likely to remain calm and equable.

For the most part, people such as you would do well in a demanding position, or one that required a good deal of trust and calm.

I wonder whether a third party reading the Total Person would believe that the person, so described, could bring Victorian Chemicals back from the grave. We had the company, but the first challenge was to keep it alive. The Total Person was fully needed.

As was once expressed on a farmers' programme on TV—

"You should never go broke spraying oil around Australia."

8   **Ee-muls-oyle Kept Us in Business**

Who has despised the day of small things?[1]

Don't waste time reinventing the bicycle.[2]

Judy and I sat in the village square, with the afternoon sun at our backs. We were extolling the benefits of Ee-muls-oyle grape-drying oil, in a circle of thirty to forty Greek farmers. Their wives and children were listening as they went about their business, looking out the windows of the houses that surrounded the square. In our travels, we have visited many villages in the hills of Crete, with their quaint names, long histories, and beautiful vistas. But the one we liked best is Profitis Ilias (προφήτης ηλίας), or the "Prophet Elijah." In these out-of-the-way spots, I have a habit of turning to Judy and saying, "Drying grapes has got us into some unexpected, quaint places!"

It is necessary to clear the air on the difference between a sultana and a raisin. Shakespeare set the tone with the following question:

> What's in a name? That which we call a rose
> By any other name would still smell as sweet.
> So Romeo would, were he not call'd
> Retain that dear perfection ...[3]

Dare we misquote Shakespeare by saying, "That which we call a sultana or a raisin would taste just as sweet"? For more than a hundred years, both sultanas and raisins have been grown from the Thompson Seedless cultivar. In the United States, they are known as raisins; whilst in Australia and South Africa, as sultanas. Other countries have their own names, such as Ak-Kishmish in Russia and Chekirdeksiz in Turkey. Its popularity and domination throughout the world is largely the result of its seedless character, thin skin, and crisp texture.

Every story has a beginning, and this one began many, many moons ago. Dried grapes—which is basically what this chapter is about—entered the food chain as a staple of Egypt's New Kingdom, from about 1550 B.C., as sultanas or raisins. They can be seen displayed on wall paintings in friezes during the Ramesside period. Further reference is made to them in 1445 B.C., in the history of the Israelite Exodus from Egypt.[4] Production of the end product was simple: grapes were left on racks in the sun to dry. A mature grape on the vine contains around 85 per cent water, and it was recognized that once the moisture was lowered to around f15 per cent, while keeping the skin intact, the dried fruit would store indefinitely for future consumption. This technique of drying takes about three to four weeks, depending on whether currants, sultanas, or raisins are being produced from the various root stock. This simplest method continues to be used today in America's San Joaquin Valley in California, where much of the world's raisins are produced.

Around two thousand years ago, at the time of Christ, an inventor, who never left his name to posterity, published his findings on a stela. Even then, one could joke that the old academic axiom "Publish or perish"[5] was well established. His writings signified that the grape-drying step could be improved by first dipping the grapes in a water mixture of ash (from the fire) and olive oil. This traditional method continues to be used today, around the Mediterranean in countries and cultures such as Greece and Turkey. The ash was a crude form of potassium carbonate, and today a pure form is used.

In the rest of this chapter, the story homes in on the dried-fruit industry's happenings over a hundred years, in the Sunraysia irrigation area which surrounds Mildura in north-western Victoria. Outside events, such as the ten-year drought and a fight over farmers' water rights, decimated the same industry during the early 2000s. Vicchem has been involved in producing natural products for the drying of grapes into raisins for the last seventy years. We have followed the ups and downs of the industry, flourishing as the farmer during the boom years and tightening our belts at the other times.

Grapes to Sultanas

Around the early 1900s, when the Chaffey brothers introduced irrigation to Mildura, grape growing became prominent in Australia. A not-insignificant dried-fruit industry developed, which used the Mediterranean drying technique by which the grapes, the Thompson Seedless strain, were dipped in a water solution containing olive oil imported from Italy and potassium carbonate. The first recommended mixture was fifty pounds of potash crystal mixed with three pints of olive oil in one hundred gallons of water. The quality of the sultanas so produced from the Thompson Seedless grapes was variable. During the 1930s, the growers began some ad hoc research to see if they could find a more consistent drying response.

The Voullaire Brothers, Izak Johannes, Henry George, and Rudolf Marc, located at Redcliffs outside Mildura, were one of the key marketers of a drying oil. They advertised in the local *Sunraysia Daily Newspaper* on January 14, 1935:

> Voullaire's Eemulsoyle, the perfect Olive Oil Emulsion,
> the result of years of research. Voullaire's Eemulsoyle
> is the economical and efficient emulsified olive oil for
> cold temperature dips. Once used, always used. Your
> shed takes orders and will carry stocks.

They were sufficiently satisfied by the sales response for them to apply for the trade mark, EE-MULS-OYLE (#66095) on June 5, 1935. The description of its use was "Fruit dipping preparation put up and sold in one, two and four gallon metal containers and being a chemical substance and used for viticulture purposes."

By 1937, the local farmers' co-operative, the Mildura Co-operative Fruit Company Ltd, had reacted to the Voullaire's Ee-muls-oyle product by developing its own. They employed a professional chemist, Eric Orton, who was brought across from Western Australia to develop their own product. It was made and sold locally by the Mildura Co-op, under its brand, Co-op Oil 60%. This new market entrant reduced the volume of product sold by the Voullaire brothers.

In 1938, Vicchem entered the market, when the company's founding technical director, Daniel Campbell, arranged to develop a rigorously standardized dipping oil for the co-op. It was advertised in the local newspaper on January 27, 1939, highlighting "the remarkable changes that had taken place in the development of the oil."

Shortly thereafter, the Second World War erupted, and all attention was on the war effort. Up until 1943, little more happened, except for alterations to the formulation through necessity because of the shortage of raw materials brought about by the war. One of these was the olive oil, which was not produced in Australia and had to be imported from Mediterranean countries, something that was strictly limited during the war years. The governmental CSIR, predecessor of the Commonwealth Scientific Industrial Research Organization (CSIRO), found in field trials that a superior drying product could be obtained by replacing the olive oil with a fatty ester, the chemistry[6] of which became my life. It was during this time that Vicchem researched and manufactured the esters which have been used ever since. How much this was reinventing the bicycle is open for debate, but just let's say we moved from the clunky olive oil to the much more refined and effective fatty ester which acted like a spear to get through the grape's waxy surface layer.

Development Work by the Farmers

While the Castrol Oil Company's 1980s television advertisement claimed, "Not all oils is oils,"[7] it is certainly true that not all esters or alcohols are the same. Under the war economy, it was decided to use tallow, the fat from sheep and cattle, as the source of the fatty segment. There was an abundant supply in the country from abattoir offcuts and offal, and under peacetime conditions, most of this tallow was exported. The choice of which alcohol to use was between methanol and ethanol. Methanol is made synthetically. There were no production plants in Australia so, like the olive oil, it was then not feasible to import it. Ethanol was the only choice, as again, there was an abundant natural supply in the country from the sugar fields of Queensland. The continuing use of ethanol in our esterification factory processes became of immense benefit to Vicchem seventy years later (as discussed more fully in chapter 9, in the section "What Is an Adjuvant?").

Vicchem's new formulation was commercialized by the Voullaire brothers, who promoted it as Voullaire's Ee-Muls-Oyle. The Padlock Company, a subsidiary of the Mildura Co-op, had the trade mark assigned to them for £4,500.00 on September 26, 1968. On February 7, 1977, the trade mark was then reassigned from Padlock to Victorian Chemicals, for $15,000.00. The previous management had not amortized it over the years, but maintained the $15,000.00 gross figure as an asset in its balance sheets. We accepted this figure in the valuation for the purchase and have maintained it at the same figure as a memento of the company's earliest beginnings, and, ultimately, our broader move into the world of agriculture.

While the Ee-muls-oyle had been paid for in the 1983 company's purchase, the legal tidy-up of the assignment needed to be completed at the patent office. This commenced with a statuary declaration from me in August 1985, indicating that the original certificate of registration had been lost or inadvertently destroyed.

As we started to scout around in early 1984 to consider how Vicchem's sales could be increased, the potential of our grape-drying oil product, Voullaire's Ee-muls-oyle, was reviewed. At that time, it represented 11 per cent of our sales, with roughly 20 per cent market share in the Sunraysia district.

Sunraysia was dominated between the farmer-owned Mildura

Co-op and the privately owned Irymple Packing House. Both of these concerns dominated the industry, from the supply of all the farmers' requirements (such as fencing wire and drying oils), to the ultimate purchase of the finished dried sultanas for their packing for retail sale or export. Because of this domination, the Mildura Co-op and Irymple Packing House forced Vicchem to take back any oil that was not sold to growers at the end of the season. As a result, Ee-muls-oyle acquired the nickname of Boomerang Oil.

The sultana export market has always been competitive, and the co-op used to threaten their suppliers that they would not sell a single gallon of oil if they heard we were selling our oil overseas. Notwithstanding, Vicchem had built a solid market in Persia, even though the letters of credit habitually arrived after the oil was in production and sometimes after the ship had sailed. For the year before our purchase, the oil had been produced, awaiting the letter of credit, when the Ayatollah Khomeini came to power, overthrowing the Shah and renaming the country Iran. The new regime cancelled all imports. With $60,000.00 of stock sitting on the wharves with nowhere to go, the previous management of Victorian Chemicals claimed the cause that forced them to sell their business was due to matters outside their control and that new Iranian regime and the Ayatollah.

By the time of our takeover in 1983, Vicchem's share of the Sunraysia drying-oil market had grown to about 20 per cent. There were three established processes to apply the drying oil as an emulsion, and these are still used today. The *cold dip* has been used from the beginning, and consists of simply dipping the grape bunches in the emulsion, in a dipping-box, when they were laid out to dry, either on the ground on plastic sheets or on the drying racks built with nine layers of chicken wire of one metre wide and about thirty metres long. This latter simple arrangement allows good circulation for the hot, drying winds.

Rack drying

Rack drying remains the preferred process, whereby the fresh bunches, just cut from the vine, are laid on the dying racks just mentioned. The grapes are then sprayed with a 2 per cent solution of Ee-muls-oyle and 4 per cent potassium carbonate. The ethyl oleate softens the waxy layer of the grapes, allowing the water from the grape to evaporate rapidly. The drying is normally finished in six to eight days, by contrast with those without drying oils, which take about two to three weeks. About 75 per cent of the grapes in Sunraysia are sprayed and dried in this way.

Trellis drying is the most recently developed process, where the grapes are left under the canopy of grape leaves, sprayed, and then the cane is cut back at the crown, which initiates the drying process. This is known as *summer pruning*. Once the drying is complete, the vines are mechanically shaken, and the sultanas are collected.

One of our first priorities after acquiring Vicchem was to bring our overall stock under control, in particular, the $60,000.00 level of Ee-muls-oyle from the previous management's aborted deal with Iran. Sales are the quickest and most profitable way to reduce stock;

thus, sales became a priority. Taking the first opportunity, within eighteen months after the company's purchase, Judy, Ken Allen, our one remaining salesman, and I, were having our first sales visit to Sunraysia, on October 24 and 25, 1984. This began a series of October/November visits to provide the new season's pricing and to promote the product before the upcoming season.

A revisit followed in the postseason to provide a dinner for the storemen in thanks for their input and for product promotion. The first of these dinners was held on February 5, 1985, for the Irymple Packing House, and on February 7, for the Mildura Co-op. It was a simple format, with welcoming drinks, then on to open seating in the dining room. Open seating, for Judy and me, meant we would be with the purchasing people and a few store managers. It was quaint that for the first years each company acted as if the dinner was only for them, but in the country, there are no secrets. After the main course, I would give a ten-minute speech—ha, ha, but normally around twenty minutes—the gist of which was "Let's get this show on the road." These were fun and quirky speeches that used overhead projector slides with humorous photos having more to do with the company being the new kid on the block. The attendees were more than happy, as most dinner speeches by major chemical companies went for forty minutes of sheer boredom.

Marketing Development

In those early days, Vicchem's problem was to make enough sales to survive. We were promoting out in the bush where there were lots of people who knew how difficult it was to survive, and we related to each other's struggles.

At the dinners, the men didn't want technical graphs showing the latest wonderful results for the new wonder product. They knew that no promoter would turn up without awesome results in hand. The main thing they were looking for was encouragement that Ee-muls-oyle would be reliable and top quality and that service would be provided immediately when needed. The classic story relates a farmer ringing up and complaining that our Ee-muls-oyle was "too frothy." Sales manager Ken promised he would leave immediately. Five and a half hours and five hundred kilometres later, he was with the blockee,[8] the local term for an owner of a block of land producing grapes. Ken enquired, "Where is the problem?" The customer proudly showed him a water trough with an outboard motor at full throttle whirring froth into the air. "No," said Ken. "Let me show you!" Ken refilled the water trough and lightly paddled in some Ee-muls-oyle. "That is all the stirring you need," Ken said. He then got in his car and drove the five and a half hours back to Melbourne. Service was provided.

The storemen had handled Ee-muls-oyle ever since they first joined the store. The men expected the dinner would be a flash in the pan like other chemical companies that would turn up one night to market a new product, a weedicide for example, when the marketing manager would talk for forty-five minutes, using incomprehensible tables and charts, driving them witless with boredom. But we became a fixture. Over the years, there were about four different eating houses, the favourite being Mildura's best-known watering hole, The Rendezvous, in Langtree Avenue. Our theme, which we repeated each year, was, "Please keep the Ee-muls-oyle at the front of the warehouse, so if a grower just asks for a drying oil, just throw our product into their ute!"[9] The dinners lasted for eighteen seasons, until 2002.

As mentioned earlier, the market was divided between The Mildura Co-op and the privately owned IPC. The first purchasing managers we met were so very different. The Co-op had Dennis Matthews, who was always on the search for a deal. IPC had Danny Orwell, a conservative Englishman who had sought out a new land and taken the opportunity of migrating on the promotional government £10.00 scheme. Our product opposition was from the oil companies—Mobil Oil, Ampol, and Shell—which sold their products through their service stations. We actually produced the Ampol and Shell products for them, as the quantities involved were considered too small for their own refineries to mess around with. We encouraged the co-op and IPC managers to see Vicchem as a little company which was under new management. We would push with the question, "Why does the rabbit, ninety-nine times out of a hundred, beat the fox to his burrow?" and answered by saying, "The oil companies were running for their lunch, but we were running for our lives, and it is all the difference in the world!"

The meetings of Dennis Matthews, merchandising manager of the co-op, and I have been described as two circling sharks. The situation reminded me of the time at Manly surf beach when Judy's and a shark's paths crossed. They looked at one another, turned, and went their separate ways. You may well ask, why? They were both showing professional respect! This was the same kind of respect that Dennis and I had for each other. When Dennis really understood that we were serious about the well-being of Sunraysia and not just interested making money, he really opened up and began to trust us. On the third October visit, we indicated that we would be undertaking television advertising in the local area. He proposed, if the co-op could sell more than one hundred thousand litres, would we be prepared to give them a special discount (or whatever name we felt led to call it)? Dennis was ambitious and wanted to make his name at the co-op, and he saw our product as a great opportunity. It did not take me long to agree on the discount.

As I flew home on Qantas's turbo-prop Dash 8 flight, I calculated what the financial implications from a one hundred thousand-litre sale could do for the company. The co-op came good in that season, with sales greater than the one hundred thousand litres, and that provided clearance of the Iranian excess stock, gave cash flow an impetus, and introduced us to the larger sales volumes available in agriculture.

We did go into television advertising, with a series of thirty-second commercials. Organizing advertising in Mildura was a fun experience. In a typical year, we would allocate around $9,000.00. The first $500.00 was for production, which was mainly for the TV station to seek out appropriate clips taken from stock footage. The remainder was for 111 transmissions at $77.00 each. In the long hours of the night, when maybe one man and his dog were watching the set, the commercials were run for free as fill-ins. We had variants of our ads each year.

We would present a script:

Voice-over	Visual
You have worked hard and long to get your grapes ready for drying.	Men working hard in their vineyards (Lots of sun and sweat)
Now is the time to use Voullaire's, the vegetable-based drying oil that was born and bred in Sunraysia over fifty years ago.	Grapes being dipped, rack-sprayed, and trellis-sprayed
Voullaire's is the drying oil with the proven track record of producing golden five-crown sultanas.	Great-looking sultanas
So, when buying your drying oil this year, pick up the green drum and put Voullaire's to work in your block. It is as reliable as a good old mate!	The green drum, or if available, men loading Voullaire's into their ute
Available from … … … … .	

From the above scant suggestions came a commercial. I think it went better than we actually anticipated, as it was left in the hands of the TV station staff to put together. They wanted to show us the level of their professionalism. Looking back after twenty years, we can only wonder why these advertisements actually worked among the blockees—but they did. They were also happy that we were spending money in the district. It was enough to let us brag, "We had the best commercials in the country … not doing too well in the city … but killing them in the country."[10]

"Dr Dave," Part I

Following our technical training over many years, we accumulated and perused any reports and scientific papers we could lay our hands on. The one that really caught our eye was a 1974 paper, *"Use of Oleic Acid Derivatives to Accelerate Drying of Thompson Seedless Grapes,"* by Vincent Petrucci et al., published in the prestigious *Journal of the American Oil Chemists Society* 51, 77. In the paper, Vince explained how he saw, in his visit to Mildura, that "the fruit was sprayed with a two per cent emulsion of Eemulsoyle (sic) and potassium carbonate ... The Eemulsoyle was found to contain a mixture of ethyl esters with an emulsifier; it is a proprietary product of the Victorian Chemical Company, Richmond, Australia." The results? It was found that "grapes of the Thompson seedless variety could be dried economically on the vine by using the Eemulsoyle and potassium carbonate treatment." This was more than enough for our first overseas export drive to set our homing device towards Vince Petrucci who was now a professor at the California State University, Fresno. This city is the centre for American dried-fruit production, with 250,000 tonnes gathered yearly, predominantly from the San Joaquin Valley.

I have always been fascinated by the American university system, where the professors' lives seem to be preoccupied with increasing financial donations from non-government sources, such as businesses and philanthropists. Vince soon realized that our business was travelling on the smell of an oily rag, and we would not be supporting American universities. He sent me to one of his key patrons, the Wilbur-Ellis (W-E) company, which described itself as a small private business with more than a $1 billion in annual sales. Our first contact was with Frank Saviez, Vice President of Agriculture. The conversation lasted about a quarter of an hour, with Frank being courteous but not really interested in our Ee-muls-oyle, since they were more than satisfied with their own natural sun-dried raisins. This was put even more succinctly by a manager of the California Raisin Advisory Board, who, in a few well chosen words, said, "We are never going to put your filthy chemicals on our sun-kissed raisins."

Dr Dave

In order to stop me wasting his time and, without being rude, Frank, as quickly as he could, sent me off to meet his company's research man, Dr Dave Schulteis. Dr Dave became our most priceless American contact. We really clicked, with our entrepreneurial spirits and technical backgrounds. He was W-E's technical manager, and, as they say, "the rest is history." Out of this and future meetings of minds came a product, an adjuvant that we called Hasten. This became the driver for Vicchem's future growth (as discussed further in chapter 9).

"Dr Bob" of Veterinary Hospital

From late 1985, vegetable-based canola oil began to replace animal-based tallow as our main raw material. This opened up the possibility of obtaining, the not only American, but worldwide-recognized food-grade approval from the United States Food and Drug Administration

(FDA). In retrospect, this turned out to be our most daring move yet. It was an incredibly brash initiative for us, a small—and I mean *small*—non-American company to approach the behemoth FDA with such a proposal. I am sure in addition that, if they had seen our run-down factory, the FDA would have immediately cancelled our application. I suppose, hidden deep in our psyche, was how we saw ourselves, and, therefore, how we approached the authorities with aplomb. I cannot remember any occasion or appointment where I have been nervous before or during the event.

What you see is what you are

Our application was presented to the FDA in 1986. I put the application together. It was a simple pitch, running to about forty pages. The main contention was that animal-fat esters had been used for forty years to produce more than a million tonnes of dried fruit without killing anyone, and look; now we had moved to vegetable oil esters—safer than ever! Maybe it was the time of living "in the fast lane," but when the FDA asked what danger there was to the environment when our product fell on the ground, I provided no data—we didn't have any—and explained that it was no different to a scenario of a farmer's cow that died and rotted on the ground. On other occasions, not in this instance, I had swallowed our ethyl oleate to show customers how safe it was. As organic chemists, we work within the carbon cycle of nature. In its most simplistic form, this cycle starts with all animal life which breathes in oxygen for life and exhales carbon in the form of gaseous carbon dioxide into the atmosphere. Carbon dioxide is also produced from burning wood and coal. From the atmosphere, all plant life absorbs carbon dioxide, and in the sunlight, photosynthesis takes place in the plant. This is the breakdown of the carbon dioxide into carbon, which the plant uses to grow, and into oxygen, which goes into the atmosphere for animal breathing. This cycle continues ad infinitum.

Meanwhile, back at the FDA, five years of frustration followed, attributable to a lack of staff continuity. The FDA had become a de facto training ground, in that, after a year there, many staff would leave to obtain better-paid private non-government work. What was in their favour was that they had "worked with the FDA," which really meant something in the marketplace. It seemed that, each year, we went to meet a new person.

Organizing our next FDA appointment, I had a telephone conversation with a Dr Robert Martin, then supervisor of the Division of Food and Color Additives. I thought he sounded a real live one, and so, as I was concluding the call, I said, "Have you heard of the Muppets?[11]" He tentatively replied, yes, and I could almost hear him thinking, *Why is he asking about the Muppets when he is on a costly international call?* It was actually so that I could provide the punch line, "Oh well, you will remember me when we meet, because I'm really Dr Bob of 'Veterinary Hospital.'" He laughed, and I laughed. For those of a younger generation, "Veterinary Hospital" is a recurring sketch on *The Muppet Show*, in which, each week, the veterinarian, Dr Bob, is played by Rawlf the dog, and is helped in the operating theatre by Nurse Piggy and Sister Janice. They stand over a new patient on the operating table and tell an endless series of bad jokes, without ever curing the patient.

There was the time when the dialogue ran:

> DR BOB: What's wrong with this patient?
> NURSE: He has acute appendicitis!
> DR BOB: I don't care how cute it is, it has to come out.

Or the time Dr Bob approached the operating table, singing "Blue Skies":

> NURSE: Dr Bob, you can't sing at a time like this!
> DR BOB: I'm not singing "At a Time Like This." I'm singing "Blue Skies."

Or the comments from the two old critics in the theatre box after "Veterinary Hospital" had every participant dressed as chickens:

> STATLER: These chickens certainly made a different skit.
> WALDORF: Yes, but it still adds up to the same old turkey!

This comment reminds me of how Judy often mentioned to me that she always wanted to soar like an eagle in life and sadly found she was married to a turkey! "Dr Bob" was natural casting for my personality.

"Dr Bob" of FDA

It is in my nature to respect people of all nations, and the same respect has always been returned. This quality was fully experienced when, four weeks later, big African American Robert Martin met us in the lobby of the FDA, with extended arms, and we ended up with a big hugging-match exploding with laughter, and saying to each other, "Dr Bob!"; "Dr Bob!" There is no doubt that the FDA's marble-floor entrance lobby has ever seen the same, before or since. We had a pleasant, understanding first-time meeting, and departed happily. We soon found that Dr Bob had become our champion! We believe he took our application and went around the various direct additives branch managers, saying something to the effect of "Please check out your section of this application; you'll find it is OK, and sign it off." Thus, our Ee-muls-oyle was FDA approved.

The official notification was dated April 15, 1992, and probably not noted by his bosses, but Dr Bob of the FDA kept our first contact running by calling me Dr Bob. Below is the letter that changed the history of our company:

DEPARTMENT OF HEALTH & HUMAN SERVICES   Public Health Service

Food and Drug Administration
Washington DC 20204

APR 15 1992

Dr. R. W. Killick
Managing Director
Victorian Chemical Company
P. O. Box 71
Richmond, Victoria 3121
AUSTRALIA

RE: GRAS Petition Nos. 6G0311 and 6G0312

Dear Dr. Bob:

Congratulations! As you note from the enclosed Federal

Register, your regulations finally published on

April 13, 1992. Thank you for your patience and

understanding.

Best regards to you and Mrs. Killick.

Sincerely yours,

Robert L. Martin, Ph.D.
Direct Additives Branch.HFF-334
Division of Food and Color Additives
Center for Food Safety
and Applied Nutrition

FDA approval

Go for the Jugular

Our approval had first come to us verbally, but it was enough to let us advertise in the December 1991 *Australian Dried Fruits Association News,* with an editorial article entitled "American FDA Acceptance of Ee-Muls-Oyle." In the paid advertisement below the article, we stressed the following:

Victorian Chemicals
is proud to announce technical approval by … …

THE AMERICAN FOOD AND DRUG ADMINISTRATION (FDA)
The international seal of product quality

- FIRST COMMERCIAL DRYING OIL
- FIRST WITH MODERN SPECIALISED DRYING AGENTS
- FIRST WITH NATURAL EDIBLE VEGETABLE OILS
- FIRST WITH FDA INTERNATIONAL ACCEPTANCE

VOULLAIRES "EE-MULS-OYLE" IN THE GREEN CAN

The green can did become the symbol of our operation throughout Sunraysia. A winner's marketing label highlighting "FDA Approval" was also stuck on every drum and can.

Having obtained this approval, the next step was to market effectively in Australia, using the advantage of having our FDA approval—something no one else enjoyed. Continual pushing at the Australian Dried Fruits Association Inc. resulted in them sending out the following classic letter on November 10, 1992. It proved to be not only positive for us as a company but also a game changer for the entire dried-fruit industry:

> Dear Bob,
> Re: Industry Specification for Drying Oils to be Vegetable Oil Based
>
> The Australian Dried Fruits Association has for some time been concerned about the use of tallow oil as a base for drying oils used by the industry … the USA,

in particular, has sought to denigrate the Australian sultanas in the world market ...

The ADFA is seeking an assurance from manufacturers that all components of the drying oil are food grade and in addition that the oil base is vegetable and not tallow based. The industry is seeking these assurances by November 30, 1992.

Yours sincerely

In January 1961, Bob Dylan[12] released what has become one of his most influential political songs, "The Times They Are A-changin'." Sunraysia's big change was forty years later, but suddenly it was apposite to sing the song. Grapes have three uses: for consumption as fresh fruit, for wine manufacture, and for dried-fruit production. The quantities of the grapes which flow to each end use depend mainly on the value of the end product and the cost of production. The first concern is the actual amount of grapes produced in any one year. The peak production of grapes was in the thirty years of the 1980s, 1990s, and early 2000s, after which it has been in decline all the way. The reduction of the grape quantities comes from the removal of the vines; firstly, because of the retiree population increase into Mildura, where very fertile growing blocks have been purchased for housing, and, secondly, on account of the severe ten-year drought, where water allocation to the irrigators was severely slashed. Once the vines die, the irrigator dies also, and vines are rarely replanted.

The fresh-fruit market is stable, increasing in size as the population grows. It is maintained in winter with the import of Californian fruit.

For many years, Australian vintners did not use the Thompson Seedless grapes in their wines. Once the world discovered Australian wines, and wine production increased exponentially, the vintners used the Sunraysia grapes to bulk up their volumes. For the blockee farmer, this was easy money. The bunches of grapes were cut from the vine, loaded into a large bin, and sent to the buyer, followed by down payment at the already agreed price.

The dried-fruit grower has to take the cut grape bunches, undertake the drying process, be concerned with the quality level achieved, and finally get paid, much later.

An Industry Can Die

The availability of grapes for drying dropped away, on account of the demand from increasing wine production in the 1990s and 2000s. When the Australian wine market faded, the grape producers faced the ten-year drought which delivered the *coup de grâce* for many in the industry.

In the glory days of sultana production, the average yearly production was around 70,000 tonnes, with a peak in 1992 of around 92,000 tonnes. In 2010, only 9,400 tonnes were produced. For the last few years, Vicchem has been selling around ninety thousand litres of Ee-muls-oyle, and we ask, whatever happened to our breakthrough first one hundred thousand-litre order twenty years ago? For us, it has been a salient reminder of how an industry can rise and fall in a hundred years. *Sic transit gloria mundi* continues to say it all.

For those with forensic skills, it is interesting to consider how all my future methods and style of running Vicchem for the next twenty-five years were encapsulated in the actions taken in the Ee-muls-oyle story. That includes the following:

- Being personable with the customer; that joke against yourself never goes astray.
- Applying the SWAN principle, or Sell What's Available Now. Ee-muls-oyle was long established, both in our product range and the market, but not selling particularly well. We decided to go for it.

- Applying an aggressive approach to the market by visiting the head buyers while still promoting through the storemen who were the front-line troops.
- Taking a serious product quality control became a priority for us. The previous management used to say, "Don't look at the quality, look at the price!" But that just doesn't "cut any ice" in the chemical industry.
- Being focused on the sales possibilities available in agriculture.

In the teaching of marketing, the lecturers would sometimes start with the query, "Who was the first pilot to cross the Atlantic by plane?" Most trivia buffs respond, "Lindbergh!"

Next question: "Who was the second?" And who has any idea, because coming second doesn't rate in history! (For those desperate to know, it was Bert Hinkler, across the Southern Atlantic.)

However, this provides some background on Vicchem:

- We were the first to advertise on television in Sunraysia.
- We had our first foray into innovative marketing.
- We were the first with then newly available canola vegetable oil.
- We were the first to obtain US FDA approval. (This only eventuated through our persistence with a bureaucracy and being prepared to travel overseas to contact the appropriate people, as described earlier in this chapter.)

As a final reflection here, there is the question asked at the beginning of this chapter: "Who has despised the day of small beginnings?" There were certainly people, after we bought Vicchem, who gossiped that we would not last a year! However, "mighty oaks from little acorns grow,"[13] and, to change the metaphor:

But what might happen if we found a mother lode?[14]

9 As Good as Gold

Easy to be a genius, harder to make a buck.[1]

Give me an alternative.[2]

By 1993, ten years after we had purchased Vicchem, our company continued to promote that we were "happy little rabbits living six feet underground, digging for bronze with streaks of silver; for when you find gold, the vultures gather."

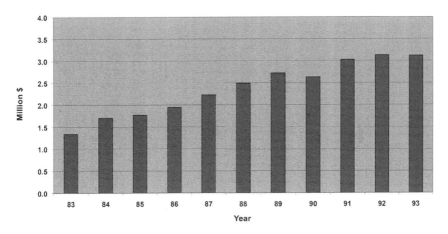

VCC sales history (I)

For our first ten years, sales marginally increased each year, reaching $3.1 million in 1993, contra the $1.3 million achieved in 1983, our year of purchase. There was a better spirit among the staff, as the company was at least making some profit. We had been able to purchase two neighbouring land blocks west and north of the factory, using personal money and that which had built up in our superannuation fund.

"Dr Dave," Part II

Meanwhile, back at the Development Ranch, we were continuing to have strong, valuable contacts with "Dr Dave" Schulteis. We had met him on our first export drive (as mentioned in chapter 8). Our first days with Dr Dave were involved, not in development, but exploring entry with Voullaire's Ee-muls-oyle into the vast 250,000 tonnes of dried-fruit production. One can see the results of our promotions if I said that the American raisins are still dried today by placing the grape bunches on plastic sheets lying between the rows. The moral we learnt then and repeated over the years was that it is as good as impossible to change traditional eating habits and farming techniques.

Dave was an "ideas man." It could be argued that he would have at least ten major projects running at any one time, and there were more projects than time available. To cover this deficiency, he would use outside help whenever he could. Dave had become frustrated, in that some of the American companies would develop products for him, and, once Wilbur-Ellis, the company Dave worked for, had approved the result, they would promote their newly developed product to opposition companies on the basis of Wilbur-Ellis's approval.

Vicchem was considered safe. We were a long way away, and Dave knew we would not go behind his back. We provided trust, a company in which there was no guile. In one of our deep and meaningful discussions over a cup of coffee, he flew the following kite to see whether it could fly:

> DAVE: Bob, is there any chance for Vicchem to make
> an adjuvant for us?
> BOB (*ever positive*): No troubles! Have you got any special
> requirements?
> DAVE: Yeah … that it works! (*laughter*)

It was a simple request, but it changed the destiny of Vicchem—and our destiny as well!

What Is an Adjuvant?

Our company's knowledge of adjuvants was limited, to say the least, when Dr Dave asked us to make a sample. In agriculture, the definition of an adjuvant is a substance that enhances the killing effectiveness of weedicides, herbicides, fungicides, insecticides, etc. In Europe, they are more usually called additives. When adjuvants were first introduced to the market in the 1960s, petroleum oils were employed, and in some measure, are still used today at the low-cost end of the market. The first change for a small number of adjuvants was to replace the petroleum oil with a vegetable oil, such as canola. Most current adjuvants use the fatty esters as the oily constituent. We knew that an adjuvant was a blend of oily material and emulsifiers to produce a product which, when added to the water in the farmer's mix-tank, forms an emulsion of the oil before spraying. Both the oil and the emulsifiers, the two essential ingredients, have varied over the years. (The chemistry of fatty esters is described in note 5 of chapter 8.)

From America that night, I rang Peter Wrigley to get the project under way and to save the few days before I returned to Melbourne. Laurie Parnaby was then our laboratory man who put new products together. Being in an unknown area, he took the simplest decision by taking our most-used ester, ethyl oleate, and the two most-used combined emulsifiers in both our textile and tanning range. He was following the old adages "Never reinvent the bicycle" and "When you are on a good thing, stick to it."[3] Two variants were prepared and sent to Dr Dave. He did not send both but chose one to forward to Professor Don Penner of Michigan State University, East Lansing, Michigan.

Obtaining the results from our first foray into adjuvants seemed to take forever, although by later standards, to which we have grown accustomed, it was quick.

I finally had Dr Dave on the phone:

DAVE: Have heard from Don Penner, and he says the product is *hot!*

BOB: What does that mean?

DAVE: It means it's good, and it is showing minimal phytotoxicity. Get some more of that material over here, and we'll go on to further trials!

A Brand Name to Remember

The Penner trials went well. In addition, we had a story to tell, with the product's main active ingredient being the ethyl oleate, by contrast with the rest of the agricultural world, which used the methyl oleate.

"Extra dead" weed

The weed under test at Michigan State University, East Lansing, Michigan, was velvetleaf (*abutilon theophrasti*), depicted in the above image. Without herbicide application, its natural growth is shown in the far left check pot. In the second pot from the left, the velvetleaf shows only half its growth, following the application of BASF's herbicide Pursuit, an Imazethapyr. When American Cyanamid's methyl ester adjuvant Sunit II is added to that application spray, the velvetleaf's growth is stunted, as shown in the third pot from the left. In the last pot to the right, the Sunit II has been replaced with our ethyl ester-based Hasten, under Wilbur-Ellis's code WE 49031, and the velvetleaf is dying, with just one leaf hanging on. The difference between Sunit II and Hasten (WE 49031) is worth a patent.

It was standard American industry practice to patent anything that looked of interest, and I agreed with Dave that we should apply for a patent, with Wilbur-Ellis and Vicchem as co-inventors. It was a moot point, and our patent attorney's advice was that it could well be argued that Vicchem was the single only inventor as a result of our choice of ingredients. I decided not to get into a long philosophical debate with Dr Dave, but, rather, to stay with the co-inventors' application. By confirming this approach, we bypassed whatever glory may have accrued to Vicchem's name. In reality, glory is ephemeral (*Sic transit gloria mundi*), whereas choosing to stay with Dave opened up much more of America's market, along with cash flow from sales of a new product.

We had a product without a name. This was solved by W-E, who had a product, Hasten, without a market. They were agreeable to moving this brand name over to the new product whilst maintaining the brand ownership in the United States. Hasten was free for us to register anywhere else in the world. Because it was their brand name, we agreed to pay a royalty fee of 1 per cent on Hasten sales over the duration of the patented period. This would be in all countries except Australia and New Zealand, which we had nominated as our home markets.

Dr Dave started to push Hasten through Wilbur-Ellis into California and Idaho, with significant sales achieved. The next major move was to the American Midwest, to a company, Wilfarm, half-owned by W-E. Our summer sales had been increasing with Ee-muls-oyle, and we felt all our Christmases had arrived in December 1995, when the month's sales passed the $1 million mark. This was followed in the January 1996, with another million dollars in sales. It was a psychological moment. *We could make and sell a million dollars in a month.* It was a long way from April 1983, our first full sales month of $89,000.00. Once a milestone has been passed, it is easier for the next, and the next and the next. ...

These million-dollar sales months were repeated a year later, in December 1996 and January 1997. Wilfarm became aggressive on pricing levels and demanded an unacceptable price reduction, with the underlying threat that if we didn't come to the party, we shouldn't be surprised if their demand for Hasten dropped off. What was further annoying was to learn that whatever they gained through the lowering of the purchase price would not be used to lower prices to the farmer to increase sales, but, instead, would go straight to increase Wilfarm's own profitability. We would not bow to the pressure, and they ripped all sales away and replaced our product with one based on the methyl ester. However, Hasten was now starting to pick up a head of steam in Australia, with its main sales achieved in the winter season.

VCC Sales History & Growth

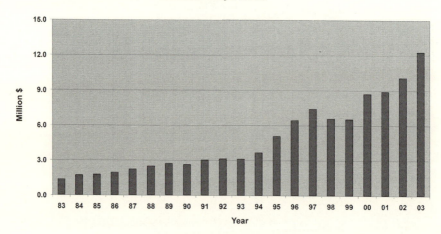

VCC sales history (II)

For this middle ten years of our ownership, sales, with the impetus of our agriculture marketing, were no longer marginally, but now seriously, increasing each year. Over the ten years from 1993 to 2003, sales had increased fourfold. Hasten had become as good as gold for us, and, as shown on the book's cover, it even provided the golden look. We were now fully ensconced in agricultural chemicals, and we were on the rise.

Not Quite a Transcendent Genius

We had our first successful patent, along with increasing sales, but does that rate me a genius? Does it make the technical group at Vicchem "a Mensa of geniuses?" What is the patent spark? It reminds me of the story when Gilbert and Sullivan were having difficulties agreeing on the plot for a new operetta; Gilbert clung to the idea of a magic lozenge which would take the players into Gilbert's own topsy-turvy world. Sullivan kept rejecting this idea as being stale and a worn-out plot line. A 1939 film about their lives shows the moment when Gilbert, pacing around his study in an aggravated mood, is startled by a Japanese sword which falls from the wall. We see him pick it up and stare at it, and his eyes begin to twinkle. In a flash, the film transports us to Japan and one of Gilbert and Sullivan's greatest successes, *The Mikado*. After cutting back to Gilbert's study, his wife, Kitty, brings in a tray of coffee for him:[4]

> GILBERT: Kitty, do you know you're married to a transcendent genius?
>
> KITTY: Willy, I never doubted it for a moment!

I confess that there are times I call Judy "Kitty," and she knows exactly that I've had one of my better ideas! The following story tells how one of our patents came together, but there was definitely no Japanese sword involved.

During the late 1990s, there was an increasing push by green activists to make petroleum products greener. The immediate possibility was to market our fatty esters to the oil companies as they, and many technical people, knew our products under the generic name of biodiesel. The terms are interchangeable, as biodiesel is mixed fatty esters, and fatty esters are biodiesel. A few of us visited one of the Independent oil companies and found the oil industry was not really interested in the green fuels. Their overriding aim was to sell petroleum-based products, and they were only going to include green products if and when the government forced them to do so. The discussion on pricing was such that it gave me the distinct impression that they would sell their grandmother down the Swanee River for a half-cent per litre.

The other possibility of greening was to include ethanol in petroleum fuels to reduce the particulate emissions from vehicle exhaust. Back in 2009, the NSW government mandated the incorporation of 4 per cent ethanol in petrol. By 2012, the government cancelled the mandate, and not even the Greens bleated. Queensland, with its large sugar cane plantations and thus ethanol availability, mandated 10 per cent ethanol in its petrol, and the fuel was known as E10. Diesel engines, are the most polluting, in regard to particulates, but ethanol was not a solution, as it was immiscible in the diesel fuel. In patenting terms, there was a need.

These were some of the thoughts mulling around in my mind when Judy and I were away in Manly. I could have been strolling down the Corso or watching a ferry leave from Manly Wharf when the first twist passed my mind that while ethanol was not miscible in diesel, it was miscible in our fatty esters. This was confirmed as I reflected that when making the fatty esters in the factory, ethanol was added to the canola oil, and it floated on the top, not being miscible. The catalyst was added, and about halfway through the reaction, the mixture became one phase, as the unreacted ethanol was miscible in the just-produced fatty esters. In addition, I knew that fatty esters were miscible in diesel/petroleum oils, as the factory often blended the two together to produce some of our specialized products. My mind put the two known facts together to provide a simple plan to add the ethanol to the biodiesel whence that mixture was added to the diesel, and we would solve the problem! I was chomping on the bit to get back to the laboratory. My only desire was to say to everyone who was providing us transport back to Melbourne, reputedly in the words of Queen Victoria's classic command to her coachman, "Home, James, and don't spare the horses!" For those who prefer modern parlance, the request to the chauffeur would be, "Get this vehicle out of second gear!"

That Monday, I had our chemist, Lawrie, make up a set of samples, following my above ideas. It worked, and I did call Judy "Kitty" that night. It was elegant, and the patent was granted. The legitimate question which arises from this, of course, is why aren't we all multimillionaires? The response is, ultimately, that one simple word: money. The major oil companies only have one aim, and that is to process the oil they have from the ground. Ethanol and biodiesel just don't count in their scheme of things. Over four years, we spent more than $200,000.00 trying to make a mark in the United States, with no success. We thought there would be a possibility, with all the diesel-driven school buses which pumped horrendous amounts of dirty exhaust gases into the air intakes of other buses standing in line. Yes, there was a concern about their children's health, but, ultimately, price always trumps other benefits.

You Don't Win Every One!

Are patents worth it? The classic response has always been "yes and no." Over the thirty years in business, we have had twenty-eight patents that have reached the patent offices, at one level or another, but only five have been commercial successes.

To obtain a patent, there are three fundamental requirements. The first is to show that there is a need in the marketplace for what the patent is claiming to have solved. The second is to show that something novel or surprising has been discovered which enabled this need to be overcome. This novelty is not obvious and would not have been expected from a person with standard knowledge in the discipline. Finally, the invention has to be usable.

Our development work has covered a broad sweep of our oleochemical world. (The list of projects which, in their earliest days, were considered to have the potential to become patents are shown in the notes section.[5]) Over time, we were stymied from a full application, mainly because of prior art, the cost, or insufficient novelty. Sometimes the prior art was discovered quite late in the process, and this was the most frustrating. There have also been patents that have been granted, but they were not able to be commercialized.[6]

On the positive side, for thirty years, our development work has been to expand our product range. The lack of a patent does not stop us from taking a product to market. The thrust has been to develop, and, if a patent became apparent during the process of that development, then that was considered a bonus.

Patent Successes

Hasten has been our major success. Consequently, the truth of the old adage "Imitation is the sincerest form of flattery"[7] became true for us. The smaller opposition companies joined the adjuvant bandwagon, launching their own products with quixotic mimicry of Hasten—namely, Sprinta, Kwicken, Dasher, and Fasta. It might be flattering, but it is still annoying. We would keep a watching brief on their activities and were amazed to discover in a random analysis that a company was selling its product in northern Queensland, with a closely matching formulation to that of our Hasten.

Letters passed between our companies, asking them to desist, but they declined to do so. After a lot of argy-bargy, we moved towards a court case, but before that expensive experience, the court demanded we go into mediation, which took everything but a day. With the pressure not to go to court, I don't think that either they or we were particularly happy with the result. Our patent had claimed that our product was novel because of the ethyl content, and the result of the mediation was that they could not have an ethyl content in their product at, or over, 50 per cent. At least we still had the bragging rights of the ethyl content, and we have successfully continued to advertise the ethyl story.

The Australian Hasten patent was granted in 1993 for use with herbicides, and in 1995 for use with insecticides and fungicides. A typical product data bulletin for herbicide applications follows. On the back page of the bulletin, one of the keys to our success has been the "Cross Labelling" text box (see table 1). We have built this up year by year, when the large multinational companies launch their new products. Hasten is considered the adjuvant against which all others are compared. The table highlights the list of herbicides on which Hasten can be used, and at what usage rate. Cross labelling then works on the multinational's herbicide bulletin, which promotes Hasten as one of its preferred adjuvants for use with their own product.

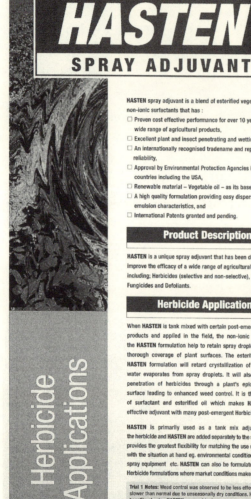

HASTEN™
SPRAY ADJUVANT

HASTEN spray adjuvant is a blend of esterified vegetable oil and non-ionic surfactants that has :

- ☐ Proven cost effective performance for over 10 years with a wide range of agricultural products,
- ☐ Excellent plant and insect penetrating and wetting properties,
- ☐ An internationally recognised tradename and reputation for reliability,
- ☐ Approval by Environmental Protection Agencies in many countries including the USA,
- ☐ Renewable material – Vegetable oil – as its base raw material,
- ☐ A high quality formulation providing easy dispersion and stable emulsion characteristics, and
- ☐ International Patents granted and pending.

Product Description

HASTEN is a unique spray adjuvant that has been designed to improve the efficacy of a wide range of agricultural products including; Herbicides (selective and non-selective), Insecticides, Fungicides and Defoliants.

Herbicide Applications

When HASTEN is tank mixed with certain post-emergent herbicide products and applied in the field, the non-ionic surfactants in the HASTEN formulation help to retain spray droplets and ensure thorough coverage of plant surfaces. The esterified oil in the HASTEN formulation will retard crystallization of herbicides as water evaporates from spray droplets. It will also increase the penetration of herbicides through a plant's epicuticular waxy surface leading to enhanced weed control. It is this dual action of surfactant and esterified oil which makes HASTEN a very effective adjuvant with many post-emergent Herbicides.

HASTEN is primarily used as a tank mix adjuvant, that is, the herbicide and HASTEN are added separately to the spray tank. This provides the greatest flexibility for matching the use rate of HASTEN with the situation at hand eg. environmental conditions, weed types, spray equipment etc. HASTEN can also be formulated directly with Herbicide formulations where market conditions make this preferable.

Trial 1 Notes: Weed control was observed to be less effective and much slower than normal due to unseasonally dry conditions. However the benefits of using HASTEN were evident.

Trial 2 Notes: HASTEN was found to be a superior adjuvant to AGRAL 90 when used with REFINE EXTRA for the weeds shown.

Trial 3 Notes: HASTEN enhanced the weed control significantly when applied with TOPIK at the sub-lethal dose of 30g/ha.

TRIAL 1
Weed Control in Winter Crops - Australia 2002
Herbicide:
HUSSAR* (50g/kg Iodosulfuron) - 200g/ha
Target: Wild Radish in Triticale
ONDUTY* (525g/kg Imazapic + 175g/kg Imazapyr) - 40g/ha
Target: Wild Oats in Clearfield Canola
Spray Rate: 70L/ha

% Weed Control 42 DAT

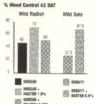

TRIAL 2
Weed Control in Summer Wheat - Canada 2004
Herbicide:
REFINE* EXTRA 75% DF (Thifensulfuron 50%, Tribenuron Methyl 25%) - 15g/ha
Crop: Wheat
Spray Rate: 100 L/ha

% Weed Control

TRIAL 3
Phalaris Control in Wheat - India 2002/3
Herbicide:
TOPIK* (Clodinafop-Propargyl 15WP) - 30g a.i./ha
Crop: Wheat
Spray Rate: 375 L/ha

% Weed Control

HASTEN Product Data Bulletin, front page

Testing and Evaluation

HASTEN is a non-ionic formulation which makes it compatible with most herbicides. In fact, HASTEN has been in use for over 10 years with many herbicides around the world and has been found to be physically compatible with major herbicide products.

HASTEN has been tested and evaluated by universities, lifescience companies, research organizations and independent researchers for many years. It has been established that HASTEN is a very effective adjuvant for improving the performance of herbicides and in many situations will outperform both emulsified petroleum and vegetable oil based products. It has also been observed that HASTEN is capable of increasing the activity of certain herbicides which may result in crop injury. Therefore in all new situations it is important to test HASTEN with the herbicide in a small area prior to applying it on a commercial scale.

Commercial Use

HASTEN is successfully used by farmers in many different countries around the world with a diverse range of agricultural products including herbicides. In Australia, HASTEN was commercialized in 1996 and is now recognised as a leading adjuvant by farmers, distributors and lifescience companies. After extensive testing many lifescience companies, including BASF, BAYER, DOW, DUPONT, SUMITOMO and SYNGENTA have endorsed and recommend the use of HASTEN on some of their herbicide labels. A list covering the use of these herbicides in Australia is provided as Table 1.

Suggestions for Use

HASTEN may be used in place of non-ionic surfactants or crop oil concentrates when permitted by herbicide labels.

Typically, HASTEN is added to the spray tank at a concentration of 0.5-1.0% when spray volumes are between 50-100 Litres per hectare. In situations where the agricultural practice is to use a higher volume than 100 Litres per hectare, HASTEN is typically used at 0.5-1.0 Litres per hectare.

The Company

Victorian Chemical Company is committed to providing quality products and professional and friendly service, that our customers can confidently rely on to add value to their businesses. In order to achieve this goal we will continue to develop, our understanding of our customer's requirements, the operations of our company and our technical expertise.

General Information

The information contained in this bulletin is of a general nature. Further information is available regarding HASTEN'S use with Insecticides, Fungicides and Defoliants. Please visit our web site at www.vicchem.com to access Label and MSDS information.

General Specifications

Appearance	Bright Clear Liquid
Specific Gravity (20°C)	0.9 g/ml
Colour	10 Gardner Max

TRIAL 4
Fallow Weed Control - Qld Australia 2002/3
HASTEN can be used successfully in GLYPHOSATE mixes especially where the mixing partner is usually recommended for use with HASTEN. The following examples come from larger studies undertaken by Conservation Farmers Inc. and published in *The 2nd Fallow Weed Management Guide*.

☐ GLYPHOSATE CT 1.5L + ALLY* 5g + HASTEN 1%
  92% Control of volunteer Mungbeans, Turnip weed and Pigweed

☐ GLYPHOSATE CT 1.5L + LONTREL* 100ml + HASTEN 1%
  86.3% Control of volunteer Mungbeans, Turnip weed and Pigweed

☐ GLYPHOSATE CT 1.2L + PLEDGE* 100ml + HASTEN 0.5%
  99% Control of Cowvine and 92.5% control of Polymeria

TABLE 1

Product	Company	Rate HASTEN per 100L Spray Volume	Product	Company	Rate HASTEN per 100L Spray Volume
Select*	Sumitomo	1.0L	Raptor* WG	BASF	0.5L
Topik*	Syngenta	0.5L	Logran* B Power	Syngenta	0.5L
Spinnaker*	BASF	0.5L	Monza*	Sumitomo	1.0L
Correct*	Bayer	0.5L	Targa* Bolt	Du Pont	1.0L
OnDuty*	BASF	0.5L	Aramo*	BASF	1.0L
Shogun*	Syngenta	0.5L	Decision*	Bayer	1.0L
Hussar*	Bayer	1.0L	Hammer*	Crop Care	0.5 - 1.0L
Midas*	BASF	0.5L	Clearso*	BASF	0.5L
Lightning*	BASF	1.0L	Atlantis*	Bayer	1.0L
Gesaprim*	Syngenta	0.5 - 1.0L	Tordon* DSH	Dow	0.5L
Blazer*	BASF	1.0L	Intervix*	BASF	1.0L
Flame* 240g/l	BASF	1.0L			

Always strictly follow label instructions before use
*Third Party Trademark

Victorian Chemical Company Pty. Limited
83 Maffra Street, Coolaroo, Victoria 3048, Australia
Telephone: (03) 9301 7000   Facsimile: (03) 9309 7966
Website: www.vicchem.com   Email: products@vicchem.com

VICTORIAN CHEMICALS
The Australian Solution

HASTEN Product Data Bulletin, back page

This was followed in 1999, with the patent that became the product called Hot-Up. It is used with a glyphosate herbicide that is sold under such brands as Round-Up and Zero." Both Hot-Up, with its solid profitability margin and good sales, and Hasten, with its continuing burgeoning sales, gave the company fiscal breathing space and time to consolidate. In the months of June over four years, company sales hit previously unimaginable monthly levels, over the million-dollar mark. The next milestone of sales over $2 million in a month was achieved in 2003.

The last three other patent successes were Outright, in 1999; Gala, in 2000; and Buffit, in 2002.

Advertise or Go Under

It is recognized that to succeed in academia, one has to write and publish those scientific papers: "Publish or perish."[8] In industry, it is not much different. Development is looking to patents wherever possible, to be followed by good marketing. Within the Australian milieu, we have worked both with the farmer and the higher echelons of the multinational companies who market the actives. Our advertising goes into the various Australian rural publications.[9]

Peer-group acceptance within the chemical and agricultural worlds was promoted at conferences at which scientific papers were presented. Our main advertising and promotion were done through the International Society on Adjuvants for Agrochemicals (ISAA), which arranges symposiums every three years. Vicchem has attended since the 1995 Melbourne symposium, and the papers we have presented appear below:

1986 Brandon, Canada
1989 Blacksburg, Virginia
1992 Cambridge, UK

1995 Melbourne, Australia

The Toxicity Response from Insecticides with Ethyl Fatty Ester Based Adjuvants, Bob Killick and Dave Schulteis

1998 Memphis, Tennessee

2001 Amsterdam, The Netherlands

Novel Glyphosate Compositions Containing Built-In Adjuvant Compounds, Robert W. Killick, Peter W. Jones, Andrew R. Killick, John D. Morrison, and Peter R. Wrigley

2004 Cape Town, South Africa

Development of a Hybrid Adjuvant for Glyphosate, Robert W. Killick, Peter W. Jones, Andrew R. Killick, John D. Morrison, and Peter R. Wrigley

Glyphosate in Oil, Robert W. Killick, Peter W. Jones, Andrew R. Killick, John D. Morrison, and Peter R. Wrigley

2007 Columbus, Ohio

2010 Freising, Germany

Adjuvants and Herbicides, Hans de Ruiter (SurfaPlus) and Bob Killick

2013 Iguaça, Brazil

Adjuvants for Foliar Nutrients, Robert W. Killick, Peter W. Jones, Andrew R. Killick, John D. Morrison, and Peter R. Wrigley

Hasten has not just been as "good as gold"; it has been the mother lode and backbone of the company. We would put it as, "*Venimus, vidimus, deus vicit.* (We came, we saw, God conquered.)"

While we started chapter 5 with a quote from the crime novels of Edgar Wallace, it is appropriate to conclude this chapter with a quote from the last paragraph of Dorothy Sayers's crime novel, *Murder Must Advertise*.[10]

Tell England. Tell the World. Eat more Oats. Take Care of your Complexion. No more War. Shine your Shoes with Shino. Ask your Grocer. Love Laxamalt. Prepare to meet thy God. Bung's Beer is Better. Try Dogsbody's Sausages. Whoosh the Dust away. Give them Crunchlets. Snagsbury's Soups are Best for the Troops. Morning Star, *best Paper by Far. Vote for Punkin and Protect your Profits. Stop that Sneeze with Snuffo. Flush your Kidneys with Fizzlets. Flush your Drains with Sanfect. Wear Woolfleece next to the Skin. Popp's Pills Pep you Up. Whiffle your Way to Fortune* ... Advertise, or go under.

But nothing is better than when the product actually works.

10 The Sheepfolds

I am carrying on a great project and cannot go down.[1]

My Father is always at his work to this very day, and I, too, am working.[2]

If it is leadership, let him govern diligently.[3]

Judy well remembers the discussions we had, before we were married, on possible plans for our future, in which I stressed that we both should be prepared to accept God's call to work "full-time" in the local church or in overseas missions. Those were the days when we were taught that the highest calling on one's life was in full-time ministry. I have kept my nose in manufacture and have never had an inkling or a twinge of guilt that I should have been away from industry.

The local church remains a bulwark. Jesus refers to Himself as the Good Shepherd[4] and the door to the sheepfolds.[5] We have belonged to only five sheepfolds during our lives. The first was Manly Baptist, as a child, which provided me with a thorough grounding in the Bible. I feel blessed that from the time I was a child I have known the Scriptures, which are able to give me the wisdom that leads to salvation through faith which is in Jesus Christ.[6]

The family moved to Seaforth in 1953, and not a five-minute walk from home was the Seaforth Baptist Church, meeting at the Masonic hall. When I went to university, Mum said to Dad, "Bob is a good boy enjoying church. Now he is at that dreadful university, *you* should go to church to show him *we* are keen. Dad dutifully came to church. Within a few months, the church built its own premises on Frenchs Forest Road, Seaforth, about a kilometre away from the Masonic hall. Interestingly,

I was not involved in any aspect of this building programme, and I can only just remember the official opening of the new church.

Within a few years, I was the church treasurer. Apart from our times in England, I served on church leadership boards, diaconates, or church councils until I was seventy-five. The other long-term ministry has been the simple greeting of people, with a smile, as they entered the building. This might not appear significant, but I have been told many times of the immense encouragement it provides to those who gather.

Two Churches in the UK

In 1962, when we arrived in New Ferry, Cheshire, England, without a car, it was most feasible to attend the local New Ferry Methodist Church. It was there that we met a sergeant of police, Cyril Harvey, his wife, Hilda, and their twin daughters, Pam and Katie. About a month before we arrived, Cyril had become a Christian and was really pleased he could rejoice with both Judy and me about his conversion.[7] The angels do, so why shouldn't we? Many were not interested that he was hungry for Bible study, and this helped confirm in us the need to set up a weekly Bible study in our home. I remembered that I had been christened a Methodist and so threw my hat into the ring to be a Methodist local preacher. It was a requirement that I had to read the *Forty-Four Sermons* of John Wesley, which had been compiled between 1746 and 1760. These I found to be most challenging. The one which provided the strongest teaching for my later responses to blessings in life was the last sermon, number 44, "The Use of Money." The first basic tenet was "Gain all you can" by honest industry and without doing damage to yourself through, for example, "working in lead mines, not having adequate rest, nor damage others through sale of liquor." The second was "Save all you can" by not wasting your gained money on, for example, a gluttonous and libidinous lifestyle, even frippery. This is certainly a delightful 250-year-old word meaning "showy or unnecessary dress." The third was "Give all you can." After we have provided for our family, and there remains an overplus (sic), then "do good to the family of believers," and if still an overplus (sic), then, "do good unto all people."[8] During the latter part of 1962, I became accredited as a local preacher in the Bebington circuit, which unleashed me into the small churches of the little villages on the Wirral Peninsula. I seem to remember that my sermons would be mostly extracted from one of Wesley's sermons. My last four sermons were preached in 1964, at Higher Bebington, on April 19; at Neston, on May 10; at Little Neston, on May 17; and, finally, at Trinity-New Ferry, on May 24. We were then on our way back to Australia.

On return to Sydney, we settled back into the work of the kingdom at the Seaforth Baptist Church, which had been our earlier spiritual home.

On our return to the UK in 1969, our rented accommodation was 8 Quernmore Close, Bromley, Kent, and we joined the Bromley Baptist Church, Kent, whose pastor was the Rev. Godfrey Robinson. He, with Stephen Winward, had written several Christian books, including *The Christian's Conduct* and *The Art of Living*. By both Australian and English standards, Bromley, with its 450 members, was considered a large church. It did provide us with the taste of all that larger congregations could do in the work of God's kingdom, and prepared us to play a larger role in the Syndal Baptist Church when we moved to Melbourne.

Syndal Baptist Church, Melbourne

We arrived in Melbourne on Friday, May 21, 1971, and stayed at the Brighton Savoy Motel. That Sunday, we went to Brighton Baptist; the following two Sundays, to the Collins Street Baptist Church in the city. Once we knew we were going to be living in Mount Waverley, we began casting around for a church. We rang the Baptist Union and were informed that we were roughly halfway between the Chadstone Church, with 30 members, to the west, and Syndal, with 150 members, to the east. There was no super-spiritual decision-making process. In the UK, we had learnt what larger membership churches can do, so Syndal was the easy choice. On the immediate Sunday following the house settlement on Friday, June 11, we joined with the fellowship of the Syndal Church. Ever since, whenever we are in Melbourne, we have always attended the services there. There was one exception, which occurred when number-two son, Peter, was courting Alison Kelly, whose father was a pastor at the Altona Meadows Church. Four times, as the courting got serious, we joined for worship at Altona Meadows and stayed for lunch.

Seven weeks later, at the church business meeting of August 4 1971, we were accepted into membership, by transfer from the Bromley Baptist Church, Kent. This was certainly speedy. Judy and I were now in our early forties, experienced in church work, and ready to give our all to the work at Syndal.

We have always had a penchant for open-house hospitality, and had our first gathering for young marrieds in August 1971. In November, we were in the swing, with a combined Christian education and diaconate dinner at home, and the preparation of World Mission of Reconciliation through Jesus Christ. We had our first Melbourne Cup Day church picnic at Jells Beach, Mornington. It was a strong sunny day, and the children's skin turned bright pink from sunburn. Judy applied raw ripe tomato over their bodies, and it did wonders. The children hated the application, and with this threat hanging over them, they never got burnt again. The monthly homemakers meeting began in February 1972, with the Rev. Neville Horn as the speaker.

We had arrived at Syndal in the last few months of the ministry of the Rev. Ern Andrews. On his departure, the church did not have an immediate person in view, so, following the union's advice, Rev. Geoff Blackburn joined us as our interim pastor. Geoff was editor of Baptist Publications, and he was expected to preach on Sunday and provide basic visitation. By the end of nine months into his ministry, there was still no pastor available for calling, and the church was asked to redouble its prayer efforts. I expressed strongly to Don Rodd, then church secretary, that in my mind, the need for more prayer was not really necessary, as we had the answer before our eyes in Geoff Blackburn. This was a left-field possibility, as Geoff had relinquished his pastoral ministry when his first wife was dying, and Jessie, his second wife, had never been a lady of the manse. For her, it would be the greater challenge. They were not young, and the question of how their ministry would be for the young people was answered by indicating it would provide the grandparental image. Dr Blackburn was inducted at a 3:00 p.m. service on Sunday, December 3, 1972. They did indeed both rise to the challenge and set our Syndal church on to the way to great accomplishments. In retrospect, I believe Jessie enjoyed her role the most.

Diaconate Days

In the meantime, and thirteen months into our membership, I was appointed to the church's governing body, the diaconate, at the annual church meeting on Wednesday, September 20, 1972. At the same meeting, Judy was appointed a deaconess. This was very speedy. Since then, I have sat for forty years like a limpet on the governing team, originally called the diaconate and which later became the church council. There were a few forced breaks to comply with church rules which prohibited a continual stay on the team.

We were blessed that by the start of 1973, our little nuclear family had transferred readily into Melbourne and was well established in the house that was going to become home for the next forty-six years and still counting. We were fully ensconced within the fellowship of the believers in the Syndal Baptist Church. Judy and I were in leadership positions and other ministries, and we were ready to put our heart and soul into the work.

At this point, I was a member of the diaconate, among a group of mature believers. In those days, the government of the church ran through a committee system, with a deacon taking the lead of each committee. I was given the role of Chairman of the Christian Education Committee, with the indomitable Dorothy Fry as the committee's secretary. Dorothy was a principal of primary schools and also ran several not-for-profit organizations. She was thus an invaluable mentor on ways to negotiate a positive way through a committee system. In later years, during some meetings, I would joke that they shouldn't complain with what they had in me, as I had been trained under their direction by "Dear Dorothy."

Diaconate meetings and work outside the meetings seemed to become ever busier, and, as deacons were not coping, male pastoral elders were introduced on October 20, 1976, to undertake the visitation workload. The deaconesses' ministry continued unabated.

Gospel Theatre

Looking back, we can see there were periods in the church's life which are easily delineated. "There is a time for everything and a season for every activity under heaven."[9] One such period occurred over the ten years from 1976 to 1986, which became the Glory Years of Music. Outside that period, the church has had concerts and musical nights, but these were ad hoc and had none of the concentration that occurred during the ten years of that period.

Although it may have been perceived as a negative, the fact was that we were an average bunch, even a real motley crew: each had differing skills and knowledge, and this allowed us to keep the various genres going. We had no prima donnas. The Gospel Theatre was spawned in the mid-1970s, when the Sunday school presented the internal play, set back during the period 755–710 B.C., within the *Hosea* musical which was set in modern times. This was part of a series of ten musicals from the pens of two Salvation Army Officers, John Gowans, librettist and John Larsson, composer. Two decades later, from 1999 to 2002, Gowans was appointed the sixteenth General of the Salvation Army, followed by Larsson as the seventeenth, from 2002 to 2006.

The aim of the presentations was an encouragement for adults and young people to present a full musical as a means of witness and outreach. The major block to present *Hosea* was that there was no tenor! So, when about twenty people met with Chas and Mia Green in November 1975, there was a swing of opinion to move to *Jesus Folk*. This musical was a series of vignettes dealing with seven ordinary people. They would tell of their problems to the Jesus Folk, who pointed them to what Jesus did in the Gospels for a connected series of Bible characters.

My role as a speak-song was that of the Man of the World—The Dodo:

> I'm as dead as the dodo, darling, I don't feel a thing anymore
> Deep down inside, I must have died, I'm cold to the very core
> I'm as cold as the concrete, darling, I'm as dull as a piece of wood
> It's years and years since I've shed tears, and I only wish I could.

The script then had the Jesus Folk Leader demanding to see the Book. From this, the Bible, they agreed the Dodo had to meet Lazarus, who had been dead but who Jesus had brought back to Life. The classic songs were "I Am the Resurrection and the Life,"[10] sung by the ladies' chorus, and the full-cast show-stopper "He Came to Give Us Life in All Its Fullness."[11] There was often discussion as to how much was good acting versus natural casting. Judy played the role of the Jesus Folk Leader, so we were always sure that we worked from natural casting. Andrew was immersed in the chorus of the Jesus Folk.

Opening nights have a tendency to jangle nerves, and there were some very apprehensive cast members and helpers who did not ask their friends in case it was all going to be too embarrassing. Yet Friday, August 6, 1976, was a resounding success and is neon marked in the annals of our church's history. All the friends were invited for Saturday night, with the performance receiving high approbation. There it could have ended, but for Robert and Pauline Arnold. Robert was enmeshed in the Baptist Union's Fellowship in Regional Evangelism (FIRE) enterprise and had a vision for building up country churches. He felt we should take the show on the road. I am not certain of his motivation, but he felt we should start at Broken Hill in NSW. He was ready to hire a plane, but one coach and several cars were found to be adequate. The *Jesus Folk* performances lasted more than three years.

The time of the Gospel Theatre was invaluable for our nuclear family, with the children growing to and through their early teens. With weekly practices and the performances, it was a period during which we learnt to play together, pray together, cry together, and laugh together within our extended family. It was a time when our children appreciated their uncles, aunties, brothers, and sisters in the faith. We were truly our own little Jesus Folk community. There were always experiences on the road. It was the practice to be billeted at the towns from which it was not convenient to return to Melbourne after the performance. On those occasions, we also took part in the local church services, where we preached or gave our testimonies. Kyabram was such a case, and we were allocated to the house of one of the town's solicitors. As a special for dinner, we each had a roast duck which he had shot in the morning and from which we had to spit out the lead shot when we were chewing the bird. I have never bothered with wild duck since.

There follows a really great list of mainly country towns where *Jesus Folk* was performed. During 1977, there was Broken Hill, March 12 and 13; Kyabram, March 26; Werribee, April 2; Police Academy, Glen Waverley, April 29; Dandenong, April 30; Murtoa, May 28; Chelsea Heights, June 4; Ringwood East Baptist, June 18; Geelong–Grovedale, September 17; Kilvington School, September 24; Syndal, October 7 and 8; Syndal, 3 p.m. November 28. In 1978, there was Warrnambool, February 25; Emerald, April 8; Bendigo, April 29; Glen Waverley,

June 24; Moe, October 28. The last year on the road was 1979, with performances at Boronia, February 24; Bairnsdale, April 7; Hopetoun-Rainbow, June 16 and 17. For the last hurrah, there was a special presentation in October 1982, at Dr Blackburn's induction as President of the Baptist Union of Victoria, with some selections from *Jesus Folk*.

A Tenor for Hosea

In the meantime, in early 1977, Ian Charlesworth, a tenor, had come to the fellowship, and, looking ahead, the Gospel Theatre could sense the possibility of performing *Hosea*. The storyline followed a local church where tensions were rife between the older members of the congregation and the youth, whose main gripe was summarized in the song lyrics arguing the complaint "they had to conform to belong?!" For the record, I played Geoff, one of the establishment heavies who continued to live in the past. The Youth Leader's marriage was not going well, and, ultimately, his wife left. Before this occurred in the musical, the warring factions had presented a mini-musical on the life of the prophet Hosea and his wayward wife, set back in the eighth century B.C.

This prophet had been ordered by God to marry a prostitute, Gomer, who abandoned him.[12] God, through Hosea, reminds the people that they are His people, and Gomer's abandonment is how they have treated Him! The people ridicule Hosea, but in song he challenges them:

> For His love remains the same, He knows you by your
> name,
> God plans for you in love, for He still cares!

Hosea buys his wife back at the slave auction,[13] but rejection by the people still continues. He again challenges them:

> If human hearts are often tender, and human minds
> can pity know,
> If human love is touched with splendour, and human
> hands compassion show
> Then how much more shall God our Father, in love
> forgive, in love forgive.

God brings them to repentance, and all respond with the show-stopping affirmation:

> With a God like this we'll face the future, for a God
> like this will set men free,
> And from this day on, we'll be His people, and from
> this day on, our God He'll be!

In God's grace, the leader and his wife are reunited, and the performance finishes with a reprise of "With a God Like This."

In our minds, we well remember four standout events on the road:

- The first was the mouse plague when we were at Rainbow/Hopetoun in western Victoria. Most of the troupe accepted the ground moving beneath their feet, but when one of the senior youth cast members held up a dead mouse by its tail in the middle of a scene, there was some consternation which came out in muffled screams. From our length of time on the road, we had enough professionalism to regroup, and the show went on.

- The second was the performance of the musical in Canberra. There was an extended stage, but no curtains. The long stage was split into three areas, using pot plants. One area was dedicated to inside the church, the second to the family home, the third to the street outside. The cast had to enter and depart through the backdrop. At the conclusion of each performance, a challenge was given for anyone who wished to make a deeper commitment to the Lord to make contact with us. That night, the response was the largest we ever experienced.

- Problems come in many forms. A peculiar one was at the Melbourne suburb of Williamstown, when our radio microphones began picking up the radio links of the passing taxis. The cast was called to prayer, and the taxi-radio link was broken.

- After some six years of playing the Gospel Theatre, the boys playing the roles of the children, and performing their show-stopping song "We Nearly Forgot to Say Thank You," found that their voices were moving to those of adults. This led to a churn of those playing these roles. Our Peter made his stage debut in front of several hundred people for a few of the performances. He is the child on the left-hand side of the photo, below.

Hosea, with Peter

The *Hosea* performances started at Syndal, on October 26 and 27, 1979. During 1980, the places visited were Syndal/Burwood Heights, February 29 and March 1; Monbulk, March 8; Rainbow/Hopetoun, April 26 and 27; Broken Hill, June 14 and 15; Syndal concert, August 2; Kyabram, September 20; Murtoa, October 11. During 1981, the presentations continued at Canberra-National Baptist Family Convention, January 16; Williamstown, March 28; Kyneton, May 3; Berwick, May 30; Dandenong, June 6; Bairnsdale, July 25; Syndal, August 9. Finally, in 1982, the last three performances were Warragul, March 13; Geelong, March 27; Yarram, April 9.

The Coming of the Holy Spirit

By 1983, age was starting to play havoc in the ranks of the cast. Daughter Jenni, for example, had already been three years in Adelaide on air traffic control training. Among the remaining original cast, there was still a desire to produce *Spirit!* Based on the book of Acts, this was a continuation of *Jesus Folk*. This sequel, *Spirit!*, deals with the coming of the Holy Spirit and the electrifying results of His presence in the early church, with the release of joy, power, and love among the disciples. It goes on to tell of the opposition which the early Christians faced; and yet, there was the bold proclamation "We must obey God rather than man."[14] For the record, I played Gamaliel,[15] who, against a hostile Sanhedrin which was demanding the disciples' death, warned them, "Be careful what you do, as God may be actually on their side."

The breakdown of prejudice is contained in the stories of the conversions of Cornelius[16] and the Ethiopian official.[17] There is the emergence of Stephen,[18] a man "full of faith and of the Holy Spirit." This leader in the church sets the scene for the first Christian martyrdom. From this event, Saul's hatred moves him to become a persecutor of the Christians. On the road to Damascus, there is his miraculous conversion, thence the Spirit taking control of his life and his going forth as an apostle. The final song, based on the letters to the churches in the book of Revelation,[19] thrusts home the point of the musical:

> What does the Spirit say to the Churches? What does
> the Spirit say to you?
> If you have ears, then hear from the Spirit, Do what the
> Spirit tells you to!

In 1983 the first performance of *Spirit!* was a selection from it sung at the Baptist Annual Assembly Missionary Rally on September 29; and the total musical was at Syndal, October 14 and 15. There were no presentations in 1984, and in the last year of the Gospel Theatre, there were performances at Geelong, March16; Castlemaine/Midlands Baptist Association, March 23; and Chadstone, March 30.

Age had taken its toll, and we had run out of puff, but over the ten years, we have said before could say again, "*Venimus, vidimus, Deus vicit.* (We came, we saw, God conquered)."

Ian and Chris Charlesworth felt it would be encouraging for the youth of *Jesus Folk*, who were now in their late teens to early twenties, to have a go at their own musicals. *Celebrate Life* was performed in 1984, and *Come Together*, in 1985. Our Jenni participated in the first.

Singing Christmas Tree

Lynda Gail Cleveland came to Syndal in 1978, from First Dallas Baptist Church, Texas, to work with a church member's direct marketing company. She waxed enthusiastically about the *Singing Christmas Tree*, which was a regular feature of the ministry of First Dallas Baptist, Texas. The summary description on the album cover states, "The music of Christmas goes forth from a choir of up to one hundred people in the tree accompanied by spectacular lighting effects and the performances are enjoyed by thousands each year."

Singing Christmas tree

The tree was a series of semicircular rising platforms which, at the base, was seven and a half metres across. This held twenty-two people, thence decreasing in size to hold eighteen, fourteen, thirteen, eleven, six, and, finally, three young sopranos at the top. This last platform was six and a half metres up from floor level. It was built around scaffolding and, when fully populated, weighed seven and a half tonnes. The scaffolding was covered by seventy square metres of chicken wire and fifteen hundred pine branches, watered nightly, stripped, and redressed after six performances. We only had the time of the overture to negotiate our way in the dark, through the scaffolding, and into our places. The American attention to detail was much appreciated when, at our allocated places, there was a stand built to our height so that all the tops of our heads were at the same level. Similarly, this one-height meant that the gold leis around our necks gave one continuous flow. For those who like statistics, the tree included thousands of light bulbs, around

700 metres of festoon lighting, 250 metres of light cable, and 70,000 watts of general lighting. There were 40 microphone audio channels and 2,600 metres of audio cable.

The music was a mixture of new and old, including "I Call Him Lord," "Away in a Manger," "Shine the Light of Jesus," "Silent Night," "God's Choir," "Go Tell It on the Mountain," and "O Holy Night."

It had taken more than a year of negotiation to obtain regulatory clearance for building, electrical, and fire safety. There were four months of intensive practice, as the words and music had to be known by heart—there were to be no cheat sheets in the Tree. By December 1982 we were as ready to go as we would ever be. For the few weeks leading up to the opening, standard practices were held on November 22, 24, and 25. The first full dress rehearsal was held on November 27. On November 28, a TV crew was present, recording the performance, and this certainly helped the concentration! The last full dress rehearsal, on November 29, was performed in front of invited guests. The tree was finally unleashed on the public on December 1.

A Bass Once in My Life

I only participated as a singer in the first two years of the Christmas Tree. Not being noted for my ability in this area, it was only achieved by being strategically located between two strong bass voices. In the photo, above, I can be located in the centre of the third row of the singers, wearing dark-rimmed glasses. Judy sang in all five seasons. My overriding highlight was being in a massed choir singing the "Hallelujah Chorus." It was an emotional experience of joy. The last three years, I was happy to be an usher. The performances were December 1 to 5, 1982; November 23 to December 4, 1983; November 21 to December 1, 1984; November 27 to December 7, 1985; December 2 to 13, 1986.

Family Night at the Theatre, described as a "musical extravaganza," was a mid-year activity to keep the Singing Christmas Tree group together. The Christian challenge at the end of the night was presented as a drama. The first season had the crucifixion of the Lord, with our son Peter in the role of one of the thieves on a cross. At the earlier part of the night, there were segments from the *Wizard of Oz*, with Judy playing the Scarecrow. The performances were August 3 to 6, 1983, and July 25 to 28, 1984.

For an old showman, they were a great ten years. However, the Glory Years of Music did come to an end, around 1986. That is not to say our church has not had concerts and musical events in the years that followed. There just haven't been major productions that run for three or more nights. As the song of the early 1960s, credited to Gene Raskin from the original Russian, says so well:

> Those were the days my friends, we thought they'd never end
> We'd sing and dance forever and a day, for we were young and sure to have our way.[20]

In the late 1990s, Judy and I began a hymn-singing group in our home, following the evening service on the first Sunday of each month. It soon established itself as a must-attend for a group of the congregation.

Church Secretary

Jumping back chronologically to the annual meeting on September 29, 1979, I was appointed church secretary after seven years on the diaconate. At the same meeting, our Jenni was appointed youth committee secretary. In the church government at that time, the church secretary was the lay leader of the church, whose main role was to interface with the senior pastor on behalf of the fellowship. Dr Geoff Blackburn, the first pastor I worked with in this role, was twenty-three years older than I and provided great mentoring. When he retired in April 1986, I provided leadership which led to the appointment of Bill Brown, our then youth pastor, as our senior pastor. The Brown family had joined the fellowship in 1971, the same year that we joined, and we have worked together for the last forty-six years. Bill, after graduating with a bachelor of science in education from Monash University, started teaching at Westall High School and became youth pastor at the church in a voluntary capacity. In February 1977, he was inducted as full-time assistant pastor, with two days a week to undertake his bachelor of divinity at Whitley College being ultimately ordained in October 1981. As the old joke asks, "What is the most difficult instrument to play in an orchestra?" Simple answer: "Second fiddle!" This provided a great continuing learning balance over many years between being "first fiddle" at Victorian Chemicals and "second fiddle" at the church, answerable to Bill.

Each secretary has brought into the ministry his own God-given skill set. The Bible expects leadership to be undertaken with "diligence"; that is, with "constant and earnest effort."[21] This is one of my strengths. It is reinforced in my parallel life as a businessman, where the Bible highlights, "be not slothful in business."[22] I have been fortunate to have known the Scriptures since I was a child, which made me wise to salvation, but I have been blessed to have been granted further wisdom to apply this Bible knowledge into the day-by-day vagaries of life. There are many books for extra reading, but two 300-page books which are of value are *How Should We Then Live?*[23] by Francis Schaeffer, and *How Now Shall We Then Live?*[24] by Charles Colson and Nancy Pearcey.

I believe I brought two important traits into the secretaryship, both of which I also had in the secular world: the ability to understand how money moves, and a penchant for acquiring surrounding property, with the freedom this provides both businesses and church ministries. The church has undertaken four major building projects since its commencement in the Williams home in 1954. The purchase of lot number 46 in 1954, and lot numbers 47 and 48 in 1955, allowed the building of the multi-purpose original church hall in 1957, which is now used as the Karinya[25] Counselling Centre. Lot number 45 became available and was bought in 1963. Finally, before we arrived, the sanctuary and the education block were built in 1968, on lot number 45, and they act now as the East Auditorium, the Resource Centre, and the Clack Room. The last room was so named to remember Bill Clack, our first pastor, who ministered part-time.

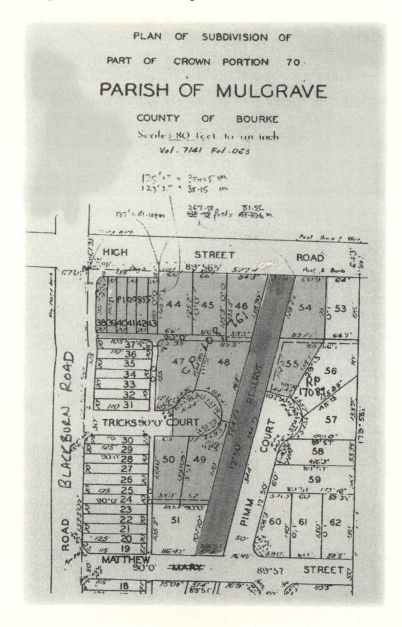

Church land area

When our family arrived in 1971, the church had a solid land grouping of lot numbers 45, 46, 47, and 48, with access from High Street Road and Tricks Court. Under the leadership of Dr Blackburn, membership had been burgeoning during the 1970s, and late in the decade, the processes were set in place for the extension of the sanctuary, to the west. A special meeting was held on March 26, 1980, with some uncertainty on account of even the lowest tender being 25 per cent above the earlier estimates. However, when one of the respected members of the diaconate unexpectedly spoke against the proposal, there was going to be no extension. The diaconate reconsidered the project, and several months later had a revamped plan that eliminated the proposed gallery, changed the open central courtyard to become a western cry room for young children, and streamlined other features. This superior overall concept was passed on November 26, 1980, with gratitude. Lot number 45 was cleared, with the sale of the church house, and the new owners had it relocated up in the country. These western extensions were opened for God's glory on June 6, 1982.

Neighbouring Properties Are Important

In the meantime, as part of the church's master plan to buy neighbouring property, we were able to purchase 1 Pimm Court (lot number 55) for $36,000.00, on September 5, 1979. This is now our church Food Bank. After two years of negotiation and a visit to the Administrative Appeals Tribunal, the church was granted a lease for the easement, called Reserve in the Plan, for a peppercorn yearly rent of $200.00. This was followed by 4 Tricks Court (lot number 50) for $69,000.00, on April 18, 1984, and was used for several ministries before being demolished in 2008 as part of our major car park. In 1988, we bought 3 Tricks Court for $175,000.00. The completion of the master plan was achieved in January 2008, with the purchase of 592 High Street Road (lot number 54) for $575,000.00.

There have been various plans on property, and it is interesting that in the late 1970s, there was our first mention of the Mobil site in the committee minutes: "The corner Mobil site at 200 Blackburn Road was briefly considered but not included as it was considered too expensive. It was also felt that church development was more likely to be southerly parallel to the Easement rather than westerly." There was a flurry in 1988, when Mobil indicated it was considering selling. There was a lot of discussion, but within a few months, Mobil decided to pull the site off the market and turn the petrol station into a repair and lube shop. If it worked out to be profitable, Mobil was planning to spread similar projects throughout the city. It was not a success.

After ten years, it was constitutionally required that I retire. Graham Brattle became secretary at the annual meeting of 1989, serving for two years. After a few months, he found it an unexpected challenge, commenting, "Bob, you have made it all look so easy, but it's not." The big difference was that I had years of experience behind me. I returned as church secretary at the 1991 meeting, and retired constitutionally again, six years later, at the 1997 annual meeting.

Life Centre Building Programme

By 1995, the church was splitting at the seams, and there were continuing property development meetings seeking ideas about how that might be overcome. Attendances at 10:00 a.m. and 7:00 p.m. were to capacity, Christian education could not expand, and off-street parking was inadequate.

On October 1, 1996, Mobil advertised twenty-one of their petrol station sites around Victoria for sale, which included the 1,884-square-metre property (lot numbers 38, 39, 40, 41, 42, 43, and 44) adjacent to our church. Mobil's experimental lube trial had not reached expectations. It takes time for a church to make a snap financial decision, so I took the initiative of putting a $400.00 deposit to the real estate agent on behalf of the church, using my personal cheque. The diaconate soon caught up, and the deposit was raised to $2,000.00. We kept discussing and negotiating. We talked with Mobil directly and flew a kite of $400,000.00. Mobil indicated that this was a little on the low side, and so, on Monday, November 18, 1996, we formally offered $440,000.00. Mobil replied on Wednesday, accepting our offer. I remember Friday night, November 22, vividly. I phoned around a group of our church people who I felt might be able to provide financial assistance. Judy and her friend Betty Simonsen were having a cup of tea after dinner, and I would come back in suppressed excitement to report another person had guaranteed a lump sum. I was emotional. It went on and on, with differing amounts, but all of significance. Halfway through, I began chuckling with each following phone call, with every person responding positively. I have never had another time like that night when it was all go! The Spirit of God was so obviously at work. Just under $200,000.00 was promised within ten phone calls. It also meant that we could go confidently to the church meeting, prepared to answer the guaranteed question, "Where is the money going to come from?" The church meeting on November 26 gave its blessing to proceed.

September 2001 could be described as the start of the Life Centre Building Programme, with contact made with six architects, and thence Atelier Wagner Architects appointed in April 2002. Six years of work finally saw the Life Centre's first worship service at 9:30 a.m., on Sunday, August 10, 2008. The Lord particularly blessed us for the previous ten years. The church had been fortunate to obtain tax-deductible giving status, and we were able to link this in with the Sonshine Foundation, which is described more fully in chapter 11. The foundation was able to carry a heavy load in repaying the costs of the Life Centre.

It is true that our Lord is ever at work and we also have been able to be at work with Him. The following quote was much used during our teenage years, in what we saw as summarizing much of Jesus's teaching:

"Be involved in God's work and He will look after yours."[26]

11 To a Land Flowing with Milk and Honey

Parting is such sweet sorrow[1]

...to a land flowing with milk and honey[2]

The Bible records the events around 1445 B.C., which became the Israelites' Exodus from Egypt to the Promised Land. Because of disobedience, a journey which could have taken a few days took forty years, to reach the land flowing with milk and honey. Fortunately, we were able to reach our land of blessedness in less than forty months. The first part of the journey is recorded in the last pages of chapter 1. In summary, the new millennium had begun with Victorian Chemicals in the doldrums. The Richmond plant was by then seventy years old, and we were fighting to stop its degradation into a pile of junk. Our locale was metamorphosing from industry to residential, and to cap it off, we had a shopping mall as our neighbour. For me, there was a hard-to-understand aversion to suggestions that we might move to a more amenable location. It was best summed up in my normal response that "it would be over my dead body." (Much of what is described in this chapter appears also in earlier chapters.)

Coolaroo Purchase

However, in 2002, the Lord gained our full attention, with three signs that solidified our thinking that we were going to have to leave our Richmond factory home of twenty years. The collapsing pallet and the changing milieu of Richmond were not game changers—but the work accident was. The backwash of the accident was the partial closure of the Richmond factory under the governmental WorkSafe Authority. In retrospect, this turned into a blessing, since, to supplement our limited production, third-party sourcing had to be undertaken. One of the third parties was Cognis, which became a supplier of ethyl oleate from its Coolaroo factory, from September 4, 2002. We soon learnt that the Coolaroo plant would be mothballed by Christmas. If—and *if* was a big word—we could acquire the factory, it would be the Golden Ball of Opportunity. We were soon reminded that the bigger the prize, the more snares, nets, gins, traps, and pitfalls there are to reach that prize. The main underlying problem lay in Australia's Cognis board's disinterest in selling to any competitor. In November, I short-circuited the Australian intransigence and went to the Cognis leadership in Germany. While I thought we were on a roll, Cognis Australia was still playing negative hardball. Persistence had got us a meeting with Helmut Heymann, one of the triumvirate who ran Cognis, and who, on April 1, 2003, confirmed that Germany would be pleased to sell to us. For those who like coincidences in life, this was twenty-one years to the day that the previous owners of Vicchem had put it up for sale. However, the negotiations would still have to be through the Australian management, and they had three months to put their act together.

We woke on August 1, 2003, with subdued excitement as we awaited the meeting with Tony Popper, the Australian CEO of Cognis, to hear his presentation for the sale of Coolaroo. However, there was no sale, but a lease proposal, which was certainly a disappointment. The earliest I could get together our think tank, more specifically known as the Breakfast Club, was three days later. There was agreement that the lease proposal would never work, since one can't have major plant sitting on land that one doesn't own. I visited Tony on August 6, to inform him that the lease proposal was not an acceptable way forward.

The rest of August and September were quiet, with both Vicchem and Cognis at an impasse. Head Office Cognis in Europe had agreed to the sale, while Tony was trying to finesse to a lease deal. We, on the other hand, by no stretch of the imagination wanted to be involved in a lease arrangement. We simply wanted a clean sale, as did Europe. This resulted in a series of internal meetings and the odd discussions with Tony. As chapter 12 relates the story, at 5:00 p.m., on Thursday, September 25, on the other side of the city, confirmation had been received from Henkel that they would sell us their 4.5-hectare chemical industrial site at Dandenong. The relationship between Henkel and Cognis was a close one. In August 1999, Henkel had set up the operationally independent unit known as Cognis, with manufacture at Coolaroo, whilst retaining all the existing staff. In November 2001, it was sold, with the once-Henkel staff to private equity funds, also known as venture capital. These venture capitalists were hungry for the release of money from their acquired assets, such as Coolaroo, and indeed they were selling similar sites in South Africa, Europe, and the United States during the same period.

One can argue that coincidences happen in life; or, as Christians, we can say that God guides in hidden ways. What did happen was that late morning on Friday, September 26, the nexus was broken! Tony rang to say he was willing to consider selling the manufacturing half of the property to us. It has always been my conviction that, within the camaraderie of the Henkel-Cognis ranks, the message of our Dandenong purchase had directly winged its way back to Tony. There is the old adage "A bird in the hand is worth two in the bush," and I could see Tony musing that, now Bob was purchasing the Dandenong chemical industrial site, he might well lose Bob, the only bird he had, and there was no one else waiting in the bush. How would he be able to tell Helmut, who had agreed to the sale, that the sale had fallen through on account of tardiness and a lack of desire to sell the land?

That Friday night, Judy and I were amazed over the turn of circumstances. As Judy so succinctly put it, "We were praying and working that we might have a replacement factory for Richmond, and the Lord has given us two!"

A month later, at 8:30 a.m., on October 21, I presented to Tony and his fellow director, Ian Pattison, our proposal to purchase the manufacturing half of the site. Late in the afternoon, Cognis rang to accept the offer. On November 23, they provided a signed agreement of intention to sell lot 2 of a subdivision of 83 Maffra Street, Coolaroo. The maxim we had worked to was "Always be prepared to take half of what you really want ... then work on the half you missed."

To cap off a semi-successful year with half the plant tied up, we got away from it all. It started with a week on the Gold Coast at Coolangatta, Queensland, then four days back in Sydney, which included the wedding of Judy's niece, Kerri. We then left on December 15, for a round-the-world business trip, including Christmas with our daughter, Jenni, and her family, in Montgomery, Alabama. The holiday break was capped off with a New Year's week cruise on the *Carnival Conquest*, out of New Orleans and around the Caribbean.

Mid-January 2004, we returned refreshed for the year ahead. The Bible recounts the story of Naomi, who, because of drought, went to live among the Moabites. There she became a widow and was bereft of her two sons who also died there. She was bitter when she returned to her homeland, Israel, but her faithful daughter-in-law, Ruth, was with her. They arrived in Bethlehem "as the barley harvest was beginning."[3] This expression indicates a coming time of hope and blessing, and we use it within our family to today. We say we are returning at the time of the barley harvest! It is one thing to have the harvest promised, but the reaping still has to be undertaken—the Breakfast Club was working overtime. As mentioned before, the Breakfast Club was a group of good thinkers, including our bank and key senior managers, with Ian McCubbin providing the legalese.

On the Tuesday after Easter, April 13, the half-site contract was signed at the offices of Cognis's solicitors, Allens Arthur Robinson. The contract included a nominal $1.00 year's lease for the office building which was on our half of the division. In retrospect, I now wonder where we were ever supposed to have our own management offices. On the day the contract was signed, Peter Wrigley and John Morrison led a team into the factory to undertake a risk study. Cognis had left minimal documentation, and we were literally starting from the bottom up—but we were in the factory!

Within a few weeks, with the ink on the contract hardly starting to dry, matters had begun to unravel for Cognis, with the potential of two high-cost impositions if they proceeded. They firstly had received information from the planning authorities that they would be demanding a firewall be built along the subdivision line between the co-joined warehouses. The estimated cost was over $500,000.00. The second was the cost to split the various services: potable water, storm water, waste, electricity, and sewage, which all came onto the site at the south-east corner of the block that Vicchem was to buy. Further hundreds of thousands of dollars were mentioned for the relocation works.

On May 12, with Tony's imminent retirement, Roger Taylor, manager of Cognis's Betatene Division, took over the day-to-day decision making for Australia. On the day I was told of the high costs with which Cognis could be slugged, I reintroduced the possibility of our purchase of the total site. The Bible[4] tells the story of the persistent, importunate widow who continually came to the judge to obtain justice for herself. The judge, who claimed to fear neither God nor man, finally gave her what she wanted before, as he said, she will wear me out![4] I am not a widow, but I am persistent. Cognis asked for a formal offer. It is never easy to pluck an offer figure out of the air. We talked with real estate agents and also obtained a plant valuation by the Dominion Group, which included an estimated new replacement value, the market value for the existing use, and an auction realization. After much discussion, consensus was reached on a seven-digit offer. Twenty years after we had bought that proverbial pile of junk, the price had increased well above tenfold, but we were after a large factory, on a clean site, with German engineering.

The prize

Marginal haggling with a minor increase in the offer price always seems to be part of the grist for the mill in all our negotiations. On July 9, Roger Taylor rang to let us know that Cognis had agreed in principle to sell the whole site to us, which would be ratified at the board meeting in Germany, in July 19.

The purchase of Coolaroo was approved.

At the end of July, Helmut called in for lunch during his last visit to Australia. It was a time of back-slapping and hilarity. He was really pleased for us that the sale had worked out to all that we desired. After weeks of preparation in liaison with our bank, the final "Proposal to Purchase Coolaroo Manufacturing Site," which ran to a hundred pages, was formally presented to the NAB on October 13. This soon received the tick of approval, and the final contract for the total site was signed at a 1:00 p.m. meeting on November 5. The settlement took place at noon on December 29, 2004. This assured Cognis that the governmental bureaucracy would complete the transfer and they would avoid land tax, which is paid on the basis of whoever owns the property on December 31; the payment then covers the whole year.

Following our entry into the site on April 13, the first necessity was to understand the piping to the various vessels throughout the factory. The various pipes carried water, gas, steam, condensate, nitrogen, and vacuum to and from the vessels. The other sets of process lines carried oils (groups 1 and 2), miscellaneous (group 3), and caustic materials (group 4). The final set of pipes carried the finished goods away to storage or to the tanks ready for packing. Two engineering consulting companies helped over the period. By September of that year, the first risk assessment was complete on one vessel, which allowed the manufacture of our Summer Oil by simple blending. This was the breakthrough that lifted the spirits of the company, with all of us feeling we were going to win. The completion of the next risk assessment during November was for a vessel which allowed us to undertake a reaction to make ethyl oleate, the basic material for most of our products. The news was received with "much cheers and heavy spitting!" It meant we were truly starting to kick goals.

We had agreed that Cognis could have time to relocate, and we survived in nooks and crannies throughout the site. Roger Taylor formally handed over the keys of Coolaroo at a celebration at 11:00 a.m., on Friday, March 18, 2005. After the weekend, on Monday, March 21, Coolaroo was officially open for Vicchem business. The most symbolic step was removing the Cognis name from the high point of the main factory building and replacing it with the name of Victorian Chemicals.

Coolaroo "signed" to Vicchem

For me, as the cherry picker came away from the wall to display the company sign at the top of the building, it was the most emotional moment of any event in my business life. The official public opening was a month later, on April 22, and included our service providers, such as the bank and our attorneys, Ian McCubbin from the commercial side and Wayne McMaster from the patents' side. The Cognis administration left the offices pre-Easter, and the technicians finally washed their test tubes for the last time on May 26, so the sun had set on the Cognis Coolaroo occupation! As a passing farewell comment, they philosophized among themselves that "Bob always said that he was paying too much, but we now feel he got a very good deal." I can only say that I agreed with them fully.

As 2005 progressed, both the Richmond and the Coolaroo factories continued manufacturing in tandem. The technical team continued mapping out the factory, whilst contact was continuous with the EPA, which was pleased we would be moving a chemical factory out of

Richmond and into Coolaroo. These discussions were found to be valuable when, in May, an EPA inspector who had no knowledge of the background discussions felt he had found a gold mine of infractions which would help to make his name. After many robust discussions, the EPA issued a face-saving PAN notice which limited us to a monthly reacting production of 167 tonnes, or 2,100 tonnes for the year. To provide some perspective on this, in a prior month, we had made 400 tonnes. Richmond puttered to an end by November, and the de-commissioning started. At our Christmas break-up lunch on December 21, the full EPA licence for the Coolaroo factory was hand delivered, after a full year of negotiation.

Our hopes had been realized, with the Coolaroo factory fully operational from January 1, 2006.

Richmond Sale

Meanwhile, back at the ranch, there was the drive to achieve the maximum financial return from the Richmond site.

I had been adamant, before the Coolaroo site became available, that the company would only be leaving Richmond over my dead body. However, I was also a believer in the old adage of keeping my powder dry; thus, as early as 1997, I maintained a semi-watching brief on the value of the neighbouring properties. Wishing to justify myself, I could truly say that it was information necessary for bank discussions. For each property, we had certainly bought at the bottom of the market, and as the yuppie invasion took hold, the land values went off like the proverbial rocket. From 1992, the value doubled in the five years to 1997; in the next four years to 2001, the value doubled again; and in the next two years to 2003, it almost doubled again.

Once the settlement for Coolaroo had been realized on December 29, 2004, the selling of Richmond became an itch within our sangfroid. It was first necessary, however, for Richmond to supplement production, and this continued on and off during 2005, on account of the EPA restrictions limiting production at Coolaroo. From May, we began to seriously work on what we should do with Richmond.

When the valuation company, Charter Keck Cramer, undertook their last valuation, it was indicated that if the properties had a mixed-use zoning, rather than industrial, there would have been no hesitation to have increased the underlying land value by more than 30 per cent. The rapidly rising land values represented the changing milieu and demographics of Richmond, where, for example, the old miners' cottages which had been selling for tens of thousands of dollars in the 1980s were changing hands for the high hundreds of thousands of dollars in the 2000s. The Yarra City Council was in control of zoning. Having recognized the disappearance of industry, the council was endeavouring to clean up its various planning zones at the end of 2004. One of its independent consultants presented the document *November 1, 2004, Final Report Urban Design Framework*, which was accepted by the council. The good news was that the Doonside precinct, which included our land, was to be rezoned from industrial to mixed-use. Good news always travels fast, and this reached us very, very quickly.

From the beginnings of our reasonings, we appreciated that the make or break selling point would be the site's level of environmental cleanliness. Sadly, in the minds of many of the new yuppies coming into Richmond, the adjective *filthy* was irrevocably linked with the word *chemicals*—those "filthy chemicals." We considered four basic levels of cleanliness:

- Sell the property "as was" (a non-option if we wanted maximum return).
- Strip out what plant we wanted, then sell "as was" (still a non-option).
- Remove entire plant, demolish all buildings to ground level, then sell "as was" (another non-option).
- Undertake process number 3, to be followed by complete site remediation.

By early December 2005, it became apparent that whilst process number 4 was the costliest option, at around $120,000.00, it would provide a clean site with the best protection to any possible future environmental legal action. "It was not a cost but an investment." We could sleep at night.

Having made this decision, we independently started by punching holes in the various vessels, but this became superfluous when the removal machinery came in, and the power of hydraulics crunched the metal vessels flat. The other key removals were the underground raw material storage tanks. We elected to use Meinhardt Infrastructure & Environment Pty Ltd (Meinhardt) to provide recommendations on necessary remedial work. A desktop study of the site indicated that the historic use of the site was likely to have caused contamination of some sort, including hot spots in the soil and groundwater. We agreed to their recommendation to proceed to a phase 2 assessment, which involved soil bore holes and installation of groundwater monitoring wells to ascertain both the up-gradient and down-gradient condition of the groundwater. The results showed the site was surprisingly clean, considering the property had been a chemical production site for seventy years. There were a few hot areas, and soil remediation was undertaken through soil removal and replacement, in accordance with EPA standards. The groundwater had no problems.

I mentioned at the start of this chapter that the company would only be leaving Richmond over my dead body, but while this obviously didn't eventuate—and if one believes that the camera never lies—the photo below at least shows that I was the last to leave the site, and as three lines from the poem "Ozymandias" (fully recorded in chapter 14) states:

Nothing beside remains. Round the decay
Of that colossal wreck, boundless and bare,
The lone and level sands stretch far away.

Last to leave Richmond

During the end of 2005, we were in full discussions with five major real estate companies: Colliers International, DTZ Australia, Gray Johnson, Jones Lang La Salle, and Knight Frank. In between times, I had discussions with our neighbour on the block, but his opening offer was so low that there was no encouragement to pursue that possibility. It apparently had been pitched at the square-metre rate of some nearby flood-prone property on the banks of the Yarra. After we had sold our property, he complained that we never got back to him. This was true, but we believed that he was so convinced of his own low cost assessment that negotiations were going to be futile. We were surprised that he had not been hungrier for our land, as the acquisition of our property would have given him a complete rectangular, island block.

When tabling an updated valuation on February 2006, Charter Keck Cramer indicated that one of their divisions could be interested in purchasing the property. This was encouraging that, although the price was at the same level as the commercial real estate agents, there were significant savings, with neither marketing costs nor commission to be paid. On June 21, VOF Management Pty Ltd signed off on the deal, with settlement agreed to be paid when the final authorized report from Meinhardt was tabled. The day of settlement became August 9, 2006, and Judy and I joined with our bank manager to hold the cheques fleetingly on their way through the system. To reinforce the real estate adage of "Location, location, location," it is interesting to note that we received more money from a 5,175-square-metre piece of land in Richmond than what we paid for a complete chemical factory on a 35,000-square-metre plot, almost seven times larger than that of Richmond.

Chemistry or Property Development?

Another item in our long discussions looking into our future was whether we should retain some ownership in the site and gain more monetary return through involvement in its redevelopment. Judy gave me some great advice which continues to be used at strategic times to the present day. The roots of the advice go back to the Gilbert and Sullivan story. In this, there was an extended period in which the friends of Sullivan, the composer, kept pushing him to write grand music through which they could promote him as the Mozart of England. His cantata *The Golden Legend* was the answer, but it only had limited success. Queen Victoria, following her dubbing of Sullivan to Sir Arthur, said she would be pleased for him to present his music at Windsor Castle. Sullivan immediately expected her request to be for his high-brow cantata. "Madam," he said, "*The Golden Legend?*" "No," the Queen replied. "*The Gondoliers.*" The music intelligentsia would only ever describe the latter as a comic opera. That night, after a most successful performance, Sullivan wrote this old maxim in his diary: "The cobbler should stick to his last," a last being an iron block shaped like a foot and used in shoemaking.

So, as we were coming to a final decision on whether we should retain some ownership in the Richmond site, Judy grabbed me by the lapels, shook me like a wet rat, and said, "Never forget, the cobbler should stick to his last. You know how to make chemicals, but almost nothing about property development!" I agreed, and this was one of the best decisions we have taken. Over the years, it has been observed that their development of the site has been very slow coming. If I had not taken Judy's advice and the money had been tied up, I wonder how the various company balance sheets would have been stressed. A significant amount of the money coming from the sale of the Richmond sites has been well used to retire debt from the purchase of both the Coolaroo and the Dandenong sites.

Roughly two-thirds of the proceeds went to the RJK Property Trust, which was subject to capital gains tax, as two of the properties had been purchased after September 20, 1985. This was a serious level of money, but the problem could be eradicated if we gave real levels of money, gained by the sale, into a tax-deductible fund. This fund could do much good into the future.

Sonshine Foundation

The appropriate course was to set up a tax-deductible fund to enable us to be better stewards of the Lord's money. It was important that everything was done decently and in order. We were informed of solicitors who were well versed in preparing the necessary documentation. The senior partner introduced us to a lady who was the most capable in the practice. Sadly, my initial thought was I *really wanted an older man with experience,* which only shows how wrong one could be. The preparations went ahead, and the application went to Canberra to receive Australian Tax Office approval for our Sonshine Foundation. It was a make or break situation that the money had to be given into a tax-deductible fund by June 30, the end of the country's financial year. Days drifted into weeks; the tax office seemed tardy, and the deadline was fast approaching. Our lady encouraged us by saying that she was going up to Canberra, and the approval would come through on time.

It did.

On June 28, 2006, we were able to start making donations into the Sonshine Foundation. This has disbursed gifts over the last nine years to those Christian works that already had their own tax-deductibility status. The foundation remains a boon, both receiving and disbursing charity.

The Second Soufflé

Coolaroo, the second soufflé, was the second opportunity that only comes once in a lifetime. This Ball of Opportunity was not bronze, it was not silver, it was gold. The timing was also exquisite. Calendar years 2006 then 2007 were our first full production years at Coolaroo, which helped us to learn the plant and work up efficiencies. We were thus prepared for the financial year ending June 30, 2008, which was the boom year in Australia before the Global Financial Crisis (GFC). People were buying goods at undreamt-of levels. It was all as if there were no tomorrow. We were fortunate that, having reached the higher sales levels, when the Global Financial Crisis took hold, we did not fall back.

It reminds me of the 1989 movie *Field of Dreams,* which tells the story of a poor novice farmer in a poor community who hears a voice telling him to build a baseball stadium, with the promise that "build it and he/they will come." Fairy tales have happy endings. We had not been living in a fairy-tale world, but we had our large factory, and there was an increase of more than 40 per cent in our sales.

An organic chemist might be a frustrated chef,
but either will have skills that make a soufflé rise twice.

12 Much Shall Be Given

To everyone who has, more shall be given.[1]

Behind every successful husband is a very surprised wife.[2]

As I was working towards ending this book, I thought it would be a little disappointing if Albert Einstein did not help to move the story along. In 1905, he introduced the concept that time is relative. While there were only a limited number of people who could understand his scientific papers, he was adept at putting his ideas into layman speak. To provide a jocular explanation that time is relative, he gave the following explanation to his secretary to relay on to reporters and other enquirers:

> Put your hand on a stove for a minute, and it will seem like an hour. Sit with a pretty girl for an hour, and it will seem like a minute. That's relativity.
> Conclusion: The state of mind of the observer plays a crucial role in the perception of time.[3]

During our lifetimes, Judy and I have made three major purchases, apart from our three family homes. The time taken to realize the commercial acquisitions varied considerably. Did we learn anything of import? The one lesson that seemed to come through was that the more important the purchase, the more time that will be required to deliberate on the purchase. One can depend on that. When we purchased the Victorian Chemical Company some thirty years ago, it took one year and four months from the moment we first considered the possibility to the moment we had the company in our hands.

Whilst the first was the step of getting us into the business world, the second was acquiring the Coolaroo factory from Cognis. The time required to achieve this was two years and three months.

The third story which follows was the purchase of the Dandenong site, and the whole show was over in forty-two days. This was not critical to our future, but was insurance taken out in the middle of the sputtering negotiations to obtain the Coolaroo factory. At various points in this book, I have highlighted how unexpected telephone calls have presaged interesting times. This was no less the case when the phone rang late in the afternoon on Sunday, September 14, 2003. It was Robbie Wilson from our church, asking whether I had seen the advertisement in Saturday's *Age* newspaper regarding the sale of the Henkel chemical property in Dandenong, a suburb in Melbourne's south.

SATURDAY SEPTEMBER 13, 2003 • THE AGE

Property Commercial Market

High visibility location

The property at 270-280 Hammond Road, Dandenong, is offered with a part-site leaseback and the option to separately lease the additional building area.

Located on the corner of Hammond Road and Brooks Drive, the 4.4-hectare site includes building area of about 9820 square metres. With prominent frontage to Hammond Road and Brooks Drive, the property is highly visible to passing traffic. Zoned Industrial 2 within the City of Greater Dandenong Planning Scheme, the property is about four kilometres from central Dandenong with good access to roads, including the M1 and it is close to the planned Scoresby Freeway.

Improvements to the site include three modern office/warehouses, with one warehouse vacant at present.

The property is offered for sale with part-lease-back to Henkel Australia for a period of one year, with a further one-year option available.

The leaseback to Henkel includes two of the office-warehouse buildings, for a period of one year, with a further one-year term available at a rent of about $273,460 per annum. The vacant area could also be leased separately. The site has additional land of about 1.7 hectares for future development.

270-280 Hammond Road, Dandenong.   PICTURES: RODGER CUMMINS

David Herschell of Colliers International says the property would suit investors, owner-occupiers, and developers, because of its extensive structures and location close to arterial roads. Also, the zoning will attract those looking for properties suitable for hazardous goods storage, warehousing and operations.

The property is offered for sale by tender closing at 3pm on Thursday, September 18, at the offices of Colliers International, 700 Springvale Road, Mulgrave. It is expected to sell for about $4.5 million.

For more details contact David Herschell at Colliers International on 8562 1111.

Dandenong advertisement

I had known Robbie from church, but not all that well. He had provided a listening ear to my various philosophical discussions on my frustrations of negotiating with the German company Cognis. Robbie had been company secretary with a German company several years earlier, and he empathized earnestly. I said I would like to see the advertisement, and we agreed to meet at the church, both of us living equidistant from it, to the east and to the west.

Dandenong Purchase

Robbie had only seen the particular advertisement on the front page on the property section of the *Age* as he was folding up the weekend papers to be thrown out. He and I chatted at length about the advertisement. Under normal circumstances, Judy and I would not have considered looking at another property whilst we were negotiating for the purchase of Coolaroo. However, those negotiations seemed bogged down, and the mood was that we should look out for any rabbit down any burrow. I also wondered whether this could be insurance if the Cognis Coolaroo negotiations died. By acquiring an already existing chemical site, we would have to be ahead, and we had to at least see what was really on offer.

The advertisement promoted a 4.5-hectare site with EPA approval and industrial number 2 council rating. One of Cognis's continuing, nagging objections to selling Coolaroo to us was that they did not want to sell to a competitor chemical company. We had been a sort-of competitor, but that only begged the question, to whom does one sell a chemical plant, if not a chemical company? To anchor whether this was again going to be a threat, the next morning, Robbie, on our behalf, rang the agent to enquire whether Henkel was prepared to sell to us, a chemical company. The message came back from David Lambert, Henkel's operation manager, who was responsible for the sale: if we had the money, we could purchase; he was not worried about to whom it was sold! The sale was by tender, and we had from that Monday, September

15, until 3:00 p.m. on Thursday week, September 25, to submit the tender.

As a strong understatement, let me say that tenders are not my ideal way of purchasing. We inspected the site and undertook long financial reviews, at which time one of my long-established traits came to the fore, and I said, "Take me to your leader!" An appointment was thus arranged for that Friday afternoon, when David Lambert, David Herschell (the real estate agent from Colliers), Peter Wrigley (Vicchem's general manager), and I met at Henkel's Kilsyth offices. After the greetings, pleasantries, and review of the process, I said, "David, what are you looking for?" He replied, "The company wants the figure we have suggested, and a two-year lease-back." I held out my hand and said, "Well, I can agree with that." David started to lift his hand to shake on the deal when real estate agent David forcefully interposed, "No, no, no!" He then controlled himself and much more quietly continued, "I would advise my principal that we are in the middle of the tender process, and we should wait for the end of the process." The meeting finished amicably.

On Thursday, September 25, the tender was finalized, with us making an offer in line with the previous conversation. The lease-back term meant that Henkel would lease the property from us for the first two years. This was most convenient, as it allowed us time to work through our plans for the site. We made an increase to the figure indicated previously by David, to make sure he would know we were serious and not being cute by lowering his quoted price. At 5:45 p.m., Agent David rang to say that we had the property! He indicated his amazement that Henkel had not gone into the traditional bartering, with Henkel bluffing the two buyers that had provided the highest tenders to go to an even higher selling price. On Friday, September 26, we went to Colliers to sign the contract.

A few weeks later, when we were having a lunch together, I said to David, "We had agreed to the purchase on that first Friday we met, hadn't we?" He replied, "We certainly had." And so it was, the lack of a handshake notwithstanding.

But back on that Thursday night, Judy and I looked at one another, struggling to realize we had bought a 4.5-hectare chemical site in ten days. For our minds, and to let us know that the Lord had a sense of humour, Cognis rang the next morning to tell us they would sell the manufacturing half of the Coolaroo site to us. And so, after chasing one rabbit, we suddenly had two big bunnies.

We have continued to lease the Dandenong property to third parties to the present day.

During the years, we have often pondered the mechanisms of the way our Lord provided guidance. In this case, to what was to become a providential acquisition, we noted that we were driven to explore the opportunity as to what we actually wanted, since Coolaroo was not happening. The second aspect was that the Dandenong property became available as a result of decisions made on the other side of the world. Henkel's German head office had issued an edict that no Henkel subsidiary could have more than one factory in a country. This might be pragmatic in Germany, but not Australia, with its tyranny of distance and its vast size, larger than all of Europe. Finally, it was interesting that Robbie, the person who introduced us to the possibility, had appeared out of left field. He was relatively unknown, not even working in the business.

Unexpected presents are somehow the most pleasing.

Growing Family

Children are a reward of the Lord.[1]

Grandchildren are the crown of the old grandparents.[2]

As family custom would have it, we *had* to have a concert as part of my seventieth birthday celebrations. The surprise for the night was the song and dance item put on by the grandchildren.

Seventieth birthday—"I-i-i-i-it's sho-o-o-ow time!"

They had great fun in the morning, keeping their activities secret while preparing the item which had included the following song, written by Elisia and Danielle, to the tune of "Give Me a Home among the Gum Trees"[3]:

Verse 1

I've been around the world a couple of times or maybe more,

I've seen so many grandpas; you should see them all;

None compares to our grandpa whom we all adore,

And he's turning seventy.

                Two … three … four …

Chorus

There's a grandpa who's turning seventy,

Four granddaughters and two grandsons,

A chemical factory (*bang!*),

A great big party,

And a sweet smiling Alice.

Verse 2

You can see him in the kitchen,

Shuffling a deck or two, ready to play you;

Just you and him—he's sure to win.

And later on we'll settle down and go out for a show,

And watch dear Nanna sing.

                Two … three … four …

Chorus

(*repeat twice*)

The grandchildren's performance was received with rapturous applause. Mac Hawkins, our master of ceremonies, completed the item by saying, "Well, there you are, there are the grandchildren. I don't know where they have got their show talent from, I really don't!" The audience thought this was the best joke for the night, as, many times over the years they had seen us grandparents performing in full flight. Any excuse and the renowned Punch and Judy Travelling Show is underway.

It is not an impossible assumption that the grandchildren's acting genes have come down the family line.

As recounted throughout this book, Judy and I have been blessed with three children: Jenni, Andrew, and Peter.

Jennifer (Jenni) Lee

Jenni Lee was born in December 1960, at Crown Street Women's Hospital, Sydney. Judy spent ten days in hospital following the birth, for some rest and recreation. This was the standard time new mothers were given to acclimatize to new life with their babies. It was still a shock to the system when we were back at home with baby Jenni in our arms. I have determined that children are resilient, and she did survive us. Truly, she survived us well.

This reminds me of the story that the first time Jenni was going to a church camp we said, "Now, look, Jenni, you are away to camp. If anything happens, let us say you scratch your finger, just let us know; it's only a three-hour drive, and Mummy and Daddy will come up and put the Band-Aid on!" Six years later, as Peter, our youngest went on his first camp, I told him, "OK, Peter, you're off to your first camp. Now, if anything happens and you are in hospital for more than three days, just let us know, and we will send a postcard."

Judy feels this joke reflects badly on her as a mother, when, in fact, she has been a wonderful mother. Maybe the story is slightly exaggerated. Perhaps I should have said, "More than two days in hospital, and we will send a postcard!" I still hold that parents become more relaxed as the number of children in a family increases. Jenni still claims that she grew up under a strict regime of rules and regulations, while "Peter got away with murder!" I ever think back to my father, the youngest of six, who, euphemistically speaking really did got away with everything during his childhood years.

Jenni's schooling went from Balgowlah Heights in Sydney; England; America and completing her high school years at Kilvington Baptist

Girls' Grammar, Melbourne. She knew she did not want to go into traditional ladies' occupations, such as, nursing, teaching, or an office position. The possibility of being an air traffic controller somehow bubbled to the surface. While awaiting realization of her hopes, she worked in several ad hoc positions. In November 1980, Jenni was accepted into an air traffic control course. She asked our opinion as to where she should request to do the eighteen months of on-the-job training, and we advised her, "Start with Melbourne, then list your preferences alphabetically"—so off to Adelaide she went.

Mark, her future husband, had joined the RAAF in January 1977, and graduated from the RAAF Academy in December 1980, with a BSc, majoring in physics, and a graduate diploma in military aviation. He was also in Adelaide as part of Number 10 Squadron, as a navigator on a P-3C Orion aircraft, covering the southern seas. He and Jenni met at an RAAF dinner and were engaged in June 1985 and married sixteen weeks later on September 28, 1985, at Syndal Baptist Church, Melbourne. It was football's Grand Final day in Melbourne, and no self-respecting Melbournian would dare marry on that day. But Mark and Jenni were out-of-towners, as were most of the guests. They were easily able to book a reception hall for the wedding breakfast. The master of ceremonies was a mad supporter of the Essendon football team which was playing in the Grand Final. He didn't get to the wedding service, where he had no role to play, but, fortunately, he did turn up at the wedding breakfast. One could say that for his master of ceremonies role, he became the showman par excellence. He was in sparkling form because his football team had won—yeah.

The family soon settled into air force life, enmeshed in the movement from one posting to another. This included Adelaide; the Cotswolds, UK and Canberra where promotion to squadron leader followed and Jenni returned to air traffic control at Canberra Airport until she accepted a redundancy payout after their daughter, Tara, was born.

Jenni had a few major operations, and the prognosis for a baby was not good. However, in July 1990, Timothy Mark was born and almost miraculously, Tara Judith was born fourteen months later, in September 1991.

More postings continued including back to Adelaide; Newcastle; Canberra; Darwin, working at Headquarters Northern Command; Tindal Air Force Base in Katherine, Northern Territory, where Mark was promoted to wing commander. This was a good two years, since it was a command position, which not everyone in the air force is privileged to obtain. Then there was Glenbrook, in the Blue Mountains, west of Sydney followed with a year at Montgomery, Alabama. On their return to Australia the posting was at the Amberley Air Force Base, Brisbane, for five years. There were two four-month postings in the Middle East. These were both strictly confidential, but a few times, when the prime minister called in at the air force base, the family at home would be surprised to see Mark on the television, showing him around the base. Jenni would say to the children, "Isn't it nice to know where Daddy is!"

The most fortunate part in all of these placements was that, for the family, this five-year stay in Brisbane was their longest posting. Tim has attended ten schools; Tara, eight. Brisbane let them have their final years of high school at the Ipswich Boys and Girls Grammars, and the start of university in one location. Indeed, when Mark's following posting in 2009 took him to London, England, Tim and Tara stayed on in Brisbane—for them it was *Home Alone*, as the well-known movie title puts it. They shared a unit together, not far from the University of Queensland. Tim was admitted to his bachelor of information technology (IT) degree in December 2010. Tara was admitted to her bachelor of chemical engineering in December 2012. We were able to celebrate, with them both having their graduations on July 22, 2013, Tara at the 3:00 p.m. ceremony and Tim at 6:00 p.m. As the graduate lines went up to the chancellor to receive their certificates, Judy commented, "How wonderful it all looks." To which

I replied, "It seems like there is an awful lot of competition." This was true. When both started applying for jobs, there were hundreds of other applications. It also seemed perverse that if one got near an interview, the panel's first questions always related to the candidate's work experience. These were graduates straight out of university. Both Tim and Tara came to live with us in Melbourne and started to gain experience working at Vicchem.

Tim, against much competition that is the IT world, finally achieved a posting with ATOS, a French-owned IT multinational corporation.[4]

Tara also found there was strong competition for a job in the Chemical engineering world. A summary of her successful application went: The hopefuls—550, including Tara—applied for three positions at BOC.[5] This was whittled down to twenty-one, who, as necessary, were flown for further interviews in Sydney. The morning interview was undertaken by placement consultants, and she was in the nine who were taken to BOC's head office, for afternoon interviews with the higher echelons of BOC's management. She was one of the three chosen.

Mark and Jenni returned to Canberra for his last posting as Chief C4, Air Operations Centre, at Head Quarters Joint Operations Command. In April 2016 Mark retired from full time service, transferring to the Reserves and working part-time.

Andrew Robert

Andrew Robert was born at our English home, in 1963, about one year after I began my assignment at the Unilever Port Sunlight Research Laboratories at Cheshire. At that time, the English medical system assumed that if a lady had not had any trouble with the first birth, then it was expected that the second birth would be at home. Indeed, it went well. (Fuller details of that time appear in chapter 7, in the section "Andrew, Home Delivery.")

After returning to Australia, Andrew began school in Sydney, at Balgowlah Heights Primary. After I took on another overseas assignment, we returned to England, and he went to the Burnt Ash Lane Primary School at Bromley, London. On return to Australia, my work took us to Melbourne, and he finished his secondary schooling at Caulfield Grammar. Andrew was admitted in December 1983 to his BSc in biochemistry and microbiology at Monash University. As a pastime during those years, he played in a band which often ended up practising in our lounge room on Saturday mornings. The band had many names, including Apathy, Rock Salt, and Foot n Mouth. The call to the stage, however, never came. It was fortunate that the neighbouring houses were across the street, which must have certainly saved any noise complaints.

After university, while Andrew was applying for jobs, I encouraged him to join Vicchem, where he began painting the offices and helping in the laboratory before moving into a purchasing role. In October 1984, he set out overseas on a six-month short-term cross-cultural trip to a mission hospital in Guntur, Andhra Pradesh; working in the laboratory there, he found his microbiology training to be put to good use.

Andrew married Jenny Cohen in 1987. They'd met at university, where Jenny completed her BA and Bachelor of Social Work. They set up home in Richmond, where the beauty of a house is certainly in the eye of the beholder

In late 1987, after three years with Vicchem, Andrew joined Betz, an American multinational, to gain sales experience. In 1992, he won Betz's Chairman's Award, for generating exceptional return on investment for a key customer. As part of winning this award, Betz flew him to the head office in the United States, where the chairman directly presented the award. Not forgetting his Vicchem roots, Andrew made time in California to meet Dr Dave Schulteis of Wilbur-Ellis, with whom Vicchem was then laying the foundation for a long-term business relationship. By the early 1990s, Andrew and Jenny were looking for a larger house in Richmond. They set their eyes on a stand-alone weatherboard house which was around a hundred years old. As with their previous house, we were not overly excited, although it did have off-street parking and was within walking distance of the Vicchem factory.

Andrew and Jenny's firstborn was Josiah Andres, who arrived on May 14, 1991. Born three months prematurely, his passing, after twenty-one days, was a time of sadness for family and friends. There was much excitement when Elisia was born in early 1996, and again about two years later when Danielle was born in 1998. When Elisia was two years old and Danielle was six months old, the family decided to go for a drive around Australia. The journey took them up the centre, across to Kununurra, and then back down the east coast. Having enjoyed that experience very much, they decided to do it all again when the girls were eleven and nine. The girls took one term off school, and this time, after heading up the centre, they turned west, heading to Broome before going down the west coast to Perth. This trip was a terrific time for the family. True to one of the girl's teacher's prediction, for those three months, the girls learnt a lot more out there, travelling through the Outback, than in a classroom in Melbourne.

Andrew re-joined Vicchem in 1995. Together, we saw the potential for Hasten, following on from its introduction in the United States. He immediately went to work registering the Hasten formulation in Australia. When this was achieved in May 1996, it was the first esterified seed oil product in Australian agriculture. Following many years of market development, it has now become a leading spray adjuvant in Australia and other important agricultural markets.

After I stepped down from the managing director role at the end of October 2012, I appointed Andrew to succeed me, and Judy and I have been more than encouraged how positively Vicchem has progressed since then.

Peter David

On a lovely sunny afternoon in May 1967, our second son, Peter, was born in Manly, NSW, bringing us back to our Manly roots. His happy, placid disposition made him an easy, lovable child. He finished his schooling at Caulfield Grammar, at which his son, Jackson, now attends. At age eighteen, Peter joined Vicchem for a year, working in the factory and doing forklifting in the warehouse. He and a mate went on to enjoy job-hopping through many varied occupations, including garbage collection, night packing for Arnott's Biscuits, and working as porters at Rockman's Regency Hotel, now the Marriott, in Melbourne. However, it was always Peter's plan to join the fire brigade.

Peter applied in 1989, and was one of 24 people selected out of 3,500 applicants. At a recent twenty-five-year service celebration, nineteen of the twenty-four in his intake are still in the job. The fire brigade has a roster system of two days on, two nights on, and four days off, which provides significant opportunities to undertake other activities, including golf, tennis, and, of course, quality time with his family. Peter has loved his job and the flexibility it has offered. He received a bravery award after an incident where he went into a house to rescue a woman who had been shot while the offender had not then yet been apprehended.

Back in 1988, Peter met Alison, and they were married in 1992, at Syndal Baptist Church. In 1988, Alison received her certificate of applied art for interior decoration. Thence, in 1995, she obtained her bachelor of education visual arts, majoring in ceramics, from the University of Melbourne. Around this time, she participated in several ceramic exhibitions. At present, she is working on-call as a part-time schoolteacher.

Their first child, Shania Mae, with a shock of bright-red hair, was born in 1997. There would be no mix-up at the hospital in her case. She definitely takes after her father, with strong networking skills and a love of all sports. Shania has just finished her first year nursing training course. She also shows a keen interest in real estate, possibly taking after her Aunty Jenni.

Shania's brother, Jackson Sidney, arrived in 1999. Like his sister, Jackson excels at sport, particularly hockey. He was selected in the Hockey Firsts for Caulfield in year 8—a rare achievement. He also does well academically, with strong interests in science and geography. This year, 2017, is his last year in High School. In the early days when he was playing football, Jackson was renowned for using his small size to confuse the opposition. He would often burst from the bottom of a melee and scamper down the field to the goal, bouncing the ball, with the hordes following behind.

The family loves to travel and had their first big three-month excursion to Cape Tribulation, south of Cooktown, in northern Queensland, towing a caravan when the children were six months and two years old. A few years later, they went around the world, through Vietnam, China, the United States, and the United Kingdom. These, plus other trips overseas, have meant that the kids are well travelled, enjoying many other cultures. In the last year, the travel has come to a halt, as there has been the excitement, yet frustration, of building their own home in Blackburn, with spectacular results!

We have been thrilled to see the development of our second son into a man who has an amazing capacity to enjoy life and serve others. He has involved himself in his community over many years, in coaching and mentoring roles. He makes friends wherever he goes and has the ability to make people feel appreciated and valued. His job has allowed him to spend much time with Shania and Jackson, passing on these values.

Milestone Year

As I mentioned earlier, I have always enjoyed mathematics, and it can be fun when patterns emerge. For example, 2013 was my seventy-fifth birthday, Andrew's fiftieth, Mark (our son-in-law)'s fifty-fifth, the company's eightieth, and our thirtieth year of ownership. Only a mathematician might think these things important! It was agreed that we would have one celebration, with a two-week cruise to New Caledonia, Fiji, and three ports in New Zealand, on the *Voyager of the Seas*.

The following family photo was taken after the second formal dinner. In the back row, from left, is Tara, while her brother, Tim, is front right. To the right of Tara is our youngest son, Peter, and his wife, Alison; their son, Jackson, is on the bottom left, and his sister, Shania, is next to Judy, the matriarch of our family. Following further at the top right is our son-in-law, Mark, and our daughter, Jenni (their children, Tim and Tara, I've already mentioned). Standing behind Judy is our son, Andrew, with his wife, Jenny, and their eldest daughter, Elisia, on the extreme right-hand side of the photograph. Their younger daughter, Danielle, is next to me.

The Milestone Year of 2013

We have indeed been blessed to be a blessing!

14 Heading for Home

You are a mist that appears for a little while and then vanishes.[1]

All the world's a stage and all the men and women merely players. They have their exits.[2]

Every journey has an end.[3]

My final apocryphal story tells of a Baptist minister who had never been to the races, but decided to go and put it down to an experience in life. Before one of the races, he noticed a Catholic priest moving his arms, as if in a ritual, before one of the horses. The horse won the race. Before the following race, he saw the same priest before another horse which went on to win its race. The minister thought that this was too good an opportunity to miss, and when he saw the procedure for the third time, he put all the money he had for the horse to win. His excitement was palpable as the horse led into the straight, and then it dropped stone dead. The minister was ropeable. He sought out the priest and in no uncertain terms expressed his displeasure. "Ah," said the priest. "You must be a Protestant if you can't tell whether I am giving the horse a blessing or the last rites."

Keeping within the racing parlance, it is very true that by seventy-nine, I have certainly turned for home, with the finishing line lying somewhere up the straight. This point ties in with the simple quote which I have always appreciated: "Every journey has an end." There are as many variations to this quote as one wants to spend time searching for on the Internet. Being an aficionado of Gilbert and Sullivan, I like its use in the trio's song, "Faint Heart Never Won Fair Lady," from the operetta *Iolanthe*. (The full lyrics are in the notes section, the third reference.)

With the end thus in sight, I do stop and reflect on what is past. I can say that I would not have changed any aspect of my life, nor pined for opportunities missed. I have contentment in all that has eventuated.

Will I be missed? I would like to believe that I would be missed, at least to some degree. Judy and I often reflect about friends that have gone on ahead. Memories of each remain, and that is the legacy that we all leave. Vicchem can continue, but who can predict for how long, in an ever-uncertain and -changing world. When we bought Victorian Chemicals more than three decades ago, there were eleven other chemical companies of our ilk in Victoria. There are now three of us. I am ever mindful of the proud, boastful rulers over the years who said their dynasties would last forever. Percy Shelley wrote of such in "Ozymandias"[4]:

> I met a traveller from an antique land
> Who said: "Two vast and trunkless legs of stone
> Stand in the desert. Near them on the sand,
> Half sunk, a shattered visage lies, whose frown
> And wrinkled lip and sneer of cold command
> Tell that its sculptor well those passions read
> Which yet survive, stamped on these lifeless things,
> The hand that mocked them and the heart that fed.
> And on the pedestal these words appear:
> "My name is Ozymandias, King of Kings:
> Look on my works, ye mighty, and despair!
> Nothing beside remains. Round the decay
> Of that colossal wreck, boundless and bare,
> The lone and level sands stretch far away."[4]

And as for our time after the end, I have been reminded that when I was preaching, my preferred theme was the Second Coming of Jesus. This is based on Jesus's teaching to his disciples that on His ascension, He would be going to prepare our home for us before He came again to take us home, whether alive or dead. Judy and I are both at peace that the end is there and that a home awaits us. This hope is picked up well in the traditional "When the Saints Go Marching In." Judy has made the 1939 version[5] of this song her own in church concerts, with her full use of the tambourine.

The Tambourine Queen

And what advice can I leave for those that remain? Instruction that has encouraged me over the years is the understanding that all work is the Lord's. It reads in the translations of those earliest days:

> Therefore, my beloved brethren, be ye steadfast, unmoveable, always abounding in the work of the Lord, forasmuch as ye know that your labour is not in vain in the Lord.[6]

A translation in contemporary language reads:

> With all this going for us, my dear, dear friends, stand your ground. And don't hold back. Throw yourselves into the work of the Master, confident that nothing you do for him is a waste of time or effort.[7]

"And finally," as any preacher will say in a sermon for the third time, if I could write my epitaph as a summary of my life, I would be pleased to read the commendation similar to that which Jesus gave to the woman who poured ointment on His feet before His crucifixion:

He has done what he could.[8]

NOTES

Introduction

1. When any aspiring member of Vicchem's management team finds that a mistake has been made, a story is often told to cover the error. When it is obvious that the story is only a bald and unconvincing narrative that is not going to hold water, further explanations are used to attempt to further paste over the situation. The quote is the explanation by Pooh Bah, the insufferable egoist of Gilbert and Sullivan's comic operetta *The Mikado*, to divert the punishment of being boiled in oil or molten lead. To understand Pooh Bah, we have in his own words, "I am, in point of fact, a particularly haughty and exclusive person, of pre-Adamite ancestral descent. You will understand this when I tell you that I can trace my ancestry back to a protoplasmal primordial atomic globule. Consequently, my family pride is something inconceivable. I can't help it, I was born sneering."

2. Children can be easily spoilt by indulgence of their any and every whim. They may be extremely spoilt, and their characters ruined. In our vernacular, *rotten* has taken the place of *extreme,* so someone can be "spoilt rotten."

3. They just don't make movies these days like *The Hallelujah Trail* (1965). The plot's setting is that of a predicted cold winter, with a wagon train of whisky on its way to the sin-soaked city of Denver, Colorado, before the snows cut off the town. The film tells the story of how Cora Templeton Massingale, the leader of the Women's Temperance Movement, spars against Colonel Thaddeus Gearheart, the leader of the army at Fort Sumter. Cora had buried two husbands who died from alcoholic poisoning. Having lost every verbal battle with Cora, the colonel only muses as to what drove her husbands to such a death. Another time, the colonel's adjutant worries what might happen if the temperance ladies come across a bunch of blood-thirsty Indians. "We will pray," said Thaddeus, "for the Indians!" Cora and Thaddeus did fall in love, and the overhead explanatory voice summarizes that "in spite of all predictions, shaggy hair and busy beavers to the contrary, the winter of 1867 turned

out to be the driest and warmest on record. Such was the year, oh pioneer West, and the days of *The Hallelujah Trail*."

4. One of the clichés from the 1965–1970 TV sitcom *Get Smart*, based on the incompetent deeds of fictional spy Maxwell Smart, Agent 86. Clichés that have become quotable include "missed by that much," "would you believe," "sorry about that, Chief," and "and … loving it."

5. "I-i-i-i-it's sho-o-o-o-ow ti-i-i-i-ime" is a drawn-out call from an emcee to start the show.

1. Can a Soufflé Rise Twice?

1. Attributed to Heraclitus of Ephesus, around 5000 B.C., and also to Chinese sources.

2. Cognis was spawned from the German-based multinational consumer products company Henkel when, in 2001, it was purchased by venture capitalists. By 2008, sales were running at €3 billion, and negotiations commenced to sell the company to BASF. These were finalized in 2010, for an enterprise transaction value of €3.1 billion. For us, the purchase of the Coolaroo site was a lot of money; for Cognis, it was petty cash.

3. The German lack of laughter was a stereotype used by the British to put the German people down. Frank Sinatra put it his own way that "They are the most serious people on earth. They are very efficient but they don't have time for laughter."

4. The full quote from George Bernard Shaw's play *Back to Methuselah* is "Life is not meant to be easy, my child, but it can be delightful." Australians only know the first seven words of the quote, as it was regularly used by Prime Minister Malcolm Fraser, who, to help his politics, was pushing for the recognition of the hard side of life.

5. A "cork eye, or caulk eye" is a Killick expression, meaning someone who is blind, the cork or caulk filling up the otherwise empty eye socket.

6. The quote has been taken from William Cowper's 1774 hymn "God moves in a mysterious way, His wonders to perform."

7. The passage is from the book *Seeing & Believing: The Eye of Faith in the Visual Culture*. WIPF & STOCK, Eugene, Oregon (2012). The author is Dr Stuart Devenish, Director of Postgraduate Studies, Tabor Adelaide, South Australia.

8. This is the first reference to ethyl oleate, on which the future success of Vicchem became based. Discussions on organic chemistry are in note 6 in chapter 8, "Ee-muls-oyle Kept Us in Business."

9. Amos 3:3.

10. When the King James Bible was published in 1611. The translation of this verse, 2 Corinthians 6:14, is blunt: "Do not be yoked together with unbelievers."

11.. The command "Take me to your leader" commenced in science fiction cartoons, mainly as a joke. It has continued in comic form, in particular on the BBC television series *Doctor Who*. For us, it is quoted to remind us of the necessity to find the decision maker(s) in major projects. Once they are "on side," the project flows.

2. To Buy a Wasted Gold Mine

1. Shakespeare, *Julius Caesar*, act 4, scene 3. The full quote is
   There is a tide in the affairs of men.
   Which, taken at the flood, leads on to fortune;
   Omitted, all the voyage of their life
   Is bound in shallows and in miseries.
   On such a full sea are we now afloat,
   And we must take the current when it serves,
   Or lose our ventures.

2. The meaning of the expression "the exception proves the rule" is fully described in Wikipedia. An example cited is of a sign that says, "Parking prohibited on Sundays"; (the exception) "proves" that parking is allowed on the other six days of the week (the rule).

3. The poem was written during a cruise on the *Explorer of the Seas* as part of the Progressive Trivia. We had just finished the standard trivia quiz with the theme of Greek and Roman mythology when the quiz mistress, Amy, challenged us to write a poem of at least eight lines, for points. This left me fired up to use some of the questions we had been just asked as the basis of our poem:

OF MYTHS AND MEN by The Coffee Club

When one day we were called
For our brains to be mauled
No questions contained worthwhile matter
To know octopi's hearts
Are three! Shows some smarts
But it all helps our knowledge grow fatter!

To know Jason the name
Golden Fleece was his game
But King Midas was watching and waiting
One eyed was the Cyclops
Whose vision was tops
'Til losing that eye left him quite fainting

To have snakes for your hair
Made men think her fair
But Medusa was one who seduces
And now myths are so old
They leave children quite cold
When Hogwarts and Hobbits amuses

But then homework she gave
To sort bold from the brave
And to compose a poem that flatters
Our dear Amy is cute
It has made us all moot
Let's get back to the trivia that matters!

We did get second place.

4. The Latin phrase *Sic transit gloria mundi* translates "Thus passes the glory of the world." From 1409 to 1963, as a newly chosen pope proceeded from St Peter's Basilica, the procession stopped three times for smouldering flax to burn away, with the Latin phrase quoted. These words were

used to remind the new pope of the transitory nature of life and earthly honours.

5. A business *white knight* is a company that comes to the aid of another company under a hostile takeover by buying a level of shares which block the undesirable predator. This works well while the white knight remains "white."

6. A version of the song was known in 1914, but the one with an endearing popularity was the 1925 rendition, with Ray Henderson providing the score, and Sam Lewis and Joseph Young the lyrics.

7. Psalm 23:6.

8. Numbers 22:28.

9. The saying apparently originated as a stock subtitle in the silent movies of the 1900s when the cowboy was involved in derring-do out in the Badlands, and there were other strategic activities occurring back at the homestead.

10. "The day that changed my life" is an expression that has become hackneyed in use from pop songs, films, and miscellaneous poems and stories. The question remains as to how many of these days actually occur in one's lifetime.

11. "Where there's muck, there's brass" is an expression originating in Yorkshire, England, during the 1900s. Brass was a nickname for money, so simply put, where there are dirty jobs to be done, there is money to be made.

12. William Sutton had the reputation of a gentleman, with people at his robberies saying how polite he was. He was reputed to have stolen over $2 million during his forty-year criminal career, whilst spending more than half his adult life in jail and escaping three times.

13. *The Castle* is a classic Australian 1997 movie written by Santo Cilauro and Tom Gleisner, and directed by Rob Sitch. It is based on the idea that a man's home is his castle, even when a rapacious developer is after the house. Several clichés have come into common usage, such as "Tell 'im he's dreaming" when, for example, a suggested price is over the top.

14. The use of "All systems go" came into its own in the 1960s, when space flight was in its heyday. The expression was originally used after the final check when preparing to launch a rocket.

15. From the Marriage Vows in the original (1549) Book of Common Prayer.

3. In the Tailing Dumps

1. This quote is attributed to Plato, fourth century B.C., Greece.
2. Further details best found in www.businessacademy.co.nz/aca-what-are-we-about.html.
3. One of the clichés from the 1965–1970 TV sitcom *Get Smart,* based on the incompetent deeds of fictional spy Maxwell Smart, Agent 86. Clichés that have become quotable include "missed by that much," "would you believe," "sorry about that, Chief," and "and … loving it."
4. "Sitting up like Jackie" is an Australian expression meaning Jackie is obviously sitting or standing on the alert, surveying the world. It has three possible derivations, the first being the kookaburra, also known as a laughing jackass; the second being a Jackie lashtail lizard; and the third an aboriginal bush tracker whose generic name is Jackie.
5. The Broken Window Policy was first introduced in a 1982 article, and in practical usage between 1984 and 1990. It proved effective.
6. "Promoted to Glory" was coined by Herbert Booth for the funeral of his mother Catherine, and wife of General William Booth, the founder of the Salvation Army. It continues to be used by Salvationists to the present.
7. This is one of the many quotes used in toasts and blessings given to departing sailors.
8. Mark Twain (1835–1910) said, "Buy land, they're not making it anymore"; whilst Will Rogers (1879–1935) put it, "Buy land, they ain't making any more of the stuff."

4. Our Ancestors

1. Shakespeare, *As You Like It,* act 2, scene 7.
2. James 4:14.
3. Anonymous quote.
4. Dr Stuart C. Devenish, teacher, practitioner, researcher, consultant, and editor for this book. Stuart is Director of Postgraduate Studies, Tabor Adelaide, South Australia.
5. First Fleet, accessed online, www.firstfleet.uow.edu.au/s_rations.html

6. My grandfather, George Killick, married Helen Bembrick (née Southwell). The Southwell family look back to the 1838 arrival of Thomas in Australia, on the *Lady Nugent*. Their ancestry book, compiled by the Southwell Family Society Australia Inc, was called *The Southwell Family in Australia, Pioneers of the Canberra District, 1838–2007.*

7. From the Star of India log. This was an iron ship constructed later than the wooden one which transported Thomas Southwell in 1883.

   https://www.facebook.com/ryanguldemondpage/photos/a.311490095724558.1073741832.307181486155419/408209136052653/

8. As recorded in *The Methodist* (Sydney, NSW: 1892–1954), Saturday, January 19, 1929, page 14

9. Charles Haddon Spurgeon is known as the Prince of Preachers, and was pastor of the Metropolitan Tabernacle, Elephant and Castle, London. It is estimated that in his lifetime, he preached to around ten million people. Spurgeon was a prolific author who is still read and studied to the present.

10. As recorded in *The Methodist* (Sydney, NSW: 1892–1954), Saturday, May 11, 1935, page 14.

11. The introduction of the nineteen counties was an attempt by Governor Darling to limit the level of squatting that was occurring and for which the government did not have the financial resources to provide adequate services, such as police.

12. The explosives reference was in the *Burrowa News*, November 25, 1904.

13. The appointment of Grandpa Killick to justice of the peace, otherwise called the local magistrate, is mentioned in the *Burrowa News*, Friday, April 14, 1911, page 2.

14. Rotherfield-Peppard with its Old World charming buildings has fitted in well into the *Midsomer Murders* genre, most notably in the "Orchis Fatalis" episode.

15. The Peppard Cottage in Rotherfield-Peppard is much used in the 1992 film *Howards End.*

16. Exodus 20:12.

17. *Gallipoli* by Les Carolyn (ISBN 9780330426039).

18. "And the Band Played 'Waltzing Matilda'" was written by Eric Bogle to remember the fifty thousand Australian soldiers who died in battle on Gallipoli during the First World War.

19. Seven *St Trinian's* films were released. They share the stories of the dastardly deeds at the infamous dysfunctional school, an institution where the girls were in charge. In one of the last films, one of the school girls summarizes the school as "like Hogwarts for psychos."

20. The Westinghouse Corporation commenced on January 8, 1886, and went on to become one of America's major corporations. This was achieved by taking patents into the marketplace by its own developments, and from third party acquisitions. The first, in 1886, was "System of electrical generation."

21. Released in 1980, "On the Road Again" was written and sung by Willie Nelson. As the song repeats, "Just can't wait to get on the road again – Goin' places that I've never been – Seein' things that I may never see again."

22. Freda's well-known monologue was "A Pleasant Half Hour at the Beach." This had been written by Marjorie Benton Cooke, who was born on November 27, 1876. She died of pneumonia in the Philippines on April 26, 1920, at age forty-three, whilst on a round-the-world trip with her mother, her father having died four years previously. She was a prolific author, and the monologue was published in 1907. The following is a transcription from Freda's handwritten notes. As I read them now, I feel that a twenty-first-century audience would not consider the humour of the monologue to be, well, humorous. To find it funny, much depends on a knowledge of the way of life that then was, and which has gone forever.

A PLEASANT HALF HOUR ON THE BEACH
Mrs Hardenspiker with a brood of erring children
Mrs Jones her confidante
Scene: The Bathing Beach

Mrs Hardenspiker speaks:

Now Joseph Hardenspiker, if you play up like you did yesterday, you'll not go in bathing again this week.

And Aggie! – now don't pull your cap way down like that- Aggie, I want you to hold on to the rope. If you let go of the rope a single minute you come in.

And Dick, if you and Johnny pull Aggie's feet out from under her, the way you did yesterday, you'll not go in bathing again this summer; and, what's more you'll get a whipping from your father.

Oh, good morning Mrs Jones; lovely day isn't it? Run away children, and take your pleasure and remember to come the minute I call you.

I'll sit right here, by you, Mrs Jones, where I can watch them. Yes! I should say I do have trouble with my children – they nearly drive me distracted … I think children are a terrible responsibility these days, anyway, don't you? There are so many ways for them to get spoilt and killed and … …

Aggie! Aggie! You take hold of that rope. Take hold of that rope or come in!

Yes, of course, she's trying to swim, but that's just what I don't want her to do. How am I going to know where she is, if she's swimming? I want her to hold on to the rope, so I can see her. This hour on the beach nearly exhausts me. The nurse, Emma, should bring the children down to the beach at this time but she insists upon this hour for her rest. She thinks she's going into nervous prostration., All the nurses and governesses of our very best people are going into nervous prostration – so many of my best friends tell me that –

Johnny! Don't you do that – don't you dive off that boat! I don't care if it is fun; it isn't fun to me. You stay right out of the water where I can see you.

What was I saying Mrs Jones, when Johnny interrupted me? Here comes that Miss Miller, and if she hasn't got on another bathing suit! That's three this week – yes it is, I've counted them. I think she brought one trunk of nothing but bathing suits … Of course she never gets them wet, so I suppose they don't wear out. Oh, I don't think she's such a beauty! Well there's something about her face I don't like, and, my dear, she's the awfullest talker, runs on like the mill wheel, of the mill dam, or whatever it is that runs on … You know, she brought ten trunks? Unham the hotel porter told Mrs Peter's maid, and she told Emma, and Emma told me, but I can't see what she brought in them. Oh yes, she has a good figure, but then, why not? Oh yes she does, you can always tell!

Dick! Dick! Let Aggie alone. I don't want her to float. You go away and leave her alone.

Who on earth is that? Why it's Mrs G Wallington. Well! Would you think a woman with a figure like that would risk it in the water? Isn't she a sight! You never can tell what a woman will do. Oh, I don't doubt she's a very nice woman, but she has the worst children I ever met anywhere in my life. I can't allow my children to associate with them at all, and my dear, she had the nerve to tell me that she should think I'd be tempted to put my children in a reform school.

Joseph! Don't do that! Get down off that man's shoulders – you're not to dive. Has he come up yet Mrs Jones? I can't bear to look. What? It isn't Joseph at all. It's one of those G Wallington youngsters – it wouldn't hurt him to get good and drowned.

I wonder where Johnny is. Do you see him anywhere? Yes! It is hard to tell them apart in the water. I tried to get my children to wear little flags in their hair but they won't do it.

Oh Aggie! Where's Johnny? Why don't you keep your eye on your bothers, Aggie? There's Dick! Dick! Oh Dick where's Johnny? Come here to me. He'd keep me shouting all day, rather than come in and see what I want.

I asked you where Johnny was? Gone to the raft? Gone to the raft? You know you're not allowed to go to the raft! Haven't you been told every day this summer you were not to go to the raft? I know you haven't gone, but your brother John has, hasn't he? You're none of you to go near that raft – you go out there just as fast as you can and bring him in here to me.

I'll never let them go in again. I'm going to make them all come out. Aggie! Aggie! Come in now – time's up. You heard me.

I believe in telling a child to do a thing just once. I do hate a whining, nagging, woman, don't you?

Aggie Hardenspiker! Did you hear me? Don't argue just come out. Get Joseph and come at once! You don't see him? Dear me, now, is Joseph lost? Do you see him Mrs Jones? Where Aggie? Yes I think that's Joseph. Joseph! J-O-S-E-P-H ! Aggie, you call, and I'll wave. I know he sees us; he's looking right at us. Aggie, where has he gone? He threw up his arms and yelled and went down. That's the way they do when they have cramps.

Mr Jordan, will you go out to save Joseph? My son, Joseph. He has a cramp. He shrieked and went down.

Mr Crosby, will you to Joseph? Shrieked – cramps- went down! He's right over there somewhere.

What shall I tell his father, if Joseph is drowned? He'll say I didn't keep my eye on him. It would be just like that boy to try it and see how it felt to get drowned. If he's gone and done it, he'll not go in bathing again.

What? He's come up, you say? Where – I don't – there he is – there's Joseph! Why- he's grinning.

Aggie! Why? Where's Aggie? Gone in again? Aggie Hardenspiker! Did you hear me to come in? I've spoken for the last time.

Yes, I see they're bringing him in. I suppose it was one of his jokes.

Thank you, Mr Jordan! Much obliged to you. Mr Crosby … … Now Joseph Hardenspiker- what do you mean by drowning yourself right before your mother's face? Well you came as near it as you could, didn't you? I never would have gotten all worked up like this if I hadn't thought you were dead. You'll settle this matter with your father. You take your sister and go to the house.

I wouldn't let them go in at all, if it wasn't that I hate to spoil their pleasure. Do you see Dick and Johnny yet? Oh yes, here they are now.

Well Richard and John, you've behaved nicely this morning, haven't you? Making your poor mother a laughing stock for the whole beach!

You're both going to get a good whipping from you father I don't care if you didn't go to the raft, you'll get the same whipping John does, on general principles.

You'll not go in bathing again this year. What? You'd rather not than have me come along? Do you hear that Mrs Jones? That's the way a mother's sacrifice is accepted. How truly the poet spake when he said – "sharper that the serpent's rattle is the tooth of an ungrateful child!"

Richard and John - to your father. (Followed with rapturous applause from the audience.)

5. The Year Bob Came Good

1. As explained previously, "spoilt rotten" is an Australian expression indicating that the person has been spoilt to an excessive degree.
2. The proverb "Nothing succeeds like success" was first seen in Sir Arthur Helps's 1868 book, *Realmah*.
3. "Control No. 2" is a 1934 short story by Edgar Wallace, in his book *The Woman from the East*. It is available for reading at http://gutenberg.net. au/ebooks13/1306141h.html. The short story "Uncle Faraway," also in Wallace's book, is a winner for those with a romantic streak.

4. Mother love is more fully discussed here: http://thesocietypages.org/socimages/2012/12/30/too-much-mother-love-proving-the-necessity-of-nurture

5. Psalm 23:4.

6. The Manly West Primary School was built in 1922, and is situated at Griffiths Street, Balgowlah.

7. The use of midget submarines in Port Jackson is fully covered in "Attack on Sydney Harbour" in Wikipedia.

8. The "Battle of the Coral Sea" is well recounted in Wikipedia.

9. The Battle of Midway is told in detail in Wikipedia.

10. The Australian victory over the Japanese through the Kokoda Track Campaign is recounted in Wikipedia.

11. Proverbs 27:17.

12. This quote has been attributed to Francis Xavier (1506–1552) in particular and the Jesuits in general, although some would trace the quote back to Aristotle (385–322 B.C.).

13. This quote comes from William Wordsworth's poem "My Heart Leaps Up When I Behold."

14. 2 Timothy 3:15–17.

15. 1 Peter 2:11–25.

16. After this paragraph, those who are excited about knowing more about algebra could do worse than read either *Algebra for Dummies* or *Algebra Basics for Dummies*. Further details are available on www.dummies.com/how-to/education-languages/math/algebra.html

17. As I reflect on the necessity of passing English for my entry into university, I wonder how many marks I ever received from the Shakespearean section. I have lately watched documentaries that have reviewed the messages of *The Tempest,* which include how to deal with the illusion of justice, treachery, the difficulty of distinguishing between "men" and "monsters," remorse, and the allure of ruling a colony. Well you could have fooled me! I just know that there was a wild storm, a wild beast, and a shipwrecked father and daughter. But I did pass English in the end.

18. In 1949, the Gospel Fishermen Mission, under the leadership of Godfrey and Winifred Theobald, moved from its base at Tanilba House to leased parts of the Tahlee property, to conduct youth camps and Bible teaching conferences.

19. Galatians 3:2–4.

20. 1 Corinthians 3:16.

21. The Thompson Chain Reference Bible was developed by Dr Frank Thompson, from 1890 to the first publication in 1908. The strength of the side notes was that they would follow a character or idea from the first mention to the last. There are also general topics, such as *unity*, which is then split down into subtopics, thence sub-subtopics.

22. *Piecework* was where we were paid a fixed piece rate for each element produced, regardless of how long we took to produce each item.

23. Georg Cantor (1845–1918) was a German mathematician who is best known as the inventor of *set theory*, which has become a fundamental theory in mathematics.

24. The number π has been calculated to five trillion decimal places (5,000,000,000,000). This is discussed more fully at http://www.numbrworld.org/misc_runs/pi-5t/details.html. This number is difficult to comprehend when the first hundred places are :3 .14159265358979323846264338327950288419716939937510582 0974944592307816406286208998628034825342117 0679 … There are another 4,999,999,999,900 places to go.

25. Genesis 6:4 (KJV). It is a little hard to understand this verse, but we do know that there were giants in the land in those days.

26. The School of the Prophets arose several times in Israel's history. They were a group of disciples who would gather around an established prophet. In Israel, a prophet was expected to be 100 per cent correct. Biblical precedents are found in 1 Samuel 19:18–24, 2 Kings 2:3, 5, 7, 12, and 15.

6. Formation of The Punch and Judy Travelling Show

1. Punch and Judy shows are part of traditional, popular, beachside, culture in the United Kingdom. The show revolves around Mr Punch and his wife, Judy; thus, the quote "There's no Punch without Judy."

2. The quote is taken from Samuel Johnson's *Table Talk*.

3. Irving Berlin, considered one of the greatest songwriters in American history, initially declined the opportunity to write the score for *Annie Get Your Gun*. He was worried that he would be unable to write songs to

fit specific scenes in a "situation show." He agreed to immerse himself in the book, and returned a few days later with "There's No Business Like Show Business," "Doin' What Comes Naturally," and "You Can't Get a Man with a Gun." The rest is history. Here are some indicative lyrics:

> I'm quick on the trigger with targets not much bigger
> Than a pinpoint. I'm number one
> But my score with a feller is lower that a cellar
> Oh you can't get a man with a gun
>
> With a gun, with a gun, oh you can't get a man with a gun.
>
> (She did!)

4. More details on this fascinating character appear under "Arthur Stace, making your life count for eternity" in Google.
5. This description is taken from "Mr Eternity the Sydney Legend," and is viewable on Google.
6. A typical study can be located by searching on Google, with "Teaching on the Tabernacle of Moses" and locating "An in Depth Study of The Tabernacle – NetBibleStudy.com." This runs for nine pages, highlighting how the Tabernacle prefigures Christ and His ministries. Even then, for example, it misses out on linking the Tabernacle's outer covering of badger skins (Exodus 26:14 [KJV]) with the fact that when we first "see" Christ, "He had no beauty or majesty to attract us to Him" (Isaiah 53:2).
7. Ephesians 4:5.
8. *The Honeymooners* was a situation comedy (sitcom) that only ran for thirty-nine episodes, during 1955 and 1956. With repeats, it was still on Australian television in the first years of our marriage and provided a plethora of quotes, but, above all, the name Alice.
9. Edgar Rice Burroughs began his record thus:

> I had this story from one who had no business to tell it to me, or to any other. I may credit the seductive influence of an old vintage upon the narrator for the beginning of it, and my own sceptical incredulity during the days that followed for the balance of the

strange tale. ... ... We only know that on a bright May morning in 1888 John, Lord Greystoke, and Lady Alice sailed from Dover on their way to Africa. A month later they arrived at Freetown where they charted a small sailing vessel, the Fuwalda, which was to bear them to their final destination. And here John, Lord Greystoke and Lady Alice his wife, vanished from the eyes and from the knowledge of men."

The story continues to recount the birth of Tarzan, the sad deaths of Lord and Lady Greystoke in the inhospitable jungle, and the home of the great apes among which Tarzan grew to manhood. ...

10. Alice Edith Akhurst was born in 1881 and died in 1952. She was the daughter of Sidney Akhurst and Alice Kitz, from their marriage in 1880.

11. "Alice in Wonderland" has become the common usage name of Lewis Carroll's book *Alice's Adventures in Wonderland,* published in 1865. It has not been out of print since then, whilst Lewis Carroll is the nom de plume for Charles Dodgson. The last few lines of the book seem to sum it up well: "Lastly, Alice's elder sister pictured to herself how this same little sister of hers (Alice) would, in the after-time, be herself a grown woman; and how she would keep through all her riper years, the simple and loving heart of her childhood: and how she would gather about her other little children, and make *their* eyes bright and eager with many a strange tale, perhaps even with the dream of wonderland of long ago: and how she would feel with all their simple sorrows, and find a pleasure in all their simple joys, remembering her own child life, and the happy summer days." Our Alice has had continuing summer days—it has indeed been a wondrous life.

12. Ephesians 5:21.

13. The ancient Greek philosopher Xenophon wrote that praise is the most pleasing of all sounds, whilst "Praise from Sir Hubert" is the way to describe praise that has special value and significance for a person. Sir Hubert was Sir Hubert Stanley, one of the leading characters in *A Cure for the Heartache,* a book written by Thomas Morton and published in 1810. Sir Hubert was rarely heard to praise, but when he praised, he praised genuinely and with a true critical sense! His words were not merely music

to the ears; they were "a cure for the heartache." Thus, "Praise from Sir Hubert is praise indeed."

14. The original poem was written by Jack Moses, and as with many traditional songs, there are variations in the lyrics, including these words. He lived from 1861 to 1945, and in his later years, claimed to be the last of the bush troubadours.

15. Liberace, christened Wladziu Valentino Liberace, built up his only style of music presentation with the approach of "I don't give concerts, I put on a show." Another classical comment was "I play classical music with the boring bits left out." As he became more popular and wealthier, the critics panned him ferociously. His three rejoinders were "I cried all the way to the bank"; "I laughed all the way to the bank"; "I bought the bank!" He gravitated to television as a duck to water, and the critics described it as "schmaltz," freely translated as "excessively sentimental." In any audience, he made sure that Mom (his mother) was in the front row. He was then ever more schmaltzy, singing to her lyrics such as "There Is Nothing in This World I Wouldn't Do for You, for You." Above all, he was a showman.

16. Katisha, "as tough as a bow with a will of her own," had worked hard to be engaged to the only son of the Mikado, and thus the daughter-in-law-elect. A termagant, elderly and ugly, she claims she is an "acquired taste" and that beauty resides not in the face alone! She has, for instance, a shoulder blade that is a miracle in loveliness, people coming miles to see it. It should be appreciated that it was thus natural casting for me to play her in our vignette.

17. The article appeared in the "Social Round About," circa page 68 of the *Australian Women's Weekly*, on Wednesday, August 3, 1960.

7. End of Training

1. Anonymous quotation
2. John 5:17 (NLB).
3. This quote has a multitude of sources. The first appears to be Virgil (70–19 B.C.), with "as the twig is bent, the tree inclines." The next usage, in English, is from Alexander Pope, in 1732.

4. Poison gas had not been used before the First World War, but with the static nature of trench warfare, it was introduced to demoralize, injure, and kill the entrenched defenders, against whom the indiscriminate and general slow-moving nature of gas clouds would be most effective. There was tear gas, mustard gas, and lethal agents, from phosgene to chlorine.

5. The most informed biography of Professor Adrien Albert (1907–1989) is in *The Australian*

6. Chemical formula of anadine

7. *The Masters* is the fifth novel in C. P. Snow's series Strangers and Brothers. Whilst its setting is unnamed, critics claim it resembles Christ's College, where Snow was a fellow. It is the analysis of the electors' motives and political manoeuvring that keep the reader's interest high.

8. Shakespeare, *Romeo and Juliet*, act 2, scene 2.

9. *Gaudy Night* by Dorothy L. Sayers was first published in 1935 by Victor Gollancz Ltd, Great Britain. It is a romance in which Harriet Vane agrees to marry Lord Peter Wimsey.

10. Augustine of Hippo, also known as St Augustine, lived from A.D. 354 to 430. He was an early Christian theologian and philosopher. Before his conversion, he was a "wild boy" around town and is well known for the prayer "Give me chastity and self control—but not yet."

11. Genesis 50:20 summarizes the life story of Joseph, who had been spoilt with his "coat of many colours," and later sold by his brothers into slavery at the house of the captain of Pharaoh's bodyguard in Egypt. He was falsely accused by the captain's wife and ended in jail. There, he rose to be steward of the jail, and after several years, and by fortuitous circumstances, became next to Pharaoh, to save the country over a seven-year drought. The words were spoken to the brothers when they came seeking food.

12. Port Sunlight was a model village of more than nine hundred buildings (the building of which commenced in 1888) and named after the company's top-selling product, Sunlight soap. As Judy would add, it was definitely not named for the weather. The aim was to accommodate those who worked in the soap factory and help them to have a healthy, happy lifestyle which would be good for all concerned.

13. Paul, recognizing that his end was near, charged Timothy in the second epistle that he would carry on the work, by being faithful in his duties (1:6), holding on to sound doctrine (1:13, 14), avoiding error (2:15–18), accepting persecution for the gospel (2:3,4; 3:10–12), and putting his confidence in the Scriptures and preaching it relentlessly (3:15–4:5).

14. Remember the third Gilbert and Sullivan operetta, *The Pirates of Penzance,* with its wild plot lines of "noblemen who have gone wrong"; the hero was born on February 29, and as such, could not leave the pirates, as he was indentured until his twenty-first birthday and at the time of the show, he was only five and a quarter. He was a slave to duty.

15. The quote is taken from short sermon number 1452, "The Sick Man Left Behind," from the sick room of C. H. Spurgeon, on January 12, 1879. It is located in the book of C. H. Spurgeon's sermons, *Metropolitan Tabernacle Pulpit, Sermons Preached and Revised by C. H. Spurgeon during the Year 1879,* vol. 25 (Pasadena, TX: Pilgrim Publications, 1972).

16. The story tells of Damocles, an obsequious courtier of King Dionysius, a fourth-century B.C. tyrant of Syracuse, Sicily. Damocles exclaimed that with all the wealth and power around him, Dionysius was truly extremely fortunate. Dionysius put Damocles onto his throne, but with a huge sword hung above his head, held up by only a single hair of a horse's tail. Damocles soon begged the king to be allowed to depart, realizing that with great fortune and power come great responsibilities. The story is used to denote the sense of foreboding in a precarious situation. Would I even have a job when I got back to Australia?

8. Ee-muls-oyle Kept Us in Business

1. Zechariah 4:10.
2. An old research maxim is "Don't reinvent the wheel." In this case, *wheel* has been substituted with *bicycle.* Either way, the saying stresses not

to duplicate a basic method or that which has already been created or optimized by others.

3. Shakespeare, *Romeo and Juliet*, act 2, scene 2.

4. Numbers 6:3.

5. "Publish or perish" is a phrase used within academia to describe the pressure to publish results in order to further the careers of academicians.

6. This is where a touch of organic chemistry appears in the memoirs, which cannot be unexpected in a story of a chemical company. To most people, the word *organic* means "natural," so when gardeners talk about using an "organic fertilizer," they mean something natural, like compost or manure, instead of human-made or synthetic fertilizers. To a chemist, however, *organic* means a product based on the element carbon. Carbon is unique in that it sits halfway between the "strongly electrical" ionic elements, thus forming non-ionic covalent bonds, whereby the carbon atoms bond with each other to form chains and rings. When twelve atoms form a chain, it is the basis of coconut oil. Fourteen atoms in a chain is the basis of palm oil; eighteen carbon atoms form the basis of most vegetable oils and animal fats.

The carbon atoms also bond with other elements, such as hydrogen, nitrogen, and oxygen, to form the basic units of most biochemicals. To a carbon atom to which is added one oxygen atom (and an attached hydrogen), the range of the alcohols is produced. Vicchem uses the 4 "lower" alcohols, starting with one carbon and increasing through two, three, and four carbon atoms:

CH_3-OH	methanol	known as wood alcohol, and poisonous
CH_3CH_2-OH	ethanol	known as alcohol, and the one drunk by humans
$CH_3CH_2CH_2-OH$	propanol	provides the distinctive odour in antiseptic wipes
$CH_3CH_2CH_2CH_2-OH$	butanol	known for its characteristic odour,

to

$$CH_3(CH_2)_nCH_2\text{-}OH$$

where n, the number of carbon atoms, continues to increase

Organic chemistry remains fascinating in that, by the addition of another oxygen atom to the last carbon atom, an organic acid is formed:

$CHOOH$	formic acid	causes the sting in ant bites
CH_3COOH	acetic acid	the key ingredient of vinegar
CH_3CH_2COOH	propionic acid	often used as a preservative
$CH_3CH_2CH_2COOH$	butyric acid	derivatives have most pleasant aromas and tastes
$CH_3(CH_2)_nCOOH$	stearic acid	when n equals 16; these are known as fatty acids

(Ever since the purchase of Vicchem, Judy has referred to me as "a fatty acid man.")

The last segment of organic chemistry knowledge required for Vicchem is that an ester is obtained when an organic acid and an alcohol are reacted, in a process called esterification. Because we start with a *fatty* acid, our reacted products are known as *fatty* esters.

7. "Not all oils is oils" was the punch line of the television advertisement used by the Castrol Oil Company. Its current theme is "It's more than just oil. It's liquid engineering."

8. The term *blockee* had a long history in Sunraysia but reached a higher acceptance level with an article entitled "'Blockees' win homesteads, properties from wasteland," in *Australian Women's Weekly*, January 22, 1958. It starts "Meet the "blockees." They are not yet in the dictionary, but they should be some day, because they are part of contemporary Australian history."

9. Ute is an abbreviation used in Australia for a utility vehicle that has the front cabin for a driver and passengers, and a cargo tray behind.

10. A traditional joke from Daryl and Ozzie the Ostrich, out of their TV show *Hey, Hey, It's Saturday*. The show reached cult status, and ran from 1971 to 1999.

11. The Muppets were initially created by Jim Henson in the 1950s, with Kermit the Frog appearing in advertising and cameos in various shows. They gained fame on *Sesame Street*, which first aired in 1969. By 1976, the full troupe had developed into its own stand-alone show. The group of puppet characters were known for their absurdist (cf. appendicitis joke), burlesque, and self-referential style of a variety sketch company. It was always sho-o-o-ow ti-i-i-ime!

12. Bob Dylan was born in 1941, and his recording career covered fifty years, appealing to the American Civil Rights movement and the counter-culture of the time. His other acclaimed song of the 1960s is "Blowing in the Wind."

13. "Mighty oaks from little acorns grow" first appeared in Geoffrey Chaucer's "Troilus and Criseyde" (1374). There are many variants.

14. Gold rushes mostly start with the discovery of alluvial gold in the bed of a river. From this, the miners work upstream to discover the location of where gold is still in the bedrock. This source seen as the mother of the gold was dubbed the "mother lode," from which real riches would be obtained.

9. As Good as Gold

1. A Vicchem maxim often quoted.
2. A frequent plaintive quote from Bob.
3. Mortein insecticide was advertised with a simple drawing of an enlarged mosquito hanging onto the tail of a fleeing dog: "when you're on a good thing stick to it."
4. A few words from the 1953 film *The Story of Gilbert and Sullivan*, which featured Robert Morley as Gilbert and Isabel Dean as his wife, Kitty.
5. There were patents which, for many and several reasons, were not granted:

Crystallizing Promoters Whilst the new products worked, we recognized they would not be cost effective.	18.11.1991
Fuel Blends (ester alcohol) (401) The blends were not stable under high humid conditions (this problem was later overcome in another patent).	15.07.1994
Sugar Enhancement in Grapes An effect could be evidenced, but there was excessive variation year to year.	24.03.1998
Carrier for Spores The CSIRO was developing the use of spores to control plague locusts, but they had a limited life span. Coating with oily materials did not improve the life span sufficiently.	11.05.2000
Carrier for Spores This second attempt, five months later, was still inadequate for patent approval.	13.10.2000
Herbicide Composition This was our first attempt to include glyphosate into an oil rather than a water medium.	10.04.2001
Agrochemical Composition (UV) Some actives are sensitive to sunlight, and the aim was to provide UV protection. We did not proceed to an application on account of prior art from Japan.	15.10.2001
*Process for Production of Fatty Acid Esters	13.12.2001
*Process for Manufacture of Fatty Esters *These two patents were pulled from the process, as we felt that it was preferable to maintain the secrecy of our discoveries within house, since, in the patent process, the discovery has to be disclosed, and unapproved use by third parties in private factories is everything but impossible to prove. We also found another more profitable use for the "waste" fatty oils.	13.12.2002

Product for Dust Control and Freeze Control Project was going well, but stopped when close prior art was found by Nalco.	08.03.2005
Improved Glycerol-Containing Product This was the second application for dust and freeze control, trying, unsuccessfully, to skirt the prior art. Agricultural Composition This was a third application in this case for a divisional patent for dust and freeze control, but prior art continued to prove the stumbling block.	18.11.2005
Coalescing Agent for Coating Compositions This failed on account of a predated patent that highlighted the same chemicals in the same paints, even though for another purpose. There were also manufacturing problems in the factory.	17.05.2011

6. There was another set of projects for which patents were granted, but which, for several reasons were not able to be exploited, mainly because of commercial considerations. Their priority dates are included, below, to provide an indication of our activities over time:

Fuel Blends (ester alcohol)	17.07.1993
Corn Drying	15.07.1994
Fuel Blends (alcohol mixture)	05.05.1999
Herbicide Composition (G-Oil)	17.10.2000
Fuel Blends (water tolerance)	07.05.2001
Fuel Blends no. 1	07.05.2001
Fuel Blends no. 2 (water tolerant) (563)	07.05.2001

7. Maxim attributed to Rev. Charles Caleb Colton (1780–1832), as his most famous quote.
8. As noted earlier, "Publish or perish" is a phrase used within academia to describe the pressures to publish results and theories in order to further the careers of academicians.
9. Advertising over the years has been undertaken in *Rural Press*, *Rural Business*, *Australian Grain*, and *Dried Fruit News*.

10. From the last lines of the Lord Peter Wimsey detective yarn *Murder Must Advertise,* by Dorothy L. Sayers, first published in 1933.

10. The Sheepfolds

1. Nehemiah 6:3.
2. John 5:17.
3. Romans 12:8.
4. John 10:14.
5. John 10:1–4.
6. 2 Timothy 3:15.
7. Luke 15:10.
8. Galatians 6:10.
9. Ecclesiastes 3:1.
10. John 11:25.
11. John 10:10.
12. Hosea 2:1–13.
13. Hosea 3:1–2.
14. Acts 5:29.
15. Acts 5:33–39.
16. Acts 5:33–39.
17. Acts 8:26–39.
18. Acts 6:8.
19. Revelation 2:7, 11, 17, 29; 3:6, 13, 22.
20. Attributed to Gene Raskin, who put English lyrics to a Russian romance song. It was made popular by the Mary Hopkin rendition.
21. Romans 12:8.
22. Romans 12:11 (KJV).
23. *How Should We Then Live?* by Francis A. Schaeffer (ISBN 0-89107-292-6).
24. *How Now Shall We Live?* by Charles Colson and Nancy Pearcey (ISBN 0-551-03258-8).
25. Karinya means "peace."
26. Verses from the Bible that are applicable include Matthew 6:25–33 and Luke 12:22–32.

11. To a Land Flowing with Milk and Honey

1. Shakespeare, *Romeo and Juliet*, act 2, scene 2.
2. Exodus 3:17.
3. Ruth 1:22.
4. Luke 18:2–5.

12. Much Shall Be Given

1. Luke 19:26.
2. This is a variation of the quote from Maryon Pearson (1901–1989): "Behind every successful man is a very surprised woman." I believe it is even more so when they are married.
3. This quotation is explained at http://thinkexist.com/quotation/ put_your_hand_on_a_hot_stove_for_a_minute-and_it/145963.html.

13. Growing Family

1. Psalm 127:3.
2. Proverbs 17:6. This slightly free translation turns "old men" into "old grandparents."
3. Popular Australian song written in 1974 by Wally Johnson and Bob Brown, who was also known as Captain Rock. The music was used as the theme song for TV's very popular *Burke's Back Yard*.
4. BOC supplies compressed bulk gases, chemicals, and equipment around the globe. It is a member of the German Linde Group.
5. ATOS is a French multinational providing managed services, particularly information technology. In Australia, it has major clients in defence, other maritime, law enforcement, government, and regulatory authorities.

14. Heading for Home

1. James 4:15.
2. Shakespeare, *As You Like It*, act 2, scene 7.

3. From the Trio's song "Faint Heart Never Won Fair Lady," from Gilbert and Sullivan's operetta *Iolanthe*, one of my favourites. Here are the lyrics, which contain many proverbs:

Lord Mountararat

If you go in
You're sure to win –
Yours will be the charming maidie:
Be your law
The ancient saw,
"Faint heart never won fair lady!"

All

Never, never, never,
"Faint heart never won fair lady!"
Every journey has an end –
When at the worst affairs will mend –
Dark the dawn when day is nigh -
Hustle your horse and don't say die!

Lord Tolloller

He who shies
At such a prize
Is not worth a maravedi,
Be so kind
To bear in mind –
"Faint heart never won fair lady!"

All

Never, never never
"Faint heart never won fair lady!"
While the sun shines make your hay –
Where a will is, there's a way –
Beard the lion in his lair –
None but the brave deserve the fair!

Lord Chancellor

I'll take heart
And make a start —
Though I fear the prospect's shady —
Much I'd spend
To gain my end —
"Faint heart never won fair lady!"

All

Never, never, never,
"Faint heart never won fair lady!"
Nothing venture, nothing win —
Blood is thick, but water's thin -
In for a penny, in for a pound
It's Love that makes the world go round!
Nothing venture, nothing win -
Blood is thick, but water's thin —
In for a penny, in for a pound —
It's Love that makes the world go round!

4. Wikipedia provides the background and origin of the poem as a friendly competition between Percy Shelley and fellow poet Horace Smith.

5. "When the Saints Go Marching In" is a traditional hymn that grew in the American slave fields during the late 1800s to reinforce the future hope of the Christians. During 1937, Luther Presley wrote four verses, while Virgil Stamps composed the music and melody to tie in with the traditional chorus melody. Here are the lyrics:

Verse 1
I'm just a weary pilgrim, Plodding thru this world of sin,
Getting ready for that city, When the saints go marching in

Chorus
When the saints go marching in, When the saints go marching in
Lord I want to be in that number, When the saints go marching in

Verse 2

My father loved the Saviour, What a soldier he had been,

But his steps will be more steady, When the saints go marching in

Verse 3

And mother may God bless her, I can see her now as then,

With a robe of white around her, When the saints go marching in

Verse 4

Up there I'll see the Saviour, Who redeemed my soul from sin,

With extended hands He'll greet me, When the saints go marching in

6. 1 Corinthians 15:58 (KJV).
7. 1 Corinthians 15:58 (TM).
8. Mark 14:8